The United States Council

The United Nations Security Council has struggled to determine which rules should govern global security in the post-cold war world. This book describes the rules governing international security decision-making and examines the different understandings of collective security held by the permanent veto powers on the Security Council.

Using a constructivist theory of global security, it analyzes major Security Council disputes since the cold war, such as Iraq, Somalia, Rwanda, Haiti, Bosnia and Kosovo, as well as current global security issues including Darfur, North Korea, Iran, Afghanistan and the War on Terrorism. Challenging the claim that 9/11 fundamentally changed world politics, Brian Frederking argues that the events exacerbated already existing tensions between the veto powers of the UN Security Council and emphasizes the many ways in which these powers disagree about how to pursue collective security.

Frederking reasons that contemporary security threats require multilateral political cooperation, and the Security Council is vital to coordinating the actions of the international community to meet these threats. While the Security Council often harms global security by failing to act, the United States also often harms global security by acting unilaterally without Council authorization. Global security requires the veto powers to navigate a middle path between Council inaction and American unilateralism.

Addressing a key issue in world politics, this book will be of interest to students and researchers of American foreign policy, security studies and international organizations.

Brian Frederking is an Associate Professor of Political Science at McKendree College, Lebanon, Illinois, USA.

Praise for *The United States and the Security Council*

Brian Frederking's new book should appeal not only to advanced undergraduate and graduate students, but to anyone interested in international organization, U.S. foreign policy, or global politics in the age of terror. In this volume, Frederking expertly engages debates over power, rules and institutions to highlight a "security-hierarchy" paradox which plagues U.S. policy toward the UN Security Council. Highlighting tensions between unilateral temptations and multilateral imperatives, Frederking provides incisive case studies of evolving approaches to peacekeeping, international justice, sanctions, regional conflicts, and terrorism. In the process, he demonstrates the contributions of an elegant theoretical synthesis to understanding the emergent global order.

Wesley Widmaier, St. Joseph's University, USA

In today's world, the Security Council is a conspicuous site for the play of power politics – this is anarchy in a nutshell. Yet the Security Council does its business by making rules, and these rules matter. Brian Frederking deftly dissects and resolves this apparent paradox by showing how these rules constitute the hegemonial and hierarchical arrangements that give the post-cold war era its distinctive structural properties. Frederking has got it right. Global security, states and power are all social constructions, talked into existence, linked by rules and expressed in forms of rule.

Nicholas Onuf, Florida International University, USA

The United States and the Security Council

Collective security since the cold war

Brian Frederking

 Routledge
Taylor & Francis Group

LONDON AND NEW YORK

First published 2007 by Routledge
2 Park Square Milton Park Abingdon Oxon OX14 4RN

Simultaneously published in the USA and Canada
by Routledge
270 Madison Avenue, New York, NY 10016

*Routledge is an imprint of the Taylor & Francis Group, an informa
business.*

Typeset in Times New Roman by Prepress Projects Ltd, Perth, UK
Printed and bound in Great Britain by Antony Rowe Ltd, Chippenham,
Wiltshire

British Library Cataloguing in Publication Data
A catalogue record for this book is available from the British Library

Library of Congress Cataloging in Publication Data
Frederking, Brian.
The United States and the Security Council : collective security since the
cold war / Brian Frederking.
p. cm.
1. Security, International. 2. United Nations. Security Council. 3. United
Nations--United States. I. Title.
JZ5588.F75 2007
341.23'23--dc22
2007006059

ISBN 10: 0-415-77076-9 (hbk)
ISBN 10: 0-415-77075-0 (pbk)
ISBN 10: 0-203-94472-0 (ebk)

ISBN 13: 978-0-415-77076-7 (hbk)
ISBN 13: 978-0-415-77075-0 (pbk)
ISBN 13: 978-0-203-94472-1 (ebk)

Contents

Acknowledgments

Many people have supported me in this project. The following is inevitably incomplete. I hope I have not forgotten too many.

I want to thank my colleagues who have offered me encouragement and friendship, including Lily Ling, Karin Fierke, James Scott, Ralph Carter, John Ishiyama, Marijke Breuning, Ryan Hendrickson, and Wesley Widmeier. I particularly want to thank Gavan Duffy, Hayward Alker, and Nick Onuf for their intellectual guidance. My colleagues at McKendree College have also given me tremendous support. I benefited tremendously from the comments of Rebecca Bostian, Martha Patterson, Peter Will, Brian Parsons, Jackie Kemp, John Greenfield, and many others.

The most important contributors to this project are my students. I could not have written this book without the inspiration and research assistance of my students. I particularly want to thank Paul Woodruff, Mark Wonnacott, Sarah Haefner, Greg Mennerick, Erin Conner, Mike Artime, and Max Sanchez Pagano. Other students contributing research assistance include Kaitlyne Motl, Phil Butler, Nicole Taylor, Lorna Neumann, and Jeff Quirin.

I want to thank McKendree College for the Fall 2006 sabbatical that made possible the finishing of this project in a reasonable amount of time.

Finally, I want to thank Debbie, Noah, and Caleb for their encouragement.

Abbreviations

ABM	Anti Ballistic Missile Treaty
AU	African Union
BWC	Biological Weapons Convention
CEDAW	Convention on the Elimination of Discrimination against Women
CTBT	Comprehensive Test Ban Treaty
CTBTO	Comprehensive Test Ban Treaty Organization
CRC	Convention on the Rights of the Child
CRMW	Convention on the Rights of Migrant Workers
CTC	Counter-Terrorism Committee
CWC	Chemical Weapons Convention
DRC	Democratic Republic of Congo
ECC	Extraordinary Chamber for Cambodia
ECOMOG	Economic Community of West African States Monitoring Group
ECOWAS	Economic Community of West African States
IAEA	International Atomic Energy Agency
ICC	International Criminal Court
ICCPR	International Covenant on Civil and Political Rights
ICESCR	International Covenant on Economic, Social and Cultural Rights
ICJ	International Court of Justice
ICTR	International Criminal Tribunal for Rwanda
ICTY	International Criminal Tribunal for Yugoslavia
ISAF	International Security Assistance Force
KPCS	Kimberley Process Certification Scheme
LRA	Lord's Resistance Army
NATO	North American Treaty Organisation
NPFL	National Patriotic Front of Liberia
NPT	Treaty on the Non-Proliferation of Nuclear Weapons
OAS	Organization of American States
OAU	Organization of African Unity
OPCW	Organisation for the Prohibition of Chemical Weapons
RCD	Rally for Congolese Democracy
RPF	Rwandan Patriotic Front

RUF	Revolutionary United Front (Sierra Leone)
SCSL	Special Court for Sierra Leone
SCR	Security Council Resolution
SPLM	Sudanese People's Liberation Movement
START	Strategic Arms Reduction Treaty
UN	United Nations
UNITA	National Union for the Total Independence of Angola
UNMOVIC	United Nations Monitoring, Verification and Inspection Commission
UNPROFOR	United Nations Protection Force
UNSCOM	United Nations Special Commission
WMD	weapons of mass destruction

Introduction

Imagine a world in which the most powerful countries have not allied against each other for two decades. They do not consider each other the primary threats to their security. They agree that the most important security threats are transnational problems such as the proliferation of weapons, terrorism, and the humanitarian implications of civil wars. They understand that they cannot protect their citizens from these threats by acting alone. They work together through international organizations and construct a collective security system in which states obligate themselves to follow certain rules to achieve security against these transnational threats.

Now imagine a world in which one country spends as much on the military as all other countries combined. It believes that the values of its domestic system are universal. Its foreign policy is to prevent any country or group of countries from challenging its position. A central goal is to export its economic and political institutions to the world. It refuses to ratify many treaties regarding human rights and the proliferation of weapons. It announces a doctrine of preemption that goes beyond all previously accepted notions of self-defense. And then it invades and occupies a country that was not directly threatening it.

We live in both of these worlds, the world of *security interdependence* and the world of *United States military supremacy.* Both worlds are historically unique. The most powerful countries are usually allied against each other, not working together to solve transnational problems. And no country has achieved this great a military preponderance for such a long period of time. However, these two worlds are also in tension with each other. United States military supremacy inevitably provides incentives for unilateral action, and security interdependence requires multilateral cooperation. Is world politics primarily about security interdependence, requiring countries to agree to a common set of rules? Or is world politics primarily about United States military supremacy, with the most powerful country having the material capability to act alone? How do we reconcile these two worlds so that we can achieve global security?

This book explores these questions by analyzing the actions of the UN Security Council since the cold war. Often the members of the Security Council have collaborated to deal with transnational security threats, sometimes in unprecedented ways. When they disagreed, it was usually because the United States relied on its military supremacy rather than political cooperation to achieve security. Conflicts arose when other Security Council members resisted United States assertions of a privileged, hierarchical position in world politics. The struggle to reconcile tensions between security interdependence and United States military supremacy is at the heart of contemporary world politics.

The permanent members of the Security Council – China, Russia, France, the United Kingdom, and the United States – are engaged in a heavily contested process to replace the cold war rivalry with collective security rules to deal with post-cold war transnational security issues. They sometimes disagree about the substance of the rules. They sometimes disagree about how to enforce agreed-upon rules. And sometimes the United States is ambivalent about the whole notion of adhering to common rules to achieve global security. But the overarching theme of contemporary world politics is a debate about how to implement collective security rules in a world of both United States military dominance and security interdependence.

The heart of this debate is whether the best path to global security is a hierarchical system led by the militarily dominant United States or a less hierarchical system characterized by political cooperation among the permanent members of the Security Council. Should the United States embed itself in international institutions and embrace a rule-based international order so that others see the system as legitimate? Or is a world of "global governance" an unnecessary and inappropriate straitjacket for a militarily dominant state? Should the United States use its military superiority to provide global security and in return expect others to accept that certain rules (arms control, human rights, Security Council authorization to use force, etc.) do not apply to the United States? Or does asserting these exceptions erode the legitimacy of United States leadership and weaken the multilateral support that the United States needs to handle transnational security issues?

Within the world of military dominance, the United States wants to maintain its position and protect its national interests. Within the world of security interdependence, the United States wants to create a legitimate multilateral order with itself as the recognized leader. But living in these two worlds creates tensions for the United States. If it unilaterally acts to protect its dominant position, then it risks undermining its role as the legitimate leader. If it increases its domestic legitimacy by pursuing narrow notions of self-interest, then it neglects to increase its global legitimacy by acting in the common good. If it maintains order, legitimizes global rules, and prevents challenges to its position through international institutions, then it obligates itself to follow those rules even when it is not in its short-term interest to do. And if it violates those rules, then it undermines the very order that serves its long-term interests.

This conundrum is the *security–hierarchy paradox*. Hierarchy is an attribute of world politics in which one or more states can issue directives to the majority of states, but the majority of states cannot issue directives to the more powerful states. The security–hierarchy paradox is that both too little hierarchy and too much hierarchy can undermine efforts to achieve global security in a world of security interdependence.]Post-cold war global security requires a certain amount of hierarchy: global rules prohibiting the proliferation of weapons, terrorism, and human rights violations; global monitoring and verification institutions; and ultimately global enforcement measures against those who fail to comply. A world with too little hierarchy – a world of sovereign nation states without common rules and institutions – cannot counter transnational security threats. Global security requires powerful states to direct the others to follow common rules.[The United States can thus undermine global security by not supporting the development of common global rules]

But too much hierarchy can also undermine global security. The United States often invokes hierarchical relationships by emphasizing its military dominance over the realities of security interdependence, relying on the unilateral use of force, and asserting that certain rules do not apply to its own policies. American assertions of hierarchy are usually counterproductive. Military power alone – even the military capability of the most powerful country in the history of the world – cannot provide security in the post-cold war world of security interdependence. If the United States pursues too much hierarchy by asserting that the rules do not always bind its own policies, then it risks alienating those whose cooperation it needs to deal with contemporary security issues. American hegemony – the dominant position of the United States in world politics – is based not only on material capability but also on the role that it plays in the world. Hegemony is not an attribute of a particular country; it is a mutually recognized and legitimate authority relationship. Hegemony requires legitimacy and consent, and asserting that global security rules do not bind the United States undermines American hegemony.

The United States must recognize this paradox. Global security requires the United States to reconcile its military dominance with security interdependence. It must pursue the appropriate level of hierarchy in world politics. It must encourage others to follow common rules that are necessary to counter transnational security threats, but it must then also follow those rules. Other countries cannot force the United States to do so – the nature of hierarchy is that directives are one-way streets. Other countries can, however, decline to cooperate with the United States, which in a world of security interdependence harms both American and global security interests. If the United States follows global security rules, then others will acknowledge its leadership as legitimate. If the United States asserts exceptions to the rules and pursues too much hierarchy, then it reduces the legitimacy of the international order that supports its interests.

Many others make similar arguments (Kegley and Raymond 2007, Jervis 2005, Luck 2003, Cronin 2001).[What this book contributes is a comprehensive examination of how post-cold war United States actions on the Security Council illustrate the security–hierarchy paradox] Every chapter includes concrete examples of the relationship between global security and American assertions of hierarchy. The first two chapters discuss the construction of collective security since the cold war. Chapter 1 lays the theoretical groundwork by developing a rule-oriented constructivist theory of global security and the concept of the security–hierarchy paradox. Chapter 2 discusses different "visions" of collective security, including theoretical debates advocating and criticizing collective security, as well as the particular system established by the UN Charter. It also provides the context for later discussions about Security Council disputes by analyzing the divergent preferences of the permanent members of the Security Council about how to implement collective security.

The next four chapters discuss various collective security tools used by the Security Council in the post-cold war world. Chapter 3 discusses the evolution of peacekeeping since the cold war, providing many examples about the complex nature of contemporary peacekeeping. Chapter 4 discusses economic sanctions, providing many examples of the variety of sanctions used by the Council. Chapter 5 discusses the use of force, the ultimate collective security enforcement mechanism, focusing on examples in Iraq and Haiti. Chapter 6 discusses judicial tribunals, an innovative mechanism developed in the post-cold war period, particularly the International Criminal Court.

The final three chapters discuss major substantive areas of collective security rules developed since the cold war. Chapter 7 discusses weapons proliferation, including the work of the UN Monitoring, Verification and Inspection Commission (UNSCOM) in Iraq, nuclear proliferation in India and Pakistan, and the crises regarding North Korea and Iran. Chapter 8 discusses human rights, including Security Council action in Bosnia, Kosovo, Rwanda, and Sudan. Chapter 9 discusses terrorism, including Security Council action regarding Afghanistan, Iraq and the United States "war" on terrorism. A concluding chapter summarizes the argument that world politics since the cold war is characterized by the security–hierarchy paradox.

1 The rules of global security

To understand the security–hierarchy paradox, one needs to analyze world politics like a constructivist. Unfortunately, there is very little agreement about what constructivism means. Instead of reviewing these theoretical debates (Finnemore and Sikkink 2001, Checkel 1998, Hopf 1998, Adler 1997), this chapter discusses one particular constructivist approach: rule-oriented constructivism (Onuf 1989, 1998; Kubalkova 2001, and Kratochwil 2001; Frederking 2003). It then presents a rule-oriented constructivist theory of global security. This theory provides the structure for the argument that contemporary world politics is characterized by the security–hierarchy paradox.

Rule-oriented constructivism

The two main arguments of rule-oriented constructivism are: (1) the structures governing world politics are primarily social rather than material; and (2) communicatively rational agents use speech acts to construct the social rules governing world politics. Most constructivists adhere to the first argument. The second argument distinguishes rule-oriented constructivism.

The first argument is ontological, asserting what is important to understand reality. Constructivism is not a theory of world politics. It is an ontology asserting the primacy of social facts, or facts that exist because all the relevant agents agree they exist (Searle 1995). Rule-oriented constructivists call social facts "rules," arguing that rules such as sovereignty, property, human rights, deterrence, and collective security govern world politics.

Rules are both constitutive and regulative. Rules are constitutive because they tell us what is possible. Rules are regulative because they tell us what is permissible. Rules enable agents to act; they tell us the nature of the situation that we are in, who we and others are, and what goals are appropriate. The regulative nature of rules is easy to understand: rules tell us what to do. The constitutive nature of rules is less easy to see: rules constitute reality by defining agents and contexts. They make action possible by telling agents how to understand themselves, their situation, and their choices within that situation. Global security rules make security policies possible in the way that the rules of tennis make double faults possible or the rules of chess make castling possible. They constitute reality. We would not be able to understand action without them.

There are three different types of rules: beliefs, norms, and identities. Beliefs are shared understandings of the world. Shared beliefs make truth claims about the world; to criticize a belief is to say that it is untrue. Shared beliefs make action possible because agents agree on the nature of the situation. Shared beliefs about how the world works (markets, security, terrorism, the environment, etc.) are fundamental rules of world politics (Adler and Haas 1992). For example, beliefs about whether security is based on military capability or political relationships tell states what is possible and permissible regarding arms control policies (Frederking 2000).

Norms are shared understandings of appropriate action. Norms make appropriateness claims about relationships; to criticize a norm is to say that it is inappropriate. Norms both guide action and make action possible, enabling agents to criticize assertions and justify actions. Norms about how we should treat others (human rights, democracy, equality, hierarchy, colonialism, etc.) are fundamental rules of world politics (Kratochwil 1989). For example, norms about the appropriateness of weapons of mass destruction (WMD) influence the range of possible war-fighting and deterrence policies (Price and Tannenwald 1996).

Identities are shared understandings of ourselves and others. Identities make sincerity claims about agents; to criticize a conveyed identity is to say that it is insincere. Identities enable us to make sense of our actions and the actions of others. Identities about who we are and who others are (enemies, allies, friends, "rogue" states, etc.) are fundamental rules of world politics (Wendt 1999). For example, identities about racial superiority influence decolonization policies and humanitarian interventions (Crawford 2002).

Rule-oriented constructivists ask: What are the rules? What are shared beliefs about how the world works? What are shared norms about how to treat each other? What are shared identities about who the agents are? Of course, agents often contest the rules; much of world politics is disputes about beliefs, norms, and identities. Rule-oriented constructivists explain conflict by stating the competing rules preferred by different agents. For rule-oriented constructivists the essence of world politics is the construction of politically contested rules.

Constructivism challenges theories of world politics with a material ontology asserting that what is most important to understand reality is the material world. Students of world politics are familiar with the differences between neorealism and neoliberalism. But what they have in common is a material ontology. Neorealism emphasizes military power, focusing on the material distribution of capabilities among states in an anarchical system and the policies necessary for states to be secure in that system. Neoliberalism emphasizes money, focusing on the influence of markets and the institutional arrangements necessary for states to maximize wealth.

Using a material or a social ontology greatly influences how one understands world politics. For example, assume that a country has acquired nuclear weapons. For realists, what matters is that this state's acquisition of weapons alters the balance of power. The state automatically becomes a potential threat to others. Such a changing distribution of capabilities within an anarchical system will cause states to try to restore equilibrium. A realist would expect others to respond by increasing their own military capability, altering alliance patterns, or enhancing deterrence policies. The state's acquisition of nuclear weapons changes the material structure, thus altering states' interests and policy preferences.

Within a social ontology, however, the distribution of capabilities alone does little to help us understand this situation. Material structures have meaning only within the context of social rules. What a state acquiring nuclear weapons means depends on existing norms, beliefs, and identities. So a constructivist asks: What are the rules? Do states believe that nuclear weapons increase stability because they deter the aggression of others? Or do states believe that nuclear weapons decrease stability? Is the state an enemy or a friend? Is it North Korea or the Netherlands, Iran or Ukraine? Do prevailing norms encourage or discourage the possession of these weapons? Does the acquisition of nuclear weapons "break the rules"? Constructivists ask these kinds of questions to illustrate the importance of social structures in world politics.

The second rule-oriented constructivist argument is that communicatively rational agents use speech acts to construct social rules. This argument begins with speech act theory, which asserts that language constitutes social action by invoking mutually recognized social rules (Austin 1962; Searle 1969). For example, saying "I do" in a marriage ceremony is a meaningful act because it invokes the rules of marriage. A touchdown creates six points and a promise creates an obligation because those acts invoke rules of football and promising. In the same way, states' security policies invoke rules of global security.

Four major types of speech acts are assertions, directives, commitments, and expressions. Assertions convey knowledge about the world; examples include "democratic governments do not go to war with each other" and "free trade maximizes economic efficiency." Directives tell us what we must or should do and often include consequences for disregarding them; examples include domestic laws, Security Council resolutions, and uses of force. Commitments are promises to act in a particular way; examples include treaties, contracts, and international trade. Expressions convey a psychological state; examples include apologizing, boasting, criticizing, or welcoming.

For rule-oriented constructivists "rules derive from, work like, and depend on speech acts, and language and rules together (they can never be separated) are the medium through which agents and structures may be said to constitute each other . . . To study international relations, or any other aspect of human existence, *is to study language and rules* (Kubalkova 2001: 64, my emphasis)." Language connects agents (speech acts) and structure (rules). When we perform speech acts, we invoke social rules because those rules have the form of speech acts. When we speak, we (re)create the world.

Rules – shared beliefs, norms, and identities – have the form of speech acts. Shared beliefs take the form of assertions that make truth claims about the world. Norms take the form of directives and commitments that make appropriateness claims about how we should treat each other. And identities take the form of expressions that make sincerity claims about who we and others are. These connections show that when agents perform speech acts, they necessarily invoke social rules. Speech acts have meaning only within an already existing structure of social rules.

For rule-oriented constructivists, agents perform speech acts, convey claims, interpret and evaluate the claims of others, and act on the basis of shared claims. Agents are communicatively rational. Communicative rationality defines a rational act as one that effectively conveys claims and invokes rules so that others correctly interpret it (Habermas 1984, 1987; Risse 2000). Communicatively rational speech acts convey implicit claims of truth (beliefs), appropriateness (norms), and sincerity (identity). This dialogic process of agents conveying and evaluating the claims of each other's speech acts constructs and reconstructs social rules.

Communicatively rational agents evaluate whether claims of truth, appropriateness, and sincerity are warranted. Agents can either challenge or accept an implicit claim of a speech act. For example, suppose a teacher asserts the following to her class: "The United States Civil War occurred in the 1900s." The class may not challenge the speech act and add it to their notes (!). Or the class could challenge the sincerity claim: the teacher wanted to see if they were paying attention. Or the class could challenge the truth claim: the Civil War was not fought in the 1900s. Or the class could challenge the appropriateness claim: teachers should not give false information to their students. In each case the students invoke – and reinforce – rules about the student–teacher relationship.

The same possibilities structure political interaction. Suppose one country directs another to destroy its WMD within six months. The other country could accept the claims and comply with the directive; it could challenge the sincerity claim (you really want a pretext to invade); it could challenge the normative rightness claim (you should not determine our military capabilities); or it could challenge the truth claim (we cannot possibly disarm within six months). This way of analyzing interaction puts language, rules, and argumentation at the heart of agency. It enables us to generate the rules governing a particular interaction by studying the implicit contents of speech acts (Frederking 2003; Duffy *et al.* 1998).

We can also treat non-verbal acts as if they were speech acts. Of course, something unspoken is not literally a speech act. However, non-verbal acts often make claims and invoke rules. The use of force is an extremely important example of a communicatively rational non-verbal act. For example, during the cold war the superpowers understood each other's missile deployments to invoke deterrence rules (Frederking 2000). But missile deployments do not necessarily invoke deterrence rules. They could alter the strategic balance or expand a sphere of influence. A missile deployment is understood as a deterrent only when all agree that certain rules govern the interaction. In this way speech acts, both verbal and non-verbal, construct social reality. How agents justify and interpret the use of force helps constitute reality.

Rule-oriented constructivists take rules and language seriously. Rules make agents and agents make rules through language: "Constructivism challenges the positivist view that language serves *only* to represent the world as it is. Language also serves a constitutive function. By speaking, we make the world what it is" (Onuf 2002: 126). Language is not a neutral medium; language is itself action. Rule-oriented constructivists thus have an interpretive view of social science (Alker 1996). To understand an act, one must know an agent's contextual understanding of the situation. One must know the reason for the action; which social rule is the agent invoking with this act? To explain an action, one refers to the rule the agent is following.

When rule-oriented constructivists see world politics, they see communicatively rational agents operating within the context of already constructed, and contested, social rules. These agents perform speech acts to (re)construct the rules that govern world politics. These rules are politically contested because they are inevitably hierarchical; all rules privilege some agents over others. Most other analysts of world politics see strategically rational actors operating within a material structure. These actors adapt to changes within that material structure and choose actions that attempt to maximize power or wealth. Those who emphasize a material ontology argue that constructivists mistake effect for cause: material structures are the "real" causes of the social rules that constructivists emphasize.

Constructivists do not dismiss the reality of the material world. Power and money are real. But a particular set of material circumstances can never determine the social rules that govern interaction. We always interpret the material world. We always have choices about how to act. We use our judgment. The material world only has meaning for us within the context of social rules. We cannot avoid being embedded in our social context. Our social context influences how we interpret the material world more than the material world influences our social context. In this way the social world is more "real."

Understanding world politics requires taking beliefs, norms, and identities into account. Yet we do not have a language to express that understanding of world politics in a systematic way. This book is an attempt to move toward that goal. To appropriately understand global security, we need to ask: What are the rules? What rules do states use to justify their security policies? Do states agree about how to organize themselves and solve their security problems? Or is there conflict about which rules should govern us? For rule-oriented constructivists, answering these questions leads to a greater understanding of world politics.

A rule-oriented constructivist theory of global security

Constructivism asserts that social rules govern world politics, but it does not tell us what those rules are. What follows is a rule-oriented constructivist theory of global security. It articulates rules that guide security policies and make security policies possible. These rules help us understand our own security policies and the security policies of others. They enable us to justify and criticize security policies. And they help us understand the debates about global security since the end of the cold war.

During the cold war everyone understood the rules. The United States and the

Soviet Union were rivals. Both had a sphere of influence in Europe. Both relied on nuclear deterrence. Both vied for greater influence in the Third World. Both championed their domestic economic system. Both perpetuated the conflict by supporting proxy wars. We have not had a consensus about what the rules of global security are since the cold war ended. (Indeed, we continue to use "post-cold war world" because we do not agree on what to call the contemporary era.)

So what are the rules of global security? The rule-oriented constructivist theory of global security presented here asserts that four different security arrangements constitute global security: wars, rivalries, collective security, and security communities (Frederking 2003). A security arrangement is a coherent set of rules that regulate and constitute security policies. The fundamental rules of each security arrangement are in Table 1.1.

The first security arrangement is war. Wars can be conventional conflicts between states, civil wars, hegemonic wars, anti-colonial wars, preemptive wars, or wars between states and transnational groups. The use of force does not necessarily invoke war rules; the use of force can also invoke rivalry or collective security rules. It depends which security arrangement is operative. Did the United States invasion of Iraq invoke war or collective security rules? Whether the world interprets United States uses of force to primarily protect its own narrow interests or the broader concerns of global security is central to many post-cold war security debates.

Table 1.1 Global security arrangements

	War	*Rivalry*
Rule 1 – Identity	We are enemies	We are rivals
Rule 2 – Autonomy	We do not recognize your autonomy	We recognize your autonomy
Rule 3 – Security	Survival is achieved through relative (alliance) military capability	Security is achieved through relative (alliance) military capability
Rule 4 – Deterrence	You must surrender	Do not attack me
Rule 5 – Use of force	Force is necessary to win the war	Force is sometimes necessary to defend oneself
	Collective security	*Security community*
Rule 1 – Identity	We are fellow citizens	We are friends
Rule 2 – Autonomy	Autonomy is limited by obligations to follow and enforce the community's rules	Autonomy is limited by obligations to follow the community's rules
Rule 3 – Security	Security is achieved through multilateral commitments	Security is achieved through good political relationships
Rule 4 – Deterrence	Do not break the rules of our community.	Do not break the rules of our community
Rule 5 – Use of force	Force is sometimes necessary to enforce community rules	Force is not acceptable

Adapted from Frederking (2003).

The second security arrangement is rivalry. Rivalry includes arrangements like power balancing, alliance systems, security dilemmas, arms races, and spheres of influence. Realists expect rivalry rules to dominate global security in a world of sovereign nation states trying to protect their security in an anarchical system. The cold war was a rivalry, but now there are no formal, antagonistic alliances of states targeting their military capability at each other. There are no arms races dominating world politics. [Of course, a rivalry between the United States, Russia and China may again dominate global security. Whether United States policies in the post-cold war world have made this more likely is a central theme in this book.]

The third security arrangement is collective security. Collective security systems encourage states to generate rules of peaceful behavior, comply with those rules, and punish those who break the rules. States have slowly replaced the cold war rivalry rules with a post-cold war collective security arrangement. This has been a highly contested process. States agree on neither the scope of the rules nor how to enforce those rules. Yet most states – even the five veto powers – tend to invoke collective security rather than rivalry rules to justify their security policies. Disputes over how to most appropriately implement collective security rules are central to post-cold war world politics.

The fourth security arrangement is a security community. Security communities resolve conflict without any threat of the use of force. States in security communities have shared values, common institutions, and a common identity. The United States, Western Europe and Japan see each other as friends and do not consider the use of force a way to resolve disputes between them. Given the history of world politics, this is a staggering accomplishment. Whether Russia and perhaps even China will someday join the Western security community is an important challenge for the future of world politics.

As Table 1.1 shows, security arrangements have five fundamental rules: identity, autonomy, security, deterrence, and the use of force. I make no claim to originality. The contents of the rules are culled from major scholars of international politics, including Alker (1996) on security systems, Onuf (1989) on mutual insecurity systems, Schelling (1960) on deterrence theory, Claude (1962) on collective security, Deutsch (1957) and Adler and Barnett (1998) on security communities, and Wendt (1999) on cultures of world politics.

The identity rule tells us who we are and who others are. If agents identify each other as enemies, then war rules apply. If agents identify each other as rivals, then rivalry rules apply. If agents identify each other as fellow citizens, then collective security rules apply. If agents identify each other as friends, then security community rules apply. [Agents often contest the sincerity of conveyed identities and dispute which social arrangement is operative.] For example, while the United States claimed to be a citizen upholding human rights norms when the North American Treaty Organisation (NATO) allies intervened in Kosovo, Russia interpreted it as a rival expanding its influence into the former Soviet empire. This kind of debate is central to contemporary world politics.

Sometimes opposed identities are built into the security arrangement. For example, while most states in a collective security arrangement are part of "the civilized world," others are "rogue states" that cannot be trusted to follow the rules. But "rogue states" are essential to a collective security arrangement. If there are no rogue states, and everyone is trusted to resolve disputes peacefully, then a security community exists. Another example is the mirrored identities often found in rivalries. Each side interprets itself as a defensive, peaceful society besieged by an aggressive, ideologically hostile rival.

The autonomy rule is the fundamental norm of security arrangements. I use "autonomy" rather than "sovereignty" so that the rule can apply to non-state actors. Like all norms, it tells us the appropriate way to treat each other. This particular rule establishes the extent to which it is appropriate to threaten or limit the autonomy of others. When should we leave others alone? And when should we intervene? The autonomy rule is intrinsically connected to the identity rule: what action is appropriate depends on the identity of the agents.

In war it is appropriate to attack if the enemy is threatening you. Agents thus do not recognize the autonomy of others, and perhaps do not recognize the right of others to exist. In a rivalry, agents do recognize the autonomy of rivals' borders or spheres of influence. While it is appropriate to build up defenses against a rival, it is also prudent to avoid worsening a rivalry until it spirals into war. In collective security, autonomy is limited by the obligation to follow and enforce agreed-upon rules. States work together with fellow citizens to protect common interests. In a security community agents develop a strong consensus about the obligation to follow agreed-upon rules. It is always appropriate to work together with friends.

Whether the autonomy rule enables intervention in others' affairs depends on whether the norm of state sovereignty or some other norm (human rights, terrorism, etc.) takes precedence. In rivalries the norm of state sovereignty takes precedence, and states are obligated to respect the territorial integrity of others. In collective security systems other norms may take precedence, and states are obligated to follow those rules. During the Kosovo crisis, for example, Russia and China emphasized state sovereignty and urged against intervention, arguing that it was a domestic matter. The United States, France, and Britain emphasized human rights over state sovereignty. The dispute revolved around how to implement the autonomy rule.

The security rule is the fundamental belief of security arrangements. It establishes a shared understanding about whether security is acquired through military capability or political relationships. This rule is intrinsically connected to the identity and autonomy rules: beliefs about how to achieve security will influence, and be influenced by, both the identity of the agents and norms of appropriate action toward others.

The belief that security is acquired primarily through military capability characterizes war and rivalry arrangements. In war, security is about survival, which often demands a military capability greater than one's enemies. In rivalries agents try to achieve security through increased military capability or joining alliances. The belief that security is acquired primarily through political relationships characterizes collective security and security communities. In collective security arrangements states act collectively to punish those who do not uphold the rules. In security communities, states engage in peaceful, multilateral decision-making.

Consider the debate about the nature of security in the war on terrorism. If the events of 9/11 were acts of war, then the United States must use military capability to defeat the enemy. War rules justify the invasion of Afghanistan, Iraq, and any other state that threatens the United States. If, however, the events of 9/11 were criminal acts violating the laws of global society, then the United States is required to cooperate with others to punish the rule-violators. The rules justify intelligence sharing, extradition agreements, and greater understanding of Islamic culture.

The deterrence rule is a fundamental norm of security arrangements. It directs others to follow the rules of the community. It includes an implicit commitment to punish any rule-violators. Again, this rule is intrinsically connected to the other rules: how to appropriately direct others to follow the rules depends on which security arrangement is operative. The war directive is to surrender so that one can avoid continued punishment. In rivalries, deterrence rules direct others not to threaten state sovereignty; military capability, alliance formation, and/or explicit threats are often necessary to invoke the rivalry deterrence rule. In collective security arrangements deterrence rules are necessary because there is no presumption that all agents will follow the rules. The implied commitment to enforce those rules is central to the global security debates since the end of the cold war. In security communities, while the directive rule is also to follow community rules, enforcing that directive is very different because the norms of non-violence and multilateral decision-making dominate.

The use of force rule is a fundamental norm of security arrangements. It establishes the extent to which force is necessary and appropriate to resolve conflict. In wars the use of force is always necessary and appropriate. In rivalries the use of force is sometimes necessary to settle disputes. As in a balance-of-power system, war is an accepted but limited practice to preserve state sovereignty and end attempts by other states to dominate world politics. In collective security arrangements the use of force is sometimes necessary to enforce community rules. In security communities the use of force is never acceptable.

Note that the use of force is consistent with war, rivalry, and collective security arrangements. The use of force in and of itself does not tell agents whether war, rivalry, or collective security rules govern their interaction. Agents must justify and interpret which security arrangement the use of force invokes at any particular time. If agents dispute which rules the use of force invokes then conflicts may develop. This is also a central theme in this book: when the United States uses force, is it invoking war, rivalry, or collective security rules?

These four security arrangements are ideal types. Existing security arrangements are offshoots of these ideal types. Without trying to be exhaustive, I will discuss eight. Three are war rules: traditional war, preventive war and hegemonic war. Three are rivalry rules: spheres of influence, balance of power, and empire. And two are collective security rules: procedural collective security and hegemonic collective security. The rules of these security arrangements are in Tables 1.2–1.4.

Three kinds of war are traditional war, hegemonic war, and preventive war (Table 1.2). Traditional war is a condition of conventional military hostilities between two or more states. In most cases states claim to be defending their territory from attack or preventing a state or alliance from dominating world politics. Examples include World War I, World War II, and the Iran–Iraq War. In other cases war is preemptive, when a state acts in self-defense against an immediate and credible security threat. The attacker does not justify the use of force with a past violation of state sovereignty. The attacker has concluded that the threat cannot be deterred and therefore preemption is necessary: "we must get them before they get us." An example is Israel's preemptive actions in the 1967 Six-Day War.

Hegemonic war occurs when a powerful state uses force against a revisionist state threatening the security of the system. It is primarily about maintaining the systemic status quo rather than defending a sovereign territory that has been attacked or protecting state sovereignty from an imminent attack. Hegemonic war has the consent of most systemic actors. They view the war as necessary to maintain global security and they interpret the hegemon as the legitimate leader of the international system. Whether wars fought by the United States and its allies are legitimate hegemonic wars (Vietnam, Panama, Kosovo, Afghanistan) constitutes much of the debate over world politics since World War II.

Preventive war occurs when a powerful state uses force to gain an advantage against a potential adversary and prevent it from challenging its position in the system. Preventive war is distinct from preemptive war because the threat is not inevitable or immediate. Instead, the preventive attacker makes a worst-case scenario and assumes that the potential adversary will attack in the future. Preventive war is also distinct from hegemonic war because most actors interpret it as purely

Table 1.2 Rules of war arrangements

	Traditional war	*Preventive war*	*Hegemonic war*
Rule 1 – Identity	We are enemies	We are enemies	We are enemies: X is the hegemon, and Y is the challenger
Rule 2 – Autonomy	We do not recognize your autonomy	We do not recognize your autonomy	We do not recognize your autonomy
Rule 3 – Security	Survival is achieved through relative (alliance) military capability	Survival is achieved through relative (alliance) military capability	Survival is achieved through relative (alliance) military capability
Rule 4 – Deterrence	You must surrender	You are threatening my sovereignty	You are threatening the security of the system
Rule 5 – Use of force	Force is necessary to win	Force is necessary for self-defense	Force is necessary to preserve the system

in the self-interest of the attacking state rather than in the interests of systemic stability. It is thus generally considered an illegal act of aggression.

It is not obvious which set of rules we should use to interpret any particular use of force. Were the United States invasions of Afghanistan and Iraq legitimate hegemonic wars to increase systemic security? Were they preemptive wars to protect United States sovereignty from immediate and credible threats? Or were they preventive wars, illegal acts of aggression intended only to punish revisionist challengers to the United States? Which rules did the United States invoke by engaging in these wars? The intentions of the United States and how others interpret United States uses of force are central to contemporary world politics.

Three types of rivalry arrangements are spheres of influence, balance of power, and empire (Table 1.3). Spheres of influence arrangements occur when powerful states recognize each other's influence within their own regions. Spheres of influence arrangements broaden the autonomy rule to include other states within the recognized sphere. Powerful states not only direct others not to threaten their sphere of influence, but also commit themselves to protect those within their sphere of influence from outside powers. In return for that security guarantee, the states within the sphere of influence agree to support the political goals of the powerful state. The cold war, for example, was partially constituted by spheres of influence rules.

A second rivalry arrangement is a balance of power. This could refer to many different arrangements: "balance of power" is a slippery concept (Paul *et al.* 2004). But generally a balance of power arrangement attempts to achieve global security through military alliances of roughly equal capability. It could exist in a bipolar system with two competing alliances, or it could exist in a multipolar system with multiple, even fluid, alliances. Balance of power arrangements are based on rules of state sovereignty and territorial integrity. The use of force is acceptable against a state or an alliance threatening those principles and invading others.

Table 1.3 Rules of rivalry arrangements

	Spheres of influence	*Balance of power*	*Empire*
Rule 1 – Identity	We are rivals: We are defensive, and you are aggressive	We are rivals: We are defensive, and you are aggressive	We are rivals: X is the hegemon, and Y is a lesser power
Rule 2 – Autonomy	We recognize your sphere of influence	We recognize your autonomy	X does not recognize Y's sphere of influence
Rule 3 – Security	Security is achieved through relative military capability	Security is achieved through relative alliance military capability	Security is achieved through relative military capability
Rule 4 – Deterrence	Do not attack me or my allies	Do not attack me or my allies	Do not attack me
Rule 5 – Use of force	Force is sometimes necessary to defend ourselves	Force is sometimes necessary to defend ourselves	Force is sometimes necessary to defend ourselves

A third rivalry arrangement is empire, in which the dominant state pursues order through coercion. It usually considers itself to be above the law it imposes. The dominant state must co-opt the leaders of a certain threshold of states because there is generally little legitimacy accorded from the weak to the strong. An empire in many cases is a contested and one-sided spheres of influence arrangement. Weaker states resist intrusion by a more powerful state into what they consider their own sphere of influence. If the weaker states join together to deter the dominant state, the security arrangement may become a balance of power.

Two types of collective security arrangements are procedural and hegemonic collective security (Table 1.4). Procedural collective security occurs when all recognized great powers authorize both the explicit rules of the community and the enforcement of those rules. Procedural collective security is institutionalized in the UN Charter powers of the five permanent members on the Security Council. Hegemonic collective security occurs when the hegemon, or those within its sphere of influence, punishes violators of Security Council resolutions without explicit authorization from all permanent members on the Security Council. Russia, China, and France often advocate procedural collective security, and the United States and Britain often advocate hegemonic collective security. Disputes about the more appropriate way to implement collective security constitute much of the debate over post-cold war security rules. Chapter 2 discusses these disputes in detail.

The rules of contemporary world politics

This theory of global security can help us understand world politics since the end of the cold war. Constructivists argue that the social world of identities, norms, and beliefs tells us more than the material world. Social rules constitute reality. Any particular distribution of capabilities – like a world of United States military dominance – can be consistent with many different security arrangements. We have to take lan-

Table 1.4 Rules of collective security arrangements

	Procedural collective security	Hegemonic collective security
Rule 1 – Identity	We are fellow citizens	We are fellow citizens
Rule 2 – Autonomy	Autonomy is limited by obligations to follow and enforce the community's rules	Autonomy is limited by obligations to follow and enforce the community's rules
Rule 3 – Security	Security is achieved through multilateral commitments (sanctions, use of force, etc.)	Security is achieved through multilateral commitments (sanctions, use of force, etc.)
Rule 4 – Deterrence	Do not break the rules stated in the UN Charter and SC resolutions	Do not break the norms of the global community
Rule 5 – Use of force	Security Council authorization of the use of force is sometimes necessary	Force is necessary whenever a rule violation threatens international security

guage and agency seriously and investigate which security arrangements agents invoke. We have to ask the constructivist question: What are the rules?

One possibility is that 9/11 and the ensuing "war on terrorism" transformed world politics into a hegemonic war. The United States is leading a coalition of states in a legitimate war against revisionist forces threatening global security. The war on terrorism is so central to world politics that other possible arrangements (great power rivalry, collective security, etc.) are secondary. Consistent with American neoconservative arguments, global order is being built on United States military power. Two limitations of this interpretation are: (1) the vast majority of humanity does not consider the war in Iraq to be a legitimate act to maintain global security; and (2) the meager multilateral support for the United States means that it cannot possibly widen its military commitments to all states that harbor terrorists. In these conditions global order cannot be based on United States military power and hegemonic war.

Another possibility is that eventually rivalry will again dominate world politics. Realist international relations theorists expect that others will eventually ally against the United States. They argue that a unipolar system is inherently unstable for two reasons: (1) the dominant state will take on so many tasks that it will eventually weaken; and (2) the dominant state is unrestrained and thus threatening to others (Waltz 2000). However, other powers have not formed an alliance against the United States; none has even significantly increased its military spending in the last decade, let alone militarily confronted the United States.

There are three main explanations for the lack of balancing (Paul 2005). One is the liberal nature of United States hegemony. Potential rivals do not believe that the United States threatens their territorial integrity. For example, it has never supported secessionist movements in Russia and China. And the United States provides either security guarantees and/or economic opportunity to all potential balancers. A second explanation is the democratic United States political system. Potential rivals know that the American public will not support "real" empire. A third explanation is the qualitative level of American military dominance. Potential rivals simply do not have the material capability to balance against the United States (Wohlforth 1999).

This does not mean that other powers see the United States as a benign hegemon. Russia and China interpret policies like missile defense, NATO expansion, and American support for Taiwan as directly threatening their interests. No potential balancer is about to give up their nuclear weapons. But instead of forming a counterbalancing alliance, they engage in "soft balancing" (Paul 2005; Pape 2005). Instead of increasing military spending or confronting the United States, they use tools like the Security Council veto power to reduce the legitimacy of United States unilateralism. They refuse to cooperate with the United States in ventures such as the invasion of Iraq. They develop regional security institutions and regional trading blocks that exclude the United States. They sell the dollar in favor of the euro. Even smaller powers can frustrate American military intervention by denying access to military bases, as Turkey and Saudi Arabia did during the 2003 invasion of Iraq.

A third possibility is that global security is dominated by rules of empire

(Ferguson 2004, Bacevich 2002, Colas and Saull 2006). Global security is moving away from multilateralism and the rule of law and toward United States unilateralism and coercion. The United States defines its interests and policies independently of others. It claims to be exempt from certain rules. Other countries are increasingly wary of the United States and work to reduce its influence in their neighborhoods. Russian hardliners resent NATO expansion, the use of force in the former Yugoslavia, and the installation of military bases in former Soviet republics to support the invasion of Afghanistan. Chinese hardliners resent the United States security guarantee to Taiwan and the presence of American troops on the Korean peninsula. Fundamentalist Islamic terrorist groups also see themselves as resisting Western influence in the Middle East. Many Europeans want to develop their own military capability and reduce American influence on the continent by marginalizing NATO.

But empire does not necessarily exist simply because the United States is militarily dominant and many countries do not see this dominance to be in their own interests. The realities of security interdependence thwart the development of an American empire. Without the consent and active collaboration of many other countries, the United States is able neither to dictate the rules nor to coerce others into following the rules. For example, the United States cannot stop North Korea from developing nuclear weapons without China, and it cannot stop Iran from developing nuclear weapons without Russia. The United States is mired in Iraq largely because the international community has done little to bail it out. And in some cases – like the International Criminal Court – the rest of the world is establishing rules and institutions without the United States. These examples hardly indicate a successful, coercive American empire.

A final possibility is that the dominant security arrangement is a form of hegemonic collective security (Ikenberry 2003). Despite its current unilateral tendencies, the United States generally attempts to enforce agreed-upon rules. The other major powers do not want a rivalry with the United States and instead prefer the United States to pursue order in a way that is in everyone's interest. Security interdependence will force the United States to (re)learn that global stability is best preserved through legitimate political institutions rather than military coercion. In order to increase the legitimacy of global security institutions, the United States will also need to submit itself to the rules generated by those institutions.

This debate over the existing rules of global security overlaps with the normative debate about what the rules should be. Which set of rules is more likely to achieve global security and protect American interests? Within the material world of United States military dominance and security interdependence, many different security arrangements are possible. Would the interests of the United States be more likely achieved by some form of empire? A hegemonic war against terrorism? A global rivalry with China and Russia? A hegemonic collective security system? The argument in this book is that a collective security system is the most appropriate security arrangement to deal with transnational issues in a world of security interdependence, and that the United States often pursues policies that are counterproductive toward constructing such an arrangement.

This argument relies on the concepts of hierarchy and legitimacy (Lake 2006). Hierarchy exists when A can issue a directive to B but B cannot issue a directive to A. One source of hierarchy in world politics is nuclear weapons: some countries can threaten others with nuclear weapons, but others cannot. Another is the Security Council: the five veto powers can issue directives to the rest of the states, but the other states cannot issue directives to the five veto powers. The directive from A is legitimate when B complies because B considers the rules invoked by the directive to be fair, necessary to maintain security, and in the interests of all. At some point, though, A's directive, and the rules invoked by that speech act, can be so hierarchical that B no longer considers them to be legitimate. When A directs B to follow a rule that A routinely violates, A's pursuit of hierarchy can undermine the legitimacy of the existing security arrangement.

Some security arrangements are more hierarchical than others (Table 1.5). Low hierarchy exists in spheres of influence, balance of power, and procedural collective security arrangements. In spheres of influence and balance of power arrangements, hierarchy exists between the major powers and the states within their spheres of influence. But there is no formal hierarchy among the great powers themselves because all mutually recognize the legitimacy of the others' spheres of influence. Relative status may come from the size of one's alliance, and there may be more or less hierarchy within a sphere of influence, but each major power is recognized as dominant in its own sphere. Similarly, hierarchy exists in procedural collective security because the veto powers have more authority than the other states. Yet there is no formal hierarchy among the veto powers themselves. All must agree before the Council can act.

Moderate levels of hierarchy exist in hegemonic war and hegemonic collective security. These security arrangements privilege the hegemon by enabling it to use force and punish rule violators, while others cannot force it to follow international law. Even with the increased hierarchy in these arrangements, there are constraints on the hegemon. It must enforce mutually agreed upon rules in a way that credibly pursues the interests of all major powers. If the hegemon ignores the interests of the other powers and pursues even higher levels of hierarchy, these arrangements can break down.

High levels of hierarchy exist in empire and preventive war. In these arrangements the rules bind everyone except the dominant state. It is free to do what it believes is necessary to maintain order. For example, while the United States claims the right to use preventive force against what it considers to be credible threats, it argues that others engaging in similar actions – India invading Pakistan,

Table 1.5 Global security social arrangements and hierarchy

	Low hierarchy	*Moderate hierarchy*	*High hierarchy*
War	Traditional war	Hegemonic war	Preventive war
Rivalry	Spheres of influence Balance of power		Empire
Collective security	Procedural collective security	Hegemonic collective security	

China invading Taiwan, or Russia invading Georgia to arrest Chechen separatists – would harm international security. This is a very hierarchical arrangement: the dominant state can limit the actions of others, but others cannot limit the actions of the dominant state. It is difficult for the dominant state to maintain the legitimacy of such arrangements. When states interpret the dominant state as invoking rules of empire or preventive war, they will resist the construction of that security arrangement.

These security arrangements, and the varying levels of hierarchy in each, help us understand global security since the end of the cold war. When the cold war ended, the major powers began a highly contested process of constructing new rules. Throughout this process, the United States has advocated security arrangements with higher levels of hierarchy. The United States has generally advocated hegemonic collective security and, if necessary, hegemonic war. The United States will not accept security arrangements with low hierarchy preferred by the other major powers – procedural collective security and regional spheres of influence. Indeed, others have often criticized the United States for pursuing policies that invoke the even more hierarchical security arrangements of empire and preventive war.

Some level of hierarchy is necessary to successfully deal with transnational security threats. Countering the proliferation of weapons, terrorism, and human rights violations requires global rules prohibiting such acts in treaty language and Security Council resolutions. It requires extensive state cooperation regarding intelligence, law enforcement, and extradition. It requires global monitoring and verification institutions. And it requires enforcement measures: sanctions, judicial tribunals, and ultimately the use of force. A world of sovereign nation states without common rules and institutions cannot counter transnational security threats. Security in the post-cold war world requires an altered understanding of state sovereignty and the global acceptance of some hierarchy. Such rules can only exist through a complicated process of multilateral negotiations, and powerful countries like the United States must encourage the rest of the world to accept them. Constructing collective security rule is easier when the rules are fair, legitimate, effective, and truly in everyone's interest.

The United States wants global rules to deal with transnational threats. But it often pursues even higher levels of hierarchy by exempting itself from those rules. The United States does so in many ways, including the following: (1) asserting that certain rules do not apply to its own policies by either failing to ratify treaties or weakly implementing them; (2) using force without Security Council authorization; (3) claiming exclusive rights to preemption beyond all previously understood notions of self-defense; (4) claiming that humanitarian intervention is justifiable when carried out by democratic states; (5) advocating sanctions as punitive measures rather than bargaining tools; and (6) advocating harsh policies of isolation and regime change for "rogue states" rather than engagement. With these policies the United States potentially pursues so much hierarchy that it could discourage others from complying with the global rules that provide both American and global security.

Throughout the post-cold war period Russia, China, and France have advocated security arrangements with lower levels of hierarchy. They have preferred procedural collective security and regional spheres of influence. They want a world based on rules and institutions that would constrain the United States. They enthusiastically embrace the idea that security interdependence is the dominant characteristic of world politics and that the major powers must work together to achieve security. They criticize the United States when they interpret it as invoking highly hierarchical security arrangements: hegemonic collective security, hegemonic war, empire, or preventive war. They fear that these United States policies undermine the cohesion necessary to maintain international order and deal with transnational security threats.

This dispute is the social reality that constitutes post-cold war global security. It is the social structure that enables states to enact, justify, and criticize security policies. When there is consensus that United States policies invoke security arrangements with relatively lower levels of hierarchy, the other major powers are supportive. When the other major powers interpret American policies to invoke security arrangements with relatively higher levels of hierarchy, they consistently criticize those policies and resist the hierarchical implications of those policies. The events of 9/11 have not changed the nature of this debate. Instead, as the following chapters will show, they deepened an already existing dispute. Following 9/11 the United States is again advocating hierarchical security arrangements, and the other powers are again resisting those arrangements. The debate about which rules should govern us has been the same throughout the post-cold war period.

This debate revolves around the relationship between hierarchy and security. What level of hierarchy is the most appropriate to achieve global security? A world with too little hierarchy – a collection of sovereign states without global rules – cannot deal with contemporary transnational security threats. There must be common rules to effectively collaborate and counter terrorism, the proliferation of weapons, and widespread violations of human rights. Security interdependence requires the development of certain rules and a process whereby powerful states direct all to follow those rules. Such a process is inherently hierarchical. But it can also be a legitimate process if the rules are fair, necessary, and binding to all.

Conversely, a world with too much hierarchy cannot deal with contemporary transnational security threats. American over-reliance on its military capability and assertions that the rules do not bind its own policies discourage others from providing the multilateral cooperation necessary in a world of security interdependence. United States military power alone cannot provide global security against terrorism, the proliferation of weapons, and human rights violations. So how much hierarchy should the United States invoke to achieve global security? When is it acceptable to put itself above the rules because it has special responsibilities as the most powerful state? And when should it embed itself in international institutions and follow the rules in order to increase the legitimacy of those institutions and prevent resistance to its dominant position?

The analysis of post-cold war global security issues in this book shows that when the United States pursues higher levels of hierarchy, it often achieves lower levels of security. The two worlds of security interdependence and military supremacy put the United States in an extremely ironic situation: it is the most powerful country in the history of the world at precisely the moment when military power alone cannot achieve security. The greatest security threats in the post-cold war world require multilateral political cooperation, not unilateral military power. Hierarchical uses of force by the United States cannot achieve security. This is part of the security–hierarchy paradox: too much hierarchy can harm American security interests.

The United States has accepted the responsibility to take the lead in establishing global security, and other states are willing to accept some hierarchy as the price of order. This relationship can continue as long as the United States does not invoke security arrangements with ever-increasing hierarchy. In the world of security interdependence, the United States can only achieve security if others cooperate, and others are more willing to cooperate in a less hierarchical security arrangement. The uproar over the United States invasion of Iraq is replaying this consistent post-cold war debate: are we better off with a more hierarchical or less hierarchical global security arrangement? At some point the ruler's pursuit of hierarchy will convince the ruled that its directives are no longer legitimate.

2 Visions of collective security

All collective security arrangements have certain rules. States identify each other as fellow citizens within a larger society, they agree to follow a particular set of rules, and they enforce those rules through multilateral action, including the use of force if necessary. Beyond this basic structure, however, many forms of collective security are possible, varying by the substance of the rules, who determines the rules, and how to enforce the rules. Collective security is a slippery concept, and this chapter delves into its complexities.

The first section analyzes the differences between pure collective security, procedural collective security, and hegemonic collective security. It also discusses the United Nations Charter, which establishes procedural collective security. The second section explains why critiques of collective security vary so widely. Realist critiques are directed against pure collective security, and radical critiques are directed against procedural and/or hegemonic collective security. The final section discusses the preferences of the veto powers regarding how to implement collective security. Russia, China, and France tend to prefer procedural collective security, and the United States and the United Kingdom are often willing to invoke hegemonic collective security. This dispute constitutes much of post-cold war world politics.

Forms of collective security

Collective security arrangements can be institutionalized in different ways. Three types of collective security arrangements are pure, procedural and hegemonic collective security. Pure collective security refers to an agreement among all states to protect their territorial integrity by establishing a legal obligation to punish those that start interstate wars. Inis Claude defined it as:

> an international system in which the danger of aggressive warfare by any state is to be met by the avowed determination of virtually all other states to exert pressure of every necessary variety – moral, diplomatic, economic, and military – to frustrate attack upon any state.
>
> (Claude 1962: 110)

Pure collective security arrangements ensure that even the most powerful states do not threaten the territorial integrity of others. They invoke an automatic legal obligation to protect the sovereignty of all states. Pure collective security has lower levels of hierarchy than other collective security arrangements: everyone is subject to punishment for violating the rules.

Procedural collective security is a political obligation among great powers to pursue stability and enforce rules that support their interests. It is an institutionalized great power concert (Vayrynen 2003). It establishes political institutions to maintain international security, not legal institutions to enforce international law. It protects the interests of the great powers without holding them accountable to community rules. For example, the Security Council cannot punish Russia for human rights violations in Chechnya, or China for proliferating weapons in Pakistan. This hierarchy leads to tensions between the great powers and all other states. If the great powers act too much like a concert, they will disregard others and risk losing legitimacy for an institution that supports their long-term interests. If other states demand that they act like a pure collective security system and follow all the rules, then the great powers will have less incentive to provide international security on the community's behalf.

Hegemonic collective security is an arrangement in which the most powerful state claims the right to unilaterally enforce agreed-upon rules. This is the most hierarchical collective security arrangement: while the dominant state asserts the right to initiate enforcement measures on its own, it denies that right to others. This arrangement can be legitimate if the vast majority of states interpret the unilateral enforcement as effectively maintaining international security. If the international community interprets the dominant state to be pursuing its narrow interests and withholds consent and collaboration, then rivalry rather than collective security exists.

The world's nations established a collective security arrangement after World War II with the UN Charter. The first purpose of the UN listed in Article 1 of the Charter is: "[T]o maintain international peace and security, and to that end: to take effective collective measures for the prevention and removal of threats to the peace, and for the suppression of acts of aggression or other breaches of the peace." Article 2 lists the principles of the UN, including sovereign equality, good faith, peaceful settlement of disputes, and – unless enforcement measures apply – nonintervention into domestic affairs. Its most explicit rule is to prohibit the aggressive use of force and threats to use force (Article 2.4).

The Charter establishes the Security Council as the organ primarily responsible for maintaining international peace and security. The Council comprises fifteen members. Five are permanent members: Russia, China, France, the United Kingdom, and the United States (Article 23). The other ten, distributed equitably among the regions of the world, are elected by a two-thirds vote of the General Assembly to two-year terms. The five permanent members have veto power (Article 27.3). The Council acts when at least nine out of fifteen members vote in favor and no permanent member votes against it. Permanent membership and the veto power establish hierarchy in the procedural collective security arrangement: the

Council cannot act unless all five veto powers agree. The rules enable the Council to authorize enforcement on all but the permanent members, who can veto any resolution directed against them. The Council cannot punish the veto powers – or any state the veto powers want to protect – for violating the rules.

The Charter gives the Security Council extraordinary powers. In Chapter V it obligates all states to enforce Security Council resolutions (Article 25). It gives the Council the power to establish other organs (Article 29). The Council has used this power to create twenty-five subsidiary organs, including judicial tribunals, sanctions committees, and working groups on peacekeeping. These bodies operate on the basis of consensus – there are no vetoes – which reduces hierarchy within the Council. In Chapter VI the Charter gives the Council its powers regarding the peaceful settlement of disputes. The Council can, for example, investigate disputes (Article 34) and make recommendations for the peaceful settlement of disputes (Article 36).

The Council's enforcement powers are in Chapter VII. The Council can determine when a threat to the peace has occurred (Article 39) and authorize a variety of enforcement measures, including sanctions (Article 41), blockades (Article 42), and the use of force (Articles 43–7). The Charter even requires states to make military forces available to the Security Council, although this has never happened (Sarooshi 1999). It prohibits the General Assembly from acting on any issue the Council is considering. The Charter thus gives the Council the power to determine threats to international security and direct all states to engage in legally binding enforcement measures. Hierarchy exists because the political decisions made by the veto powers legally bind others.

Procedural collective security works when the veto powers agree on both what constitutes a security threat and what to do about it. If the veto powers have different understandings of how to implement collective security, then the arrangement can break down. Much of post-cold war world politics is captured by the disputes between advocates of these various forms of collective security. These disputes are really about the relative levels of hierarchy in these three forms of collective security. The Charter establishes procedural collective security with medium levels of hierarchy privileging the five veto powers. Many developing countries argue that the Charter establishes too much hierarchy and want to reform the Security Council to augment the power of other states. Others, however, argue that the Charter establishes too little hierarchy by creating a legal equality between militarily and politically unequal powers. They argue that rules of global security should reflect the military dominance of the United States.

These fundamental differences manifest themselves in many ways. One dispute revolves around how to determine the rules of the community. In pure collective security arrangements, all states would participate in some type of consensual rule-making process. Efforts to elevate the importance of the General Assembly are consistent with pure collective security. In procedural collective security, the great powers would determine the rules through Security Council resolutions. In hegemonic collective security, though, other factors (regional norms or the interests of the hegemon) can sometimes determine enforceable rules.

Another dispute is about the substance of the rules to be enforced. Which rule violations warrant Security Council action? Should the Council enforce only traditional rules regarding state sovereignty? Or should it also enforce rules like non-proliferation, anti-terrorism, and human rights? This dispute does not necessarily distinguish the collective security arrangements: pure and procedural collective security rules do not necessarily enforce only state sovereignty, and hegemonic collective security rules do not necessarily enforce a broader set of rules. However, in practice this is often the case. The pure collective security emphasis on widespread participation in formulating the rules and the procedural collective security emphasis on Council authorization tends to prevent the proliferation of rules.

A third dispute is the extent to which it is appropriate to punish rule-violators. Should the Security Council merely pass a resolution condemning the violation? Should it impose trade sanctions? Should it authorize the use of force? Once again, this dispute in practice distinguishes the collective security arrangements. Advocates of the less hierarchical pure and procedural collective security arrangements are often reluctant to establish harsh punishments that could set precedents for future action against other states, whereas advocates of the more hierarchical hegemonic collective security often are more willing to establish harsh punishments.

A fourth dispute revolves around who can retaliate. Must it be an entity authorized by the Security Council, or can another entity enforce the rules without explicit Council authorization? Pure and procedural collective security rules emphasize the necessity of explicit Council authorization. Security Council resolutions' authorizing force should be interpreted narrowly to prevent states from formulating objectives that exceed the Council's clear intentions. States invoking hegemonic collective security emphasize the need for the use of force, or at least the threat of the use of force, to ensure compliance with Council resolutions. And the militarily most powerful state can most credibly use or threaten to use such force.

A final dispute is about how often to authorize the use of force to ensure compliance. Pure and procedural collective security rules state that diplomatic solutions are always preferable. The use of force should be a last resort, used only with explicit authorization from the Security Council. Hegemonic collective security rules state that the use of force is necessary whenever a violation of a Security Council resolution threatens international peace and security. Together these disputes illustrate the complexities of collective security. Without agreement on what the rules are, when to enforce them, how to enforce them, and who can enforce them, collective security arrangements are difficult to maintain.

Critiques of collective security

The many critiques of collective security differ widely. For realists, collective security is not in the interests of powerful states. For radicals, collective security is a tool of powerful states to impose their interests on everyone else. For realists the Security Council is usually irrelevant; for radicals the Council is a central institution perpetuating Western imperialism. The reason for these differences is that each one critiques a different version of collective security. When realists critique collective security, they go after pure collective security. When radicals critique collective security, they go after procedural and/or hegemonic collective security.

Realists criticize the likelihood and desirability of collective security in an anarchical world of sovereign nation states (Mearsheimer 1994/5; Betts 1992; Miller, L. H. 1999). First, they argue that collective security requires states to equate national security with international security. States must believe that an attack on anyone is an attack on all. Realists argue that states would often harm their own national security if they acted on such beliefs. Why would great powers want to get involved in local wars in areas of no strategic interest? Doing so would not only reduce their ability to protect their real national interests, but it would also harm global stability by transforming minor wars into global conflicts.

Second, realists argue that collective security requires states to give up their sovereign right to determine when to use force. Characterizing collective security as an automatic legal obligation, realists argue that states would not be able to decide when the use of force is in their interests and when it is not. Collective security in anarchical systems is thus paradoxical: a system established to protect the sovereignty of all states requires a degree of centralization that violates state sovereignty. Collective security transforms world politics so that states are no longer sovereign entities but subjects to a higher law.

Third, realists argue that collective security requires states to treat all rule-violators alike. States must be willing to punish friends as well as enemies, powerful countries as well as weak ones. Realists argue that this is very unlikely. Will states really condemn a friend that pursues aggressive policies toward another? Or agree to enforce an embargo and end commerce with a huge trading partner? Or send troops to punish a regional power? Economic sanctions have little effect without near-universal participation. And the use of force is only effective if a certain threshold of militarily powerful states is willing to contribute troops. Realists argue that politics will override law and inevitably lead to no, or at least selective, enforcement.

Fourth, realists argue that collective security requires states to denounce all uses of force to alter the status quo. Only force authorized by the collective security organization and force used in self-defense are legitimate. States must believe that all other uses of force are an illegitimate form of aggression. Realists argue that rarely will most states believe that the status quo is worth preserving. States use force to engage in "regime change." States encourage civil wars, decolonization, national independence movements, and terrorism to destabilize others. States use force to achieve a regional or global hegemonic status. Realists argue that using force to alter the status quo is common and cannot be defined as illegal and abolished.

Fifth, realists argue that collective security assumes that states will be able to distinguish between aggressors and victims. It presumes that in every conflict there are good guys and bad guys. States will know whom to punish and whom to protect. Realists argue that the world is more complicated than that. In any given conflict states will disagree over these issues. In the Israeli–Palestinian conflict, which one is the aggressor and which one is the victim? Realists argue that states will end up making political rather than legal judgments in most circumstances.

Finally, realists argue that advocates of collective security believe that collective security causes peace, when it is really peace that causes collective security. When great powers have common interests, realists admit that some form of collective security is possible. But when those conditions change and great powers again see each other as a threat, collective security will not make war less likely. It might also make war more likely because alternative security mechanisms (alliances) have not developed. Realists argue that rivalry is the normal arrangement in world politics; conflict among the great powers will inevitably thwart collective security.

Realists cite both the failure of the League of Nations after World War I and the cold war overwhelming the UN after World War II as evidence for their claims. After World War I the winning allies attempted to construct a collective security system with the League of Nations. Woodrow Wilson (1982) said that it would be "not a balance of power, but a community of power; not organized rivalries, but an organized common peace." The League failed, however, because the great powers did not have common interests. It could not even gain universal membership: unsatisfied, revisionist powers (Japan, Germany, and Italy) left the League, and the isolationist United States never joined it.

The world again tried to build a collective security arrangement after World War II with the UN. The winners – the United States, the Soviet Union, the United Kingdom, China and France – gave themselves a permanent seat and veto power in the Security Council. However, the post-war rivalry between the United States and the Soviet Union paralyzed the Security Council. Once again, the great powers did not have enough common interests to pursue collective security. Despite the occurrence of over eighty wars from 1945 to 1989, the Council recognized a threat to international peace and security only seven times, labeled the acts of only two states to be aggression (South Africa and Israel), resorted to military force once (Korea) and sanctions twice (South Africa and Rhodesia) (Koskenniemi 1998).

There are two major problems with these powerful critiques. First, they target pure collective security, an arrangement not established by the UN Charter. Realists consistently assert that collective security requires states to accept an automatic obligation to use force against all aggressors (Kupchan 1994; Kupchan and Kupchan 1995; Weiss 1993). The realist critiques do not target the concert-like behavior of the Security Council. Second, realist critiques presume a world of sovereign states concerned that other states will invade and violate their territorial integrity. This does not adequately characterize the post-cold war world. Civil wars and transnational security threats have replaced interstate war as the greatest threats to international security. Realists underestimate the reality of security interdependence.

The end of the cold war altered the meaning of security (Newman 2001, Buzan 1997). Security has traditionally referred to states and the military defense of territory against external threats. But the near disappearance of interstate war and the growing importance of Western liberal norms in the post-cold war world have led to the norm of "human security." Security is now more likely to refer to individuals. Security requires protecting individuals from disease, hunger, environmental degradation, crime, domestic violence, torture, unfair imprisonment, economic instability, or discrimination. International security requires states with domestic legitimacy, the rule of law and human rights.

The Security Council has embraced much of the human security agenda (United Nations 2004). It has said that states failing to maintain domestic order (Somalia, Cambodia, Georgia), disregarding democratic elections (Liberia, Haiti, Sierra Leone), and violating minority rights (Iraqi Kurds, Albanians in Kosovo, East Timorese in Indonesia) justify Council action. It has cited the existence of refugees and related humanitarian crises as a threat to international security in many cases, including Yugoslavia, Somalia, Haiti, Liberia, and Sierra Leone. It has passed resolutions on issues such as children and armed conflict, the humanitarian components of peacekeeping, and the role of gender in peacekeeping. Many want the Council to go further and cite AIDS and global warming as international security threats (Elbe 2006).

The shift to human security alters the meaning of sovereignty. Sovereignty is not a fixed, absolute principle. It is a social rule, and it is being (re)constructed to include a responsibility to protect human security. States cannot do whatever they want because they are "sovereign." States are increasingly binding themselves to rules that protect individuals. And in our world of security interdependence, it is in their interest to do so. Consider the realist criticism that collective security transforms local wars of no strategic interest into systemic wars by involving the great powers. However, "failed states" threaten international security by creating terrorist havens, refugee flows, and humanitarian disasters. Given security interdependence, there are no wars of low strategic interest. Some form of collective security is necessary.

While the realist critique is that collective security is not in the interests of the great powers, the radical critique is that collective security is a tool of the great powers to impose their interests on the rest of the world. While realists see the Security Council as an often insignificant institution, radicals see it as a powerful tool of Western imperialism. Radicals argue that the United States controls the UN: few peacekeeping operations can occur, and few UN agencies are effective, without American financial support. Radical critiques all emphasize that the hierarchy in the Charter system – the Council can take no collective action against the veto powers and states protected by the veto powers – makes it an illegitimate security arrangement. Why should states continue to consent to an arrangement privileging the five winners of World War II?

One radical criticism is that the Security Council only protects the narrow interests of the permanent members (Mazrui 1996). For example, the Council has authorized veto powers to use force in their own spheres of influence, including the United States in Haiti, Russia in Georgia, and France in Rwanda. A related criticism is that the Council enables the veto powers to thwart collective punishment for their own rules violations. For example, the United States vetoed resolutions regarding its invasions of Panama and Grenada and regime change policies toward Libya and Nicaragua; the Soviet Union vetoed resolutions regarding its interventions in Hungary, Czechoslovakia and Afghanistan; and Britain and France vetoed resolutions condemning their role in the Suez Crisis.

The permanent members have also used their veto power to protect allies from Council enforcement measures. The Soviet Union vetoed resolutions condemning Vietnam for its invasion of Cambodia; Britain vetoed resolutions condemning apartheid policies in Rhodesia. The most egregious examples are the United States protecting Israel and South Africa; the United States has vetoed forty resolutions targeting Israel, including sixteen since the cold war, and nine resolutions targeting South African apartheid policies. For radicals this is a biased security arrangement. Many empirical studies support radical criticisms (Mullenbach 2005). The Security Council is less likely to act when the target is a major power or an ally of a major power and more likely when a target has no alliance with a major power. Also, the Security Council is more likely to act when a major power has already intervened in the conflict.

Another radical criticism is that the UN perpetuates the Western project to export liberal internationalism into the developing world. Western hegemony is based on ideas: democratic governance, rule of law, private property, capitalism, human rights, and limited government (Puchala 2005). It advocates international law, free trade, and collective security. The role of the UN is to validate the liberal world order. The role of the Security Council is to punish (illiberal) actions of "rogue states" that threaten the (liberal) order. Radicals are not convinced that this Western project is more benign than previous Western projects. Like colonialism, liberal internationalism makes claims to universality, is insensitive to cultural differences, and rejects economic redistribution to minimize inequality.

While realists critique the legal notion of collective security and presume that politics will overwhelm it, radicals critique the political aspects of collective security and presume there are no legal limits on the Security Council. It is purely an instrument of power politics to further the interests of the veto powers. But this characterization exaggerates the power of the Security Council within the UN. The Council cannot do whatever it wants; it must adhere to the purposes and principles of the UN, including human rights, the sovereign equality of states and nonintervention into domestic affairs (de Wet 2004, Angelet 2001). For example, resolutions authorizing genocide or changing the borders of a state would be illegal. The Council is also bound by fundamental principles of international law, such as proportionality and good faith.

But how many limits are on the Security Council? Does humanitarian international law limit the ability of the Council to enforce harsh economic sanctions (Al-Anbari 2001)? Can the Council require states to act in ways that contradict their treaty obligations? Is it implicitly subject to judicial review by the International Court of Justice (Dugard 2001)? States have asked the Court to review three

Council actions: (1) whether requiring Libya to extradite the Lockerbie suspects precluded Libya's right to try its own nationals under the Montreal Convention; (2) whether an arms embargo impaired Bosnia's right of self-defense against a genocidal aggressor; and (3) whether the Council could establish the ad hoc war crimes tribunal for Yugoslavia. In the third case, the Court claimed the competence to rule on the legality of a Council act, ruling that the Council did lawfully establish the tribunal.

But more important than legal challenges, the Council is politically accountable to the members of the UN. States can withhold their consent to the Security Council as the appropriate guarantor of international peace and security if it pursues the interests of the veto powers at the expense of others. For example, the Organization of African Unity (OAU) refused to implement sanctions against Libya in 1998. The OAU concluded that the United States and the United Kingdom were abusing their authority by maintaining sanctions against Libya even after it had complied with the Council and extradited alleged terror suspects (see Chapter 4). Norms such as good faith are necessary to foster compliance, even for hierarchical institutions like the Security Council.

The veto powers and collective security

The Security Council acts when the veto powers can protect common interests through multilateral collaboration. If conflicting interests overtake the veto powers – as during the cold war – then rivalry rules exist and the Council will be unable to function. The difference in Security Council action during the cold war and since the cold war is substantial. During the cold war, the Council passed fifteen resolutions per year; since 1989 the Council has passed sixty-four resolutions per year. During the cold war, the permanent members vetoed six resolutions per year; since 1989 there has been less than one per year. From 1990 to 1994 the veto powers voted together on 282 out of 310 resolutions (Koskenniemi 1998). The Council has also passed over 90 percent of all resolutions invoking Chapter VII enforcement powers since the end of the cold war (Wallensteen and Johansson 2004).

Whether collective security or rivalry rules dominate world politics thus depends on the political relationship between the great powers. The shift away from rivalry rules and toward collective security rules began with the rise of Gorbachev in the Soviet Union. Gorbachev's "new thinking" in Soviet foreign policy challenged and ultimately ended the cold war rivalry rules (Frederking 2000). Gorbachev wrote an important *Pravda* article on 17 September 1987 advocating "wider use of . . . the institution of UN military observers and UN peacekeeping forces in disengaging the troops of warring sides, observing cease-fires and armistice agreements" (Gorbachev 1987).

The United States at the time was ambivalent about the UN (Malone 2003). Developing nations dominated many UN agencies and advocated radical economic redistribution plans. They consistently outvoted American positions in the General Assembly. They used the UN to identify South Africa and Israel – two cold war allies – as pariah states. The International Court of Justice ruled against the United States in a case brought to it by Nicaragua. There were persistent fears that a strengthened UN would threaten the sovereignty of the United States. The Security Council had not authorized a peacekeeping mission in over ten years.

Yet with the end of the cold war, the superpowers agreed to use the UN as a credible third party mediator to help resolve regional conflicts. The Security Council authorized twelve peacekeeping missions during the term of George H.W. Bush, a former UN ambassador. In 1991 Bush and Gorbachev said: "We support fully the United Nations and the enhancement of its role promoting peace, security, and justice. We affirm our commitment to the principles and purposes of the United Nations as enshrined in the Charter and condemn all violations of its principles" (in Carey 2001: 73). The veto powers illustrated their new-found collaboration by quickly responding to the Iraqi invasion of Kuwait in 1990. Before a joint session of Congress on 11 September 1990 Bush famously proclaimed:

> Out of these troubled times . . . a new world order can emerge: a new era – freer from the threat of terror, stronger in the pursuit of justice, and more se- cure in the quest for peace . . .Today that new world is struggling to be born. A world quite different from the one we've known. A world where the rule of law supplants the rule of the jungle. A world in which nations recognize the shared responsibility for freedom and justice. A world where the strong respects the rights of the weak.
>
> (Bush and Scrowcroft 1998: 370)

The veto powers cemented their new relationship with the first ever Security Council summit meeting on 31 January 1992. They charged the Secretary General to prepare recommendations to strengthen the capacity of the United Nations. Boutros Boutros-Ghali responded with the path-breaking *An Agenda for Peace*, discussed more thoroughly in the next chapter.

The euphoria about the possibilities of collective security demonstrated by the Gulf War, however, quickly diminished given the struggles in Somalia, Bosnia and Rwanda. The demise of the cold war rivalry rules did not mean that collective security rules would easily arise. It was not enough that the veto powers recog- nized their common interests in collaborating through the Security Council. They had to agree on which rules to enforce. They had to agree on which enforcement measures to use in certain circumstances. Ultimately, they had to agree on the ap- propriate level of hierarchy in world politics. Much of the post-cold war conflict among the veto powers in the Security Council revolved around different visions of how to implement collective security rules.

France, China, Russia, and procedural collective security

France, China, and Russia advocate procedural collective security. They minimize the importance of United States military dominance and argue that today's world is characterized by multipolarity and security interdependence. They believe that only multilateral efforts can solve contemporary security threats. They insist on the centrality of the Security Council in resolving international disputes. When they criticize United States unilateralism, they believe that they are defending the principles of the UN. They fear that if the UN collective security system breaks down and rivalry ensues, global security would be less stable. They advocate procedural collective security as the best way to achieve international peace and security. Of course, maintaining the centrality of the Security Council also preserves their great power status.

For Russia and China, more than France, advocating procedural collective security enables them to thwart the development of certain rules. Both Russia and China want to protect the traditional notion of sovereignty and prevent the institutionalization of Western human rights norms. Both want to protect their commercial ties to regimes considered "rogue states" by the West. Both want to resist American dominance in what they consider their own spheres of influence without directly challenging the United States.

Russia and China have particular identities, interests, and relations with the United States that influence their advocacy of procedural collective security. Russian foreign policy since the cold war has competing goals of integrating with the West, establishing its own regional sphere of influence, and checking United States dominance (Zlobin 2004). Gorbachev and Yeltsin tended to democratize, observe international norms, and economically integrate with the West. They argued that many Russian interests coincided with Western interests, including securing Russian WMD, avoiding fundamentalist Islamic regimes in Eurasia, preventing secessionist movements, and developing energy resources in the Caspian Sea.

An anti-Western backlash, however, emerged in Russia throughout the 1990s (Shearman 2001; Williams and Neumann 2000). Economic liberalization policies ended up enriching corrupt oligarchs. NATO expansion into former Warsaw Pact countries threatened Russian security interests and harmed its status and prestige. NATO's use of force in Kosovo was the turning point. Most Russians concluded that it illustrated American imperial ambitions; nationalist and communist hardliners argued that the real reason for the campaign was that Yugoslavia was the only East European country not interested in joining NATO (Tsygankov 2001). Russia believed that American marginalization of international institutions and the presence of American military bases in its periphery threatened its security.

Russia has been willing to use its position on the Security Council to support its interests in what is considers its sphere of influence. It has gained Council authorization to send troops to Moldova, Georgia, and Tajikistan since the end of the cold war. It has used its Council status to protect its interests in the war between Armenia and Azerbaijan. And in 1993 it vetoed a United States proposal to lift the arms embargo on Bosnia. Putin's foreign policy has also reemphasized the Russian sphere of influence: reestablishing economic ties, dealing with secessionist movements, and ensuring the rights of Russian minorities in the former

Soviet states. Putin is less worried about alienating the West, rebuffing criticisms about his rollback of democratic reforms, the war with Chechen separatists, and commercial ties to Iran's nuclear industry.

Like Russia, China has balanced its preference for a multipolar world respecting traditional norms of sovereignty and noninterference with its strategic imperative to pursue economic growth and avoid confrontational relations with the United States (Zhao 2004). China has long based its foreign policy on the "five principles of peaceful coexistence": mutual respect for territorial integrity and sovereignty, mutual nonaggression, noninterference in each other's internal affairs, equality and mutual benefit, and peaceful coexistence. These principles are similar to the traditional notion of sovereignty and are not always conducive to collective security. But for China, echoing the radical critique of collective security, they are necessary to reduce Western influence in the developing world.

China's balancing act includes an identity crisis. It is losing its cold war identity as the leader of the anti-Western developing world. But should it aspire to Asian hegemonic status and (eventually) challenge the Western system? Or should it join the Western club and embrace the great power responsibility of permanent membership on the Security Council (Yong 2001)? Will China be a satisfied power or a revisionist power (Kane 2001; Johnston 2003)? It is not yet clear which path China will take. These tensions are illustrated by Chinese statements citing the two main threats to post-cold war global security: United States unilateralism and transnational issues like terrorism and weapons proliferation. The former requires deterring the United States, and the latter requires working with the United States.

In many ways China has increasingly accepted international norms since the cold war (Medeiros 2003; Lynch 2002). It established diplomatic relations with nearly thirty countries. It increased its membership in multilateral organizations and joined trade and security agreements, including the World Trade Organization. It settled border conflicts with six countries and agreed to peaceful resolutions under international law for all ongoing disputes. It greatly improved relations with Russia and India. It ratified several weapons treaties, provided aid after the 1997 financial crisis, and cooperated with the United States regarding the North Korean nuclear crisis. It voted with the other permanent Council members 91 percent of the time during the 1990s, abstaining on 28 out of the 174 resolutions authorizing enforcement measures (Morphet 2000).

China, however, remains suspicious of the West. Western countries have criticized its missile sales to Pakistan, Syria, and Iran. United States nuclear planning always includes China as a possible nuclear target. China does not believe that the American bombing of its embassy during the NATO bombings in Yugoslavia in 1998 was an accident. It is ambivalent about the war on terrorism, which has increased the number of American troops in Asia. It is critical of American plans for missile defense. It views Western arguments about democracy and human rights as a way to establish it as a pariah state to contain rather than a partner to welcome into the club (Yong 2001).

But the most important reason for Chinese suspicion is Taiwan. China considers the United States' political and military support for Taiwan to be interference in Chinese internal affairs. It blames the American security guarantees for encouraging the Taiwanese independence movement. What China considers a sovereign right to defend its own territorial integrity, the West considers an undemocratic violation of human rights. China considers Taiwan its most important strategic interest, and it has shown a willingness to use its position on the Security Council to protect those interests. It has vetoed only two Council resolutions, and both targeted countries that were friendly with Taiwan. The first would have sent military observers to Guatemala, and the other ended a peacekeeping mission in Macedonia.

France's advocacy of procedural collective security arises from a very different set of identities, interests, and relations with the United States. France has a long tradition of advocating international law, international institutions, and the authority of the Security Council. Similar to the United States, it sees itself as a country with a civilizing global mission to support human rights and universal moral values. It has been an ally of the United States since World War II. It agrees with the United States that contemporary security threats include weapons proliferation, terrorism, and human rights violations. France and the United States have a strong set of common identities and interests.

France, however, has long resisted American hierarchy. During the cold war France built its own nuclear capability so it would not have to rely on the United States. It did not participate in NATO military structures so it would not have to take orders from the United States. France continues to criticize the centrality of NATO in European security, which institutionalizes American dominance. France advocates an autonomous European military capability and foreign policy through the European Union to reduce American influence in Europe (Bowen 2005).

French criticism of United States unilateralism continued in the post-cold war world. After the United States bombed Iraq in 1998, French Foreign Minister Hubert Vedrine called it a "hyperpower." These criticisms increased dramatically when the United States adopted the doctrine of preemption after 9/11. French President Jacques Chirac argued on 29 August 2002: "[T]he world must not just organize itself around the response to the challenge made on 9/11, for we would only be playing into the hands of those whom we are fighting." Preemption is "contrary to France's view of collective security, based on cooperation between states, respect for the law and the authority of the Security Council" (Chirac 2002).

France also considers itself to have a sphere of influence in French-speaking African countries. France is Africa's largest trading partner, its largest foreign aid donor, and its largest arms merchant. French material interests in Africa have little to do with collective security. They are about global status, access to resources, and securing profits from monopolistic economic arrangements. France has supported many undemocratic African regimes that protect its interests. The democratization movement pushed by the United States often threatens French influence in the region. During the 1990s, French support for countries experimenting with democracy decreased, and French aid to dictatorships increased (Renou 2002).

An important exception to the French advocacy of procedural collective secu-rity was its support for the NATO use of force in Kosovo. Along with its NATO allies, France agreed that they should act for humanitarian reasons even without Security Council authorization. France essentially argued that it was "the right thing to do." In this case morality trumped law and human rights trumped proce-dural collective security. However, the French argued that the NATO operation in Kosovo was a unique case. It was an exception and not a precedent invoking hegemonic collective security rules.

The United Kingdom, the United States, and hegemonic collective security

The United Kingdom also performs a delicate balancing act to reconcile conflict-ing identities and interests. Is it primarily a strategic partner of the often unilateral United States? Or is it primarily a European power that embraces multilateralism? The British agree with France, Russia and China that security interdependence dominates contemporary world politics. They recognize that many issues are be-yond the control of national governments acting alone and multilateral collabora-tion in international organizations is necessary to achieve security. And like the other veto powers, it has an interest in a Security Council-centered system be-cause its veto would enable it to, in the words of Foreign Minister Douglas Hurd, "punch above its weight."

Tony Blair and the ruling Labour Party have liberal internationalist beliefs that support multilateralism (Vickers 2003). They endorse collective security as a more stable approach to world order than a balance of power. They argue that states share a common interest in building international institutions. They advo-cate an "international community" approach in which states forgo a narrow notion of national security and work for the common good. They believe that foreign policy should be based on democratic principles and universal moral norms. They embrace humanitarian interventionism and the "responsibility to protect." They argue that all have strategic interests in dealing with failed states.

> By necessity we have to cooperate with each other across nations. Many of our domestic problems are caused on the other side of the world. . ..These problems can only be addressed by international cooperation. We are all in-ternationalists now, whether we like it or not.
>
> (Blair 1999)

But the United Kingdom also considers itself to have a "special relationship" with the United States, and this often conflicts with its multilateral tendencies (Williams 2002). While Blair argues that the United Kingdom can use its influ-ence to encourage the United States to embrace multilateralism, critics argue that the only such example is persuading the Bush administration to seek Council authorization prior to the invasion of Iraq (Wallace 2005,;Williams 2004). British lobbying has made little progress in changing American positions in other areas, including terrorism, climate change, landmines, the International Criminal Court, Guantanamo Bay, missile defense, European security and defense, the Middle East peace process, or African security issues.

Despite these policy differences and a general commitment to multilateralism, the United Kingdom routinely invokes hegemonic collective security by supporting American uses of force without Security Council authorization. Blair has argued that the Security Council does not have a monopoly of authority: in certain circumstances a deadlock on the Council should not prevent states or other international organizations from intervening to maintain international peace and security. British forces have participated in seven enforcement operations, and only three were explicitly authorized by the Council: East Timor (1999), Sierra Leone (2000), and Congo (2003). The other four – Iraq (1998), Kosovo (1999), Afghanistan (2001), and Iraq (2003) – did not have prior Council authorization, invoking hegemonic collective security.

The United States has consistently advocated hegemonic collective security throughout the post-cold war period. While it often prefers to work with the Security Council, it also asserts the right to use force without Council authorization to maintain international security. The United States thus has an ambivalent relationship with the UN. It has historically supported the organization because it legitimizes the status quo and thus the American position in world politics. The UN provides an institutional setting for multilateral cooperation among the great powers and encourages states to accept norms that are consistent with American values. However, the American conception of global order has never included giving international organizations much autonomy (Ruggie 1994). The United States supports the UN as long as it serves its interests.

American beliefs about its "exceptionalism" undermine its multilateralism (Mingst 2003). The United States assumes that its values are universal and its policies are therefore moral. It is willing to act alone regardless of the criticism of others. It elevates domestic concerns over its international obligations to such an extent that acting through international organizations is an option to be rejected if its immediate security interests dictate another path (Luck 2003). It often asserts that certain global rules (Geneva Convention rules on detainees, international inspections regarding chemical weapons, customary international law of self-defense, the necessity of Council authorization for enforcement measures, etc.) do not apply to its own actions. Hierarchy results when the United States asserts that others still need to follow those rules. Only the United States is exceptional and can claim exceptions to the rules.

The three post-cold war presidents exhibited various levels of support for the UN. G.H.W. Bush worked together with Gorbachev to revive the Security Council. He orchestrated a tremendous diplomatic coalition in favor of the 1991 Gulf War and afterward famously talked about a "new world order." In a September 1992 address to the General Assembly, he encouraged nations to train military units for possible peacekeeping duty and to make them available on short notice. He pledged American logistical, military, and intelligence support for UN peacekeeping missions. But he did not increase the use of American forces in peacekeeping missions, he could not get Congress to pay back dues to the UN, and he offered no solutions to the perpetual funding problems for peacekeeping missions.

The Clinton administration was generally more supportive of UN collective security efforts than either Bush administration. Clinton expressed initial support for UN peacekeeping, even advocating a UN rapid deployment force. He technically, although not in practice, placed American troops under the authority of the Secretary General during the Somalia mission. He tried to get Congress to pay its UN arrears. He signed multilateral treaties (International Criminal Court, Kyoto Protocol, etc.) that his successor later rejected. His UN ambassador and Secretary of State Madeline Albright embraced the realities of security interdependence:

> Only collective security can ultimately manage . . . a world where weapons of mass destruction proliferate and ethnic and regional conflicts trigger massive refugee flows, enormous economic dislocations, unacceptable human rights atrocities, environmental catastrophes, and the senseless killing and maiming of millions of civilians.
>
> (Albright 1999)

The difficulties in Somalia and Bosnia, however, dampened American enthusiasm for UN enforcement measures. And when the Republican Party took over Congress after the 1994 mid-term elections, it reduced United States support of peacekeeping missions, prohibited American forces from serving under UN command and violated the UN Charter by unilaterally reducing the United States share of peacekeeping assessments. The United States held the UN hostage by refusing to pay its back dues until the UN made a series of reforms in 1997. The Clinton administration also denied a second term to Boutros Boutros-Ghali as Secretary General.

The George W. Bush administration has taken United States ambivalence toward the United Nations to new levels. Neoconservative elements of the Bush administration have openly advocated empire, wanting to loosen multilateral commitments and establish American primacy. The "Bush Doctrine" asserts an understanding of self-defense that goes beyond previously understood notions. Bush has pursued harsh policies of isolation, sanctions and regime change rather than engagement toward rogue states such as Iran, Iraq, and North Korea. And he has continued the practice of unilaterally using force without Council authorization in Afghanistan and Iraq, spectacularly so in the latter case.

The list of treaties the United States has rejected and/or refused to ratify is quite long, including human rights treaties, weapons treaties, and many others (including the Rome Statute of the International Criminal Court, the Law of the Sea Treaty and the Kyoto Protocol to the Convention on Climate Change). Its domestic legislation implementing the Chemical Weapons Convention weakened the inspections provisions, creating for itself a separate and less rigorous verification regime. It refused to abide by Geneva Conventions regarding the treatment of its prisoners of war in Guantanamo Bay. And it has resisted the development of global rules regarding biological weapons, prison inspections, and small arms.

The most prominent examples of American advocacy of hegemonic collective security, of course, are unilateral uses of force without Security Council authorization. The United States has used force without Council authorization seven times in the post-cold war world (see Chapter 5). When the United States uses force, it argues that it must do so to uphold global security because it is the only country with the capability to do so. The United States is, in the words of Bill Clinton, the "indispensable nation." The United States does not see itself as a lawless renegade but the ultimate enforcer of international law and global security. The United States has used force against Iraq six times in the post-cold war world, and each time it invoked Security Council resolutions and the enforcement of international law to justify that force.

The United States thus also has conflicting identities and interests regarding the rules of global security. A collective security arrangement is in American interests: it solves collective action problems, it ties other states into a relatively stable order, and it is more efficient than a global order requiring the constant exercise of power. It coordinates action regarding security issues such as weapons proliferation and terrorism, and it helps institutionalize democracy, free markets, and human rights. Despite these interests, however, the United States is reluctant to enmesh itself in these institutions (Ikenberry 2003). The United States wants others to follow the rules but also to agree that it does not always have to follow those same rules because America has special obligations as the ultimate guarantor of global security. The risk is that other states will no longer consent to this arrangement unless the rules also bind the United States as well.

Conclusions

The Security Council matters. States want to be on the Council. They want to participate in Council deliberations. They recognize that Council action is often necessary to resolve a global security issue. They consider putting an issue on the Council's agenda to be a serious step. They argue vociferously over the wording of Council resolutions. But there are two necessary conditions for the Council to successfully perform its functions: (1) the five veto powers must agree how to implement collective security rules; and (2) the other countries must interpret those rules to be legitimate and contribute to the enforcement of those rules. The realist critique is that the first condition is unlikely to occur. The radical critique is that the second condition is unlikely to occur.

The following chapters will illustrate the difficulties of realizing these two necessary conditions and successfully constructing collective security. While the Security Council has acted in path-breaking ways since the cold war, veto powers have often disagreed about the nature of collective security. The dominant pattern over the most critical issues in the post-cold war world is Russia, China, and France advocating procedural collective security and the United States and the United Kingdom advocating hegemonic collective security. Russia, China, and France want the United States to recognize the necessity of collaboration in a security interdependent world. The United States wants the others to recognize the reality of its military dominance and accept its unique role and responsibility to provide global security. Each believes that their preferred rules are the most appropriate path to global security.

Achieving the second set of conditions – legitimacy, multilateral enforcement and compliance – is also difficult in many situations. Unilateral acts by the United States when the veto powers disagree often undermines the legitimacy of the Council. Inaction during genocides in Bosnia, Rwanda, and Sudan harms the Council. States sometimes continue to prioritize domestic interests over Council resolutions and fail to enforce economic sanctions or contribute to peacekeeping missions. Developing countries complain that the Council is biased in its agenda setting and enforcement measures. Still, with all these limitations, the Security Council remains the primary institution dealing with global security. States that fail to abide by its procedures pay a price in terms of burden sharing and standing within the international community. The developing world is split about whether the Security Council is a legitimate institution that merits their support or an illegitimate tool of the veto powers to preserve their own narrow interests.

These interpretive disputes over global security rules are at the heart of world politics since the cold war. They constitute conflicts over issues like Kosovo and Iraq. But they also invoke a shared commitment to collective security. Few want rivalry, and fewer want empire. Such arrangements would be less likely to counter transnational security threats like weapons proliferation and terrorism. Every veto power has a common interest in maintaining international security through a multilateral, rule-based order, and the other countries have a common interest in maintaining the veto powers' commitment to a multilateral, rule-based order. But the stability of the post-cold war collective security arrangement is constantly threatened because the veto powers do not always agree on how to implement the rules and many countries around the world do not always interpret that implementation to be legitimate.

3   Peacekeeping

Peacekeeping is the use of troops to ensure the implementation of peace agreements. It is not, however, a collective security enforcement tool. Peacekeeping missions operate on the principles of consent, neutrality, and self-defense. Enforcing collective security rules does not require consent, it identifies violators of global rules, and it punishes those violators. The Council must decide whether to adopt a neutral peacekeeping approach or a coercive collective security approach for every crisis on its agenda. The Council generally authorizes peacekeeping missions when the relevant parties agree that a third party will help resolve their conflict. The more difficult decision is whether to escalate peacekeeping missions into collective security operations when local parties renege on their commitment to implement peace agreements.

This chapter analyzes the now-routine Security Council practice of peacekeeping: it has authorized 46 missions since the end of the cold war. The first section discusses the evolution of peacekeeping, particularly the proliferation of missions and the development of complex "peace-building" missions. The second section uses examples of peacekeeping missions in Somalia and the Democratic Republic of the Congo to analyze the conditions for successful peacekeeping and the pressures for peacekeeping missions to evolve into coercive collective security operations. The third section uses Liberia as an example to discuss the important post-cold war trend of the Security Council collaborating with regional organizations to implement peacekeeping missions. The final section connects peacekeeping to the security–hierarchy paradox.

The evolution of peacekeeping

Peacekeeping missions have evolved through three different eras: "first generation" peacekeeping during the cold war, "second generation" peacekeeping in the late 1980s and early 1990s, and "third generation" peacekeeping since the late 1990s (Woodhouse and Ramsbotham 2005). First-generation peacekeeping is the classic version in which two states consent to international troops forming a buffer between them as they implement a peace agreement. Peacekeeping troops are neutral between the parties and they use force only in self-defense. This notion of peacekeeping is not in the UN Charter but was institutionalized after the Suez War in 1956. Secretary General Dag Hammarskjold called peacekeeping "Chapter six and a half" missions because they go beyond Chapter VI conflict resolution measures but are not Chapter VII enforcement measures. During the cold war, all peacekeeping missions but one (Congo) followed this model and deployed troops between the standing militaries of consenting states.

The end of the cold war brought about a new era of peacekeeping in the late 1980s and early 1990s. This second generation had three fundamental characteristics: (1) a dramatic increase in the number of peacekeeping missions; (2) a more tenuous reliance on the traditional norms of consent, neutrality, and self-defense; and (3) missions with a multidimensional scope. Each was driven by a fundamental change in world politics brought about by the end of the cold war: (1) many cold war conflicts waned and required third-party mediation to resolve; (2) civil wars and failed states replaced interstate wars as the major global security threats; and (3) "security" increasingly referred to human security as well as national security.

The second era of peacekeeping saw an explosion of missions. The end of the cold war brought about the veto power cooperation necessary to authorize peacekeeping missions precisely when many conflicts were ending (Sanderson 1998). The Security Council authorized twenty missions from 1988 to 1993 – more than the entire cold war period. In 1990 the UN spent about $490 million on peacekeeping and deployed about 15,000 soldiers. By 1993 the UN peacekeeping budget was over $3 billion, with over 75,000 soldiers deployed around the world.

Some of the more significant early peacekeeping missions include the following:

- *Iran–Iraq*. This mission monitored the ceasefire ending the war between Iran and Iraq. Military observers patrolled the 850-mile border to ensure compliance with the ceasefire for three years until Iran and Iraq signed a formal peace treaty in 1991.
- *Afghanistan*. This mission monitored compliance with agreements ending both the Soviet occupation of Afghanistan and fighting between Afghan forces and various mujahadeen groups. It monitored the withdrawal of Soviet troops, assisted in repatriation, and investigated violations of the peace agreements. The mission ended in 1990 after the Soviet troop withdrawal but without a political settlement among the various Afghan factions.
- *Namibia*. This mission monitored compliance with a peace agreement ending a long conflict between South Africa and the Southwest African People's Organization in Namibia. The peace agreement, jointly negotiated with the United States and the Soviet Union, provided for South Africa to withdraw from Namibia and a transitional period of UN administration prior to independence. The mission presided over the abolition of apartheid laws in Namibia and monitored legislative elections on the way to Namibia gaining independence in March 1990.
- *Angola*. This mission monitored both the withdrawal of Cuban troops and

compliance with a peace agreement between Angola and the National Union for the Total Independence of Angola (UNITA). It monitored September 1992 elections and declared them fair, but UNITA contested the elections, abandoned the peace process, and restarted the civil war. The mission later monitored compliance with another peace agreement signed in November 1994. This agreement bogged down when UNITA refused to disarm and join a national unity government. By 1998 the civil war resumed, and the Council withdrew the peacekeeping mission.

- *Mozambique.* This mission monitored compliance with an October 1992 peace agreement ending a 19-year civil war between the government and the Mozambique National Resistance. It was successful despite its broad mandate, including demobilizing militia groups, destroying weapons, monitoring the withdrawal of foreign forces, and assisting refugees. Mozambique held elections in 1994, and the mission ended in January 1995.

- *Nicaragua.* This mission monitored elections at the request of the Sandinista government, the first such request from a sovereign state. The observer mission was part of a broader Central American peace plan calling for an end to all support for guerillas in the region. Its mandate included disarming the contras, supervising the release of political detainees, and providing a secure environment for elections.

- *El Salvador.* This mission monitored compliance with a peace agreement between El Salvador and the Farabundo Marti National Liberation Front. Its mandate slowly expanded to include training a new police force, monitoring the human rights situation, and overseeing March 1994 elections.

- *Cambodia.* This mission monitored compliance with an October 1991 agreement signed by four Cambodian parties and 18 countries to end a 25-year civil war. In the most ambitious mission at the time, the UN sent 16,000 troops to monitor the withdrawal of Vietnamese troops and the cessation of the Khmer Rouge guerilla war. The mission had administrative authority during the transition with a mandate that included de-mining, monitoring human rights violations, maintaining order, conducting elections, disarming the warring parties, assisting refugees, and reconstructing infrastructure. The Khmer Rouge, however, would not take part in the elections. Elections were held in April 1993 without the Khmer Rouge, and the Council then terminated the mission.

As these examples suggest, UN peacekeepers increasingly entered civil wars, which complicated the norm of consent. Sometimes rebel groups viewed peacekeeping troops with suspicion, presuming they were sent to protect the government. Sometimes there were multiple warring parties, making it difficult to gain consent from everyone. As a result, second generation peacekeeping missions rarely operated in classic peacekeeping settings and could not always follow the norms of consent, neutrality, and self-defense. Their mandates often included enforcing rather than monitoring ceasefire agreements, making them more likely to evolve into coercive operations.

The emerging norm of human security also led to increasingly complex peace-keeping missions (Hampson and Malone 2002, Sens 2004). Second-generation peacekeeping routinely maintained internal security, ensured the delivery of humanitarian aid, protected civilian populations, helped repatriate refugees, and monitored human rights abuses. The widening scope of these missions increased the likelihood that peacekeeping troops could not uphold the traditional goals of neutrality and self-defense, particularly if violence erupted again. Missions with a mandate to maintain internal security had to violate the norm of self-defense when the combatants fired on each other. Missions with a mandate to protect human rights had to violate the norm of neutrality when one side started killing civilians. In second generation peacekeeping, providing for human security sometimes trumped these traditional norms.

UN Secretary General Boutros Boutros-Ghali advocated multidimensional peacekeeping in *An Agenda for Peace*. Boutros-Ghali (1992) argued that the UN must emphasize human security because individuals were more threatened by lack of basic human needs, weak economies, disease, environmental degradation, and political instability than by invading armies. States were often not a source of protection but a source of harm. Significantly, Boutros-Ghali argued that UN intervention to protect human security was not interference in domestic affairs. He recognized that contemporary peacekeeping missions could not always follow traditional norms. He also identified "peace building" as a legitimate Council action short of Chapter VII enforcement. He defined peace building as "action to identify and support structures which will tend to strengthen and solidify peace in order to avoid a relapse into conflict."

Second-generation peacekeeping was thus the first attempt to engage in what Boutros-Ghali called "peace building." Peace-building missions are complex humanitarian operations that try to address the root causes of conflict, including poverty, human rights violations, arms sales, and the absence of democracy. Common peace-building tasks are: (1) internal security and police work; (2) disarming and reintegrating combatants; (3) assisting in the return of refugees and displaced persons; (4) democratization, electoral assistance and institution building; (5) reforming the military, police, and judiciary; (6) economic development; (7) promotion of human rights; (8) conflict management and dispute resolution training; (9) de-mining; and (10) continued humanitarian assistance. The vast majority of post-cold war peacekeeping missions had mandates to perform at least half of these ten tasks.

The second era of peacekeeping ended with Somalia, Bosnia, and Rwanda (Paris 1997). The problem remained the tensions between the increased scope of second-generation missions and the traditional norms of first-generation missions. Multidimensional mandates created more opportunities for clashes with the combatants. There were more rules to break: they could thwart the delivery of humanitarian aid, systematically kill civilians or otherwise violate human rights, violate the ceasefire agreement, refuse to disarm, etc. What do peacekeepers do when there is no peace to keep? The options were to adhere to traditional peacekeeping norms and remain "neutral" while the warring parties commit atrocities (as in

Bosnia), escalate to a collective security enforcement mission (as in Somalia), or withdraw (as in Rwanda).

But the difficulties of Somalia (discussed below), Bosnia and Rwanda (discussed in Chapter 7) eroded UN enthusiasm for large-scale peacekeeping missions. The United States scaled back its commitment to peacekeeping missions after Somalia and the Republican midterm election victories in 1994. With neither the bureaucrats nor the hegemon on board, the proliferation of missions ended. From 1994 to 1997, the Council authorized only two new missions – in Tajikistan and Guatemala – and the latter lasted only four months. The number of UN peacekeepers declined from 53,000 in November 1995 to 13,000 at the beginning of 1998. In the same time period the UN peacekeeping budget dropped from $3.3 billion to below $1 billion. The burst of peacekeeping missions initiated by the end of the cold war was over.

But the Council did not give up on peacekeeping altogether. Since the mid-1990s the Council has searched for ways to reconcile traditional peacekeeping norms, the spread of human security and democratization norms, and the often brutal nature of identity-based post-cold war conflicts. The two worst humanitarian disasters in the 1990s – in Rwanda and Angola – occurred after failed attempts to implement peace agreements. In this current period of third-generation peacekeeping the Council is once again "peace building": protecting civilians from violent conflict and pursuing a human security agenda. This third era centers on a slowly building consensus that the UN has a "responsibility to protect." Like the second era, it is again characterized by the increasing scope of the mandates and a transformation of traditional peacekeeping principles. What distinguishes third generation peacekeeping is a renewed willingness to use coercive measures to achieve the mandates.

Kofi Annan led a reexamination of peacekeeping that ushered in this third generation, particularly a shift from "neutrality" to "impartiality" as a primary peacekeeping norm (Donald 2002). Instead of passive "neutrality" Annan advocated an active "impartial" approach in which peacekeepers enforced UN Charter principles in a fair and just way. In May 1998 Annan visited Rwanda and said: "In the face of genocide, there can be no standing aside, no looking away, no neutrality" (United Nations 1998). In January 1999 he told the Council on Foreign Relations in the United States: "Impartiality does not – and must not – mean neutrality in the face of evil. It means strict and unbiased adherence to the principles of the Charter" (United Nations 1999). Peacekeepers would no longer remain neutral between those that abided by the peace agreement and those that did not.

Third-generation peacekeeping began with six missions authorized between 1998 and 2000: Central African Republic, Sierra Leone, Kosovo, East Timor, the Democratic Republic of the Congo, and Eritrea/Ethiopia. After a lull of no missions in 2001–2, the Council authorized a second wave of six missions from 2003 to 2006: Liberia, Ivory Coast, Burundi, Haiti, Sudan and Somalia. All were sizeable missions with complex mandates and significant administrative responsibilities. In some cases – East Timor and Kosovo – the missions even acted as transitional governments with the power to issue laws. Significantly, nine out of these twelve missions included Chapter VII mandates giving peacekeeping troops robust rules of engagement to punish parties who violated the relevant peace agreement. Third-generation peacekeeping is consistently in a gray area between traditional peacekeeping and collective security.

⌠Another characteristic of third-generation peacekeeping is the encouragement of democratization to facilitate conflict resolution and human security⌡ The presumption is that undemocratic institutions cause war and democratic institutions encourage nonviolent conflict resolution. Second generation missions also stressed the importance of democracy, but their mandates rarely went beyond monitoring elections. Third generation missions recognize that democracy goes beyond holding elections, and they also focus on other priorities such as institution building, developing local capacities for governance, and judicial reform. However, the notion that peacekeeping operations can promote democracy is widely criticized. Many studies show that democratization actually increases the risks of civil war, and democracies following military interventions tend to be short-lived (Marten 2004).

Analyses about the overall success of peacekeeping are mixed but generally positive (Doyle and Sambanis 2006; Fortna 2004; Malone and Thakur 2001). The number of armed conflicts around the world is lower than at any time since the early 1970s. The increased number of missions since the cold war is correlated with the decreased number of civil wars and instances of genocide (Dobbins 2005). A UN report concluded that more civil wars were ended through negotiations in the post-cold war world than in the previous two centuries (United Nations 2004). One study of twenty-two missions concluded that three led to a self-sustaining peace, eleven prevented the recurrence of war without successful nation building, and eight failed to prevent a return to large-scale violence (Sens 2004). Another study, however, showed that the presence of peacekeeping troops in conflicts without a negotiated peace agreement does not make such an agreement more likely (Greig and Diehl 2005).

Obstacles to success abound: (1) developing countries sometimes interpret the missions as Western attempts to impose its political, cultural, and economic norms; (2) the missions are logistically difficult because the expanded mandates cut across the jurisdictions of many UN agencies; (3) they operate on the Western but often dubious assumption that elections and economic liberalization promote peace; (4) the states contributing troops often have different police "cultures," leading to a lack of cooperation, corruption, and sexual crimes; (5) the Council often writes resolutions with ambiguous mandates for peacekeepers on the ground; and (6) states are often unwilling to contribute troops in dangerous situations (Yilmaz 2005).

And yet the Security Council continues to authorize peacekeeping missions. Some type of collective action to ameliorate the harmful effects of conflicts around the world is necessary to achieve international peace and security. As of 2006 there were sixteen ongoing missions with over 100,000 personnel around the world. Seven are in Africa, three are in the Middle East, three are in Europe, two are in Asia, and one in the Americas. Their continued effectiveness, however, requires the political cooperation of the veto powers and economic and military resources from the developed countries. The sixteen ongoing missions cost around $5 billion per year – less than one-half of 1 percent of global military spending.

Peacekeeping and collective security

Post-cold war peacekeeping missions can easily turn into collective security operations because the troops often use force against those who break the rules by preventing the distribution of humanitarian aid, refusing to disarm, using intimidation and violence during elections, violating human rights, etc. When peacekeeping troops use force against those who violate the rules, they become combatants in the conflict. They no longer are neutral, and the local parties (if they ever did) no longer consent. In such contexts, peacekeeping missions with an expanded peace building mandate often become collective security arrangements.

Somalia

The mission in Somalia is an excellent example of a second generation peacekeeping mission that evolved into a collective security operation (Fenton 2004; Boulden 2001; Clarke and Herbst 1997). It began as a humanitarian rather than a classic peacekeeping mission. There was no functioning central government to give consent. There was no peace agreement among the warring parties to implement. The Security Council eventually realized that a neutral peacekeeping approach would not effectively achieve the humanitarian purpose of the mission and avert mass starvation. Yet the switch to a more coercive approach in such difficult circumstances proved to be fraught with difficulties and led to a tragic outcome.

Somalia has no history of centralized government. Somalis are nomads and farmers who share a common ethnic, linguistic, and religious background. They are socially organized and politically divided by kinship and clan ties. After independence in 1960 Somalia had a short-lived parliamentary democracy until Mohamed Siad Barre established a dictatorship after a coup in 1969. The Barre government favored certain clans over others, and by the late 1970s disaffected clans formed militias with bases in Ethiopia. They began periodic border raids into Somalia in 1981. A 1988 peace agreement between Ethiopia and Somalia over the disputed Ogaden territory obligated Ethiopia to end its support for the SMN and shut down the rebel bases.

The rebel clans, led by Mohammed Aideed, left Ethiopia and returned to Somalia, joined with other clans marginalized by the Barre government and began a full-fledged civil war. The rebels defeated the Somali army, and the government collapsed. When the rebels closed in on Mogadishu in January 1991, Barre fled the country. Part of the anti-Barre coalition quickly gathered and named Ali Mahdi the interim leader. But Aideed and Mahdi could not agree on the formation of a new government, and by November 1991 war again broke out between forces loyal to Mahdi and Aideed. The clan-based conflict continued with no functioning central government.

The war destroyed the limited infrastructure in the country, collapsed all political and economic institutions, and created a million displaced people. A massive drought was under way, the war destroyed much of the agriculture sector, and famine was looming. The UN issued a warning that 2 million people were at risk of starvation. The Security Council, seeing no clear connection to its responsibilities to maintain international security, reacted slowly. The veto powers were reluctant to intervene without the consent of the local parties. However, given reports of refugees flowing into Kenya, the Council established an arms embargo in January to minimize the escalation of the war (SCR 733).

Mahdi supported UN oversight of a future ceasefire agreement. On 3 February 1992 he asked the Security Council to act. The request illustrated the growing prioritization of human security over traditional peacekeeping and state sovereignty norms:

> (L)et me assure the Council that any measures – even if coercive – to resolve the current crisis in Somalia cannot and will not be interpreted as interference in our internal affairs since their effect will be the saving of human lives and the restoration of human dignity. The situation cries out for the help of the United Nations and particularly the Security Council. The Somali people are bewildered by what they see as the callous indifference of the international community, but their eyes are nevertheless focused on the United Nations. They are pleading with you to stop the bleeding of their country. Please help by acting now.
>
> (United Nations 1992: 3–4)

This request by the Somalis was extremely important in initiating Council action. The United States had been insisting on consent, and China and Russia did not want to establish a precedent encouraging the intervention into the domestic affairs of states. The problem was that Aideed was at best lukewarm about international intervention.

The UN brokered a ceasefire agreement signed by both Mahdi and Aideed on 3 March that called for an "international monitoring mechanism." Given this limited political agreement, the Council established a mission in April 1992 to monitor the tenuous ceasefire and provide humanitarian relief (SCR 746). The resolution cited both the regional and internal humanitarian implications of the war to justify Council involvement. This initial mission followed traditional peacekeeping rules of consent, neutrality, and self-defense.

It soon became apparent that the classic peacekeeping approach would not protect the delivery of humanitarian aid. Aideed increasingly grew suspicious of UN involvement, believing that the UN favored Mahdi. He was also wary of Boutros-Ghali, who, as an Egyptian diplomat, had previously supported the Barre government. He increasingly ordered his militias to loot the humanitarian aid shipments. Boutros-Ghali argued that the mission must be strengthened – armed convoys to escort the aid and disarm Aideed's militias – to carry out its humanitarian goals. Such a mandate would inevitably become a collective security mission whose purpose was to punish Aideed for preventing the delivery of humanitarian aid. The UN would become a combatant, convincing Aideed that his suspicions about the lack of UN neutrality were correct.

The Council slowly escalated the mission away from traditional peacekeeping principles. In April 1992 it sent 500 soldiers to safeguard the delivery of humanitarian aid (SCR 751). In August – without consulting the Somali factions – it increased the mission to 3,000 soldiers (SCR 775). When the militia activity and famine-related deaths continued, the United States changed its position and offered to send troops to Somalia. Domestic pressure influenced the outgoing Bush administration: both houses of Congress passed resolutions in favor of intervention, groups from across the political spectrum lobbied for intervention, and media accounts of the mass starvation influenced American public opinion.

Given the United States position, the Security Council on 3 December authorized what eventually became 37,000 troops from twenty countries to ensure the delivery of relief supplies (SCR 794). Resolution 794 was a landmark document in the post-cold war expansion of Security Council powers. For the first time the Council called an internal humanitarian crisis a threat to international peace and security. The resolution authorized the use of force to intervene into a member state to resolve a humanitarian crisis that threatened hundreds of thousands of lives. It did not refer to refugees, regional stability, or any international implications. It cited the "unique" situation of a humanitarian crisis in a country with no functioning government. It was the first recognition that the Council has a "responsibility to protect" if a member state could not do so.

Both Russia and China voted in favor of SCR 794. The Russian delegate said that "resolution of the crisis requires the use of international armed forces under the auspices of the Security Council to ensure the delivery and safe keeping of the humanitarian assistance and its distribution to the country's starving population." China opposed the intervention but went along when African states overwhelmingly supported the proposal. The Chinese delegate did not want SCR 794 to establish a precedent for future action:

> [T]he military operation authorized by the draft resolution is an exceptional action in view of the unique situation in Somalia, and its purpose is to create promptly a secure environment in a short period of time for the humanitarian relief effort in Somalia. Once such an environment is created, the military operation should cease.
>
> (United Nations 1992: 37)

The United States entered Somalia with the limited intention of ensuring the delivery of humanitarian supplies to the areas most in need. It did not want to help negotiate a political settlement or disarm the militias. Once the humanitarian crisis was over, American troops would leave. Echoing peacekeeping rather than collective security principles, the outgoing Bush administration said that the United States would engage in disarmament only with the consent of the parties. However, others in the mission – particularly France and Australia – engaged in aggressive disarmament policies in their areas of operation. There was no agreement among the contributing countries about rules of engagement. Different national contingents used different levels of force when dealing with the Somalis.

The incoming Clinton administration maintained Bush's commitment to a limited intervention and even began withdrawing troops in May 1993. The UN could claim some success – the areas of Somalia outside Aideed's control were free of starvation by the middle of 1993. In May the Council authorized an expansive peace-building mandate, including economic and social reconstruction, the reestablishment of political institutions, the repatriation of refugees, de-mining, and disarmament (SCR 814). United States delegate Madeleine Albright called the resolution "an unprecedented enterprise aimed at nothing less than the restoration of an entire country . . . This is a historic undertaking." The Council also broke new ground by stating that violations of humanitarian international law threatened international peace and security. The veto powers were now saying that Aideed, by attacking the humanitarian shipments, was violating collective security rules. Russia and China reluctantly agreed given the "unique" situation.

When the factions again began fighting each other, clashes between the militias and UN troops with a disarmament mandate became more confrontational. On 5 June, an Aideed militia killed twenty-five and wounded more than fifty Pakistani troops when they tried to inspect a weapons site. The Council responded in order to safeguard peacekeeping troops around the world, authorizing the use of "all necessary measures" against those responsible for the attack (SCR 837). The UN mission placed a bounty on Aideed. There was no going back to a neutral, mediating role. Efforts to arrest Aideed continued throughout the summer and early fall, culminating on 3 October when militias killed eighteen American soldiers and wounded eighty more. Militia members dragged one of the dead soldiers through the streets of Mogadishu while Somalis cheered.

Clinton blamed the UN for the soldiers' deaths, wrongly suggesting that they were under effective UN command. He announced that the United States would withdraw its forces from Somalia by March 1994, and the Security Council then concentrated on political reconciliation rather than arresting Aideed and disarming militias. After Somalia the Clinton administration stopped talking about expanding UN resources and issued a presidential directive limiting United States participation in peacekeeping operations. When the Republican Party won the November 1994 Congressional elections, American support for peacekeeping waned further. The shift from peacekeeping to collective security in Somalia failed, marking a turning point in post-cold war collective security. Afterward "Somalia" was a warning about the dangers of collective security enforcement without local consent. Even Boutros-Ghali concluded that the UN should not engage in large-scale enforcement measures. The Council had abandoned the expansive goals in his *Agenda for Peace.*

Democratic Republic of Congo

Another good example of the inadequacy of classic peacekeeping in complex post-cold war conflicts is the regional war fought in the Democratic Republic of Congo (DRC) (Miskel and Norton 2003; Weiss and Carayannis 2004; Ginifer 2002). Six countries and three major domestic rebel groups were involved in the conflict that began in 1998. It was a regional war with neighboring countries crossing national borders to go after domestic enemies. Both the foreign armies and domestic rebels exploited DRC natural resources to fund their activities. The war and related famine and disease caused 3.5 million deaths and displaced 6 million people. The complexity of the situation and the sheer volume of actors limited the possibility of a neutral, consent-based peacekeeping approach.

The DRC is the size of Western Europe and has over 60 million people. It has over 200 distinct ethnic groups. Despite an abundance of natural resources and a tripling of the population, the country's GDP did not increase between 1960 and 2000. The average annual income is $100. Life expectancy for men is 47 and for women 51. There are few roads, and communication between regions is difficult. The country is fragmented into ethnic fiefdoms run by warlords or tribal chiefs. During the civil war the government controlled less than one-half of its territory; there was no government presence in much of the east. Racism is prevalent in many parts of the country, particularly against the Tutsis.

The West greatly influenced the contemporary DRC. Belgian King Leopold owned it as a private commercial empire in the late nineteenth century. The boundaries were arbitrary and separated African nations into different European colonies. Colonial rule by the Belgians was particularly exploitative and harsh. After independence in 1960 the Congo engaged in the first modern democratic election in Africa's history, electing Patrice Lumumba to be prime minister. But as a follower of "African socialism" the United States deemed him on the wrong side of the cold war and helped engineer a coup against him by Joseph Mobutu – right in the middle of a controversial UN peacekeeping mission in Congo. Mobutu – who renamed the country Zaire – presided over a corrupt and repressive dictatorship, but American support continued because he supported efforts to fight Soviet- and Cuban-inspired insurgencies in Africa. Western support for Mobutu dwindled when the cold war ended, opening the way for economic chaos and ethnic strife in the 1990s.

The conflict in the DRC is inextricably linked to related conflicts in Rwanda, Uganda, Angola, and Sudan. Ethnic conflicts in these countries spilled over into the DRC. Two dominant groups in eastern DRC claim a kinship to the Tutsi and Hutu. These groups began seizing each other's land by driving off or killing the owners due to an economic downturn in the early 1990s and related conflicts between these groups in Rwanda and Burundi. In 1994 the civil war in Rwanda brought over one million refugees into the eastern regions of Zaire. They were mostly Hutu, including many who had engaged in genocide against Rwandan Tutsis. Refugee camps formed and overwhelmed local economies and governments. The Hutu in the camps formed militias that both persecuted Tutsis in eastern Zaire and began military incursions into both Rwanda and Uganda.

The Mobutu government did nothing to stop Hutu militias from forming or to protect Tutsis from them. A rebellion against the Mobutu government led by Laurent Kabila began in 1997, and the eastern Tutsis joined Kabila's movement. Kabila received support from the Tutsi-led governments in Rwanda and Burundi, who also were upset that Mobutu did little to stop the Hutu militias. The Mobutu regime had little domestic support, and Kabila easily overthrew it on 17 May 1997. Kabila named the country the Democratic Republic of the Congo. However, once in power, Kabila also did not stop the Hutu militias. The cross border raids by Hutu militias into Rwanda continued. Rwanda accused Kabila of remobilizing Hutu extremists in order to redirect the conflict out of the DRC and back into Rwanda.

Rwanda and Burundi, feeling betrayed by Kabila, sent their militaries into the DRC to go after the Hutu militias. Both argued that they were arresting those who engaged in genocide and were wanted by the ad hoc tribunal for Rwanda created by the Security Council. But the Rwandans were also providing military support for the anti-Kabila rebels called Rally for Congolese Democracy (RCD) and exploiting DRC natural resources during their incursions. Burundi, however, declared neutrality and denied supporting rebel groups in the DRC. Kabila fanned ethnic tensions in the east, declaring that Rwandan support for the RCD was part of a plan for Tutsi ethnic hegemony in the region.

Uganda also sent its military into the DRC and supported an anti-Kabila rebel group, the Movement for the Liberation of Congo. Uganda had three different internal rebel movements, all operating out of the DRC and supported by Sudan. The DRC did nothing to stop the Ugandan rebel groups because Sudan supported Kabila. Sudan's support for the Ugandan rebel groups was retaliation for Ugandan support of the Sudanese People's Liberation Movement (SPLM), a rebel group long embroiled in a civil war with Sudan. Sudan and Uganda were each supporting civil war in the other. And both were fighting their conflict through proxies in the DRC, with DRC natural resources fueling the conflict. So Uganda sent its military into the DRC to prevent Sudan from controlling certain airfields, to exploit DRC resources, and to protect the SPLA against rear attacks by the Sudanese government in their civil war.

To further complicate the situation, Angola also sent its military into the DRC. The Mobutu government had supported the UNITA rebels against the Angolan government throughout their civil war. Angola therefore gave military support to the Kabila rebellion against Mobutu. In the midst of the Kabila rebellion, the Angolan ceasefire broke down and civil war with UNITA continued. Angola did not want UNITA to use the DRC as a base to acquire diamonds and weapons. Kabila did not betray Angola's support – as he did Rwanda and Burundi regarding the Hutu militias – and forcefully acted to keep UNITA out of the DRC.

Namibia, Chad and Zimbabwe also militarily entered the conflict in support of the Kabila government. All intervened primarily to gain more access to DRC resources. For example, Zimbabwe President Robert Mugabe deployed more than 10,000 troops, over one-third of its military, into the DRC, even although Zimbabwe is thousands of kilometers away. In return for Zimbabwe's support, Kabila offered economic concessions to Mugabe, including rights to copper and diamond mines. Both Angolan and Zimbabwe troops were later crucial to the survival of the Kabila regime against the RCD rebellion in 1998. Although the rebels controlled much of the eastern regions of the DRC, they could not advance to the capital city Kinshasa. With Angola, Namibia, Zimbabwe, and Rwandan Hutu militias supporting the Kabila government (Chad withdrew relatively quickly), and Rwanda and Uganda supporting the domestic rebellion, the DRC civil war was truly a regional war.

When the civil war broke out in August 1998, there were at least nine armed groups with external connections to neighboring countries and even more internal groups, some that were part of the anti-Kabila movement and some with the backing of the DRC. The UN-sponsored peace talks in Lusaka, Zambia, with the DRC, Angola, Namibia, Rwanda, Uganda, and Zimbabwe, eventually resulted in the signing of a ceasefire agreement on 10 July 1999 calling for a UN peacekeeping mission that would oversee the withdrawal of all foreign fighters. The agreement included the recognition of DRC sovereignty and territorial integrity, the control of illicit trafficking of armed groups and natural resources across the DRC border, the disarmament of all domestic militias and armed groups, open corridors for humanitarian aid, and an "open dialogue" between all domestic parties about the future of the DRC. Both major rebel groups signed the agreement in August. The Council authorized a peacekeeping mission without Chapter VII powers to oversee implementation of the agreement, facilitate ongoing political negotiations, and deliver humanitarian aid (SCR 1291).

The parties did not comply with the agreement throughout 2000. Fighting continued in eastern DRC. Kabila refused to integrate the rebel groups into a future DRC government. The DRC went to the International Court of Justice and charged Burundi, Rwanda, and Uganda with carrying out armed activities in its territory. The rebel groups did not want to relinquish control of the territory – and the natural resources – under their control. The neighboring states did not withdraw their militaries in order to continue extracting DRC gold and diamonds. Rwanda did not trust the DRC to turn over suspected Hutu war criminals to the Rwanda tribunal. Then in June 2000 fighting broke out between Rwandan and Ugandan troops in the eastern DRC – even though both supported anti-Kabila rebels, they supported different rebel groups. In August 2000 the Security Council first called the situation a "threat to international peace and security" and urged all parties to implement the Lusaka ceasefire agreement.

What reignited the peace process, ironically, was the assassination of Kabila in January 2001. He was succeeded by his son, Joseph, who began good faith negotiations with all the parties on the basis of the Lusaka ceasefire. Joseph Kabila signed an agreement with Rwanda in July 2002 and with Uganda in September 2002; Rwandan troops withdrew from eastern DRC by the end of that year and Ugandan troops withdrew by May 2003. Kabila also signed an agreement with the rebel groups in December 2002 to include them in a transitional government until a new constitution was adopted and elections were held.

Fighting continued despite this political progress, and the Security Council began to move away from a peacekeeping and toward a collective security approach. In December 2002 the Council bolstered the mission to 8,700 troops and expanded the mandate to include the disarmament of domestic armed groups (SCR 1445). The political vacuum brought about by the withdrawal of Ugandan forces in eastern DRC caused renewed violence, and in May 2003 the Council authorized the deployment of European Union forces to use "all necessary means" to restore order (SCR1484). In July the Council authorized an arms embargo in three eastern regions (SCR 1493). In October it increased the mission to 16,700 troops to enforce the arms embargo and ensure the protection of civilians (SCR 1565). In April 2004 it extended the arms embargo to include all of the DRC and initiated travel and financial sanctions against those violating the arms embargo (SCR 1596).

Periodic setbacks occurred. In December 2004 fighting erupted between the DRC and a pro-Rwanda militia. In March 2005 an eastern militia killed nine UN peacekeepers from Bangladesh. In September 2005 Uganda warned that its troops might reenter the DRC after a Ugandan rebel group sought refuge there via Sudan. However, the peace process continued. All factions within the parliament adopted a new constitution in May 2005, and a national referendum passed the constitution in December. The EU and UN forces continued to disarm militias to prepare for 2006 elections. The International Criminal Court issued its first ever indictment against an eastern warlord for forcing children into active combat. The DRC held general elections in July 2006 and runoff elections won by Kabila in October, the first free elections in forty-five years. The peace building mission, the sanctions, and EU forces periodically clashing with forces in eastern DRC continue.

The Security Council and regional organizations

The Security Council has increasingly partnered with regional organizations to implement peacekeeping missions. Member states are unwilling to provide the UN with the resources to adequately deploy troops in all necessary peacekeeping missions around the world. Regional organizations have stepped into that vacuum. In most years since the cold war, there were as many non-UN peacekeeping operations as UN peacekeeping operations, and the former included more personnel (Bellamy and Williams 2005). In Africa alone during the 1990s, the Council cooperated with ten regional peacekeeping missions.

In most cases the Security Council delegates its responsibilities to regional organizations. Some missions are led by major regional organizations, such as the European Union (Bosnia, Macedonia) or the African Union (Burundi, Sudan); some by smaller organizations, such as the Commonwealth of Independent States (Tajikistan, Georgia) or the Economic Community of West African States (Liberia, Sierra Leone); and some by the NATO alliance (Bosnia). However, not all regional peacekeeping operations have a prior Security Council authorization. Given the forces that transform peacekeeping missions into collective security missions, many question the legitimacy of unauthorized regional missions because the UN Charter does not explicitly allow regional organizations to engage in enforcement without Council authorization.

These situations lead to fundamental issues of hierarchy. Do we want an arrangement in which only the Security Council can authorize peacekeeping missions and delegate its responsibilities to regional organizations? Or do we want a more decentralized world in which regional organizations can act on their own authority, particularly when the Security Council is either uninterested or dead-locked? Would a less hierarchical arrangement that empowers regional organiza-tions be pragmatic and flexible? Or would it invite a haphazard and even lawless approach to conflict resolution around the world? These issues will increase as regional organizations acquire greater capacities to intervene in local conflicts.

One early example was the intervention by the Economic Community of West African States (ECOWAS) into Liberia in 1990, which did not receive Council au-thorization until 1993 (Olonisakin 1996). Liberia was founded in 1821 as a place to resettle free American slaves in Africa. Throughout the history of Liberia these American settlers, at less than 5 percent of the population, held disproportionate power over indigenous groups. The economic exploitation included slavery and forced labor. Indigenous Liberians were prevented from running for office unless they had adopted Christianity for three years.

In 1980 there was a coup led by Samuel Doe, a native Liberian. Doe imple-mented his own repressive policies that created ethnic rifts among native Liberi-ans. Doe's tribe and its allies benefited from the regime, and other groups were marginalized. Opposition to the Doe regime was widespread; unsuccessful coup attempts were followed with reprisals against the perpetrators and their tribes-men. In December 1989 Charles Taylor began another rebellion by the National Patriotic Front of Liberia (NPFL). A typical post-cold war civil war began: brutal fighting without regard to the laws of war, large-scale massacre of civilians, and humanitarian emergencies. By October 1990 there were more than 600,000 refu-gees.

The Security Council, preoccupied with the Iraqi invasion of Kuwait, did not respond to the crisis. So ECOWAS negotiated a ceasefire agreement and, at the request of the Liberian government, sent troops called the ECOWAS Monitoring Group (ECOMOG) in August 1990. Its initial mandate was purely humanitarian: to protect citizens in Monrovia. ECOWAS originally intended to act according to the peacekeeping principles of neutrality, consent, and self-defense. However, Charles Taylor and the NPFL were suspicious of Nigerian influence in the ECO-MOG forces and viewed the intervention as an attempt to protect the Doe regime. The NPFL immediately engaged ECOMOG in combat, and the peacekeepers became an actor in the war.

In September ECOWAS changed the ECOMOG mandate to a collective se-curity operation: it was to enforce the ceasefire agreement and secure the co-operation of the warring parties. In violation of the UN Charter, ECOWAS did not consult with the Security Council prior to authorizing enforcement measures. But the Security Council made no statement protesting ECOWAS actions. The more robust ECOMOG forces managed to restore order and sponsor peace talks between the NPFL and the Doe government. Three agreements in 1991 and 1992 all failed over the issue of disarmament: the NPFL would not disarm until another other major rebel group agreed to. Taylor also would not hand over weapons to the Nigerian-dominated ECOMOG.

In October 1992 the NPFL broke the ceasefire and again attacked both Liberian and ECOMOG forces. In November the NPFL rebels murdered six American nuns. It took the death of six American citizens to put Liberia on the Security Council's agenda, which responded by imposing an arms embargo on the territory held by the NPFL (SCR 788). The Council did not criticize the ECOWAS decision to send in troops, implicitly endorsing the regional collective security mission. The embargo had little effect, though, as weapons continued to pour in through Sierra Leone and the Ivory Coast. In March 1993 the Council instructed the Secretary General to negotiate with ECOWAS regarding the deployment of UN observers to help implement the ceasefire agreement (SCR 813).

The Doe government and the NPFL signed a peace agreement on 25 July 1993 calling on the UN and ECOWAS to help with its implementation. The Security Council authorized a UN mission in September (SCR 866), the first peacekeeping mission conducted jointly with a regional organization. It did not have a robust enforcement mandate: it was to monitor compliance with the peace agreement, observe the election process, coordinate humanitarian assistance, and report major violations of international humanitarian law. Its unofficial mandate was also to monitor ECOMOG, which was accused of looting and human rights violations. The more coercive aspects of the mission – creating buffer zones, sealing the borders, and disarming the parties – were left to ECOMOG.

Coordination between the UN and ECOMOG was poor. ECOMOG soldiers often restricted the movement of the UN monitors so they could not verify their activities, in violation of the peace agreement. When the UN asked ECOWAS to ensure that ECOMOG comply with the agreement, the soldiers on the ground ignored commands from their political leadership. Another problem was that ECOMOG did not have the resources required to fulfill its duties. The NPFL demanded that ECOMOG have fewer Nigerian soldiers, and when the Nigerians began to withdraw there was no one to take their place. In this environment the warring factions violated the peace agreement throughout 1993 and 1994. In addition to constant and widespread killing of civilians, the rebel groups recruited child soldiers and kidnapped UN observers, ECOMOG soldiers, and humanitarian personnel.

The Security Council continued to emphasize diplomatic means rather than authorize more coercive enforcement measures. The parties negotiated an amazing fourteen peace agreements between July 1993 and August 1997. After four years of war the parties finally agreed to democratic elections observed by ECOWAS, the OAU and the UN. Charles Taylor was elected president, ostensibly ending a war in which 150,000 civilians were killed and 850,000 became refugees. The Security Council changed the mandate of the UN mission to peace building: the UN was now promoting national reconciliation, respect for human rights and economic reconstruction.

But as in many other cases, merely holding elections does not resolve political conflict. After the election rebel forces opposed to Taylor's rule continue to ignite violence. And Taylor himself exacerbated regional conflicts in a variety of ways. He supported the Revolutionary United Front (RUF) in neighboring Sierra Leone, allowing Liberian territory to be used to ship both "blood diamonds" out of Sierra

Leone and weapons to the RUF. He also supported rebel movements in Guinea and the Ivory Coast; West African politics became dominated by cross-border military activities. Taylor's support for the RUF in Sierra Leone was so destabilizing that in March 2001 the Security Council authorized an arms embargo, travel sanctions, and bans on diamond and timber exports from Liberia (SCR 1343).

Liberia's domestic problems continued as well. The Taylor government excluded and harassed political opponents and its forces engaged in systematic human rights abuses. Rebel groups continued to fight, including multiple assassination attempts on Taylor. The civil war intensified in 2003, and in August the Security Council finally embraced a more assertive approach, authorizing a multinational force including United States troops to stabilize the situation (SCR 1497). The announcement that American forces were arriving spurred further negotiations and the warring parties signed yet another peace agreement on 18 August. This time the UN sent in over 15,000 troops, and the situation stabilized. Overwhelming international pressure for Taylor to resign – he was by then indicted by an international tribunal investigating the war in Sierra Leone – forced him to step down in late August.

In September 2003 the mission in Liberia became an expansive peace building effort. The operation spanned the entire spectrum of civil society, including political, military, police, criminal justice, human rights, gender, child protection, HIV/AIDS, disarmament, demobilization, humanitarian, refugee assistance, and electoral components (SCR 1509). UN forces took over all peacekeeping duties; over 3,500 African soldiers switched hats and joined the UN mission. The Council also imposed financial sanctions on members of the Charles Taylor regime in March 2004 for evading arrest by the Sierra Leone special tribunal (SCR 1532). All sanctions on Liberia except for the timber ban continue.

Regional peacekeeping missions are likely to continue when there is no consensus or will on the Security Council to intervene. This is particularly true when classic peacekeeping conditions do not exist. The Council is reluctant to authorize combat operations and is not capable of acting quickly without a standing military. Regional missions like ECOMOG in Liberia and Sierra Leone, Australian-led forces in East Timor, and NATO's involvement in Bosnia enabled peace enforcement actions that the UN could not undertake. The Liberia example suggests that regional peacekeeping missions should be incorporated into larger UN operations (Pugh and Sidhu 2003). Combatants often suspect that peacekeeping troops from nearby countries are not politically neutral. Local parties must see the peacekeeping mission as legitimate, and the UN can provide that legitimacy. As the examples in this chapter show, however, it is difficult for peacekeeping troops to maintain neutrality in post-cold war conflicts.

Peacekeeping, security, and hierarchy

Peacekeeping is less hierarchical than collective security because it is rooted in the traditional norms of state sovereignty and non-intervention. The peacekeeping norm of consent means that the Security Council cannot impose a mission when the local parties do not want one. The norms of neutrality and self-defense mean that UN peacekeeping forces cannot militarily tip the scales in favor of one side. Peacekeeping is not an intrusive, hierarchical mechanism. It can be very success-ful when the warring parties want a third party to mediate a peaceful resolution to their conflict. But post-cold war peacekeeping missions show two patterns that require a more hierarchical approach than classic peacekeeping: (1) post-conflict peace processes require expansive UN peace-building operations; and (2) if the conflict reignites, the Council needs to abandon peacekeeping and invoke collec-tive security rules to maintain security. Like other post-cold war security issues, increased hierarchy is often necessary to provide security.

The Security Council has embraced the increased hierarchy of peace building. In 2001 it defined peace building as:

> aimed at preventing the outbreak, the recurrence or continuation of armed conflict and therefore encompasses a wide range of political, developmental, humanitarian, and human rights programs and mechanisms . . . These actions focus on fostering sustainable institutions and processes in areas such as sus-tainable development, the eradication of poverty and inequalities, transparent and accountable governance, the promotion of democracy, respect for human rights and the rule of law, and the promotion of a culture of peace and non-violence.
>
> (United Nations 2001)

This expansive notion of peace building thrusts the Security Council into ac-tions that during the cold war would have been considered interference into the internal affairs of states. Peace building, the governance of failed states, and the "responsibility to protect" have collectively transformed the traditional notion of state sovereignty (Krasner 2004). State sovereignty no longer enables states to resist all outside intervention. It now obligates states to provide human security, and UN peace-building missions enforce these new rules.

The UN has issued two studies to improve third generation complex peace building missions (Ramcharan 2002). A 2000 study known as the Brahimi Re-port tried to reconcile the tensions between traditional peacekeeping and human security:

> The Panel concurs that consent of the local parties, impartiality and the use of force only in self-defense should remain bedrock principles of peacekeeping. Experience shows, however, that in the context of intra-state/transnational conflicts, consent may be manipulated in many ways. Impartiality for United Nations operations must therefore mean adherence to the principles of the Charter: where one party to a peace agreement clearly and incontrovertibly is violating its terms, continued equal treatment of all parties by the United Nations can in the best case result in ineffectiveness and in the worst may amount to complicity with evil. No failure did more to damage the standing

and credibility of United Nations peacekeeping in the 1990s than its reluctance to distinguish victim from aggressor.

(United Nations 2000: 3)

This last sentence is crucial: while peacekeeping requires neutrality, collective security requires the Council to distinguish victim from aggressor. Third-generation peacekeeping thus remains in a gray area between neutral third party mediation and coercive enforcement. It presumes that human security can be achieved through collective intervention. It challenges the traditional notion of order based on state sovereignty and nonintervention. It rejects the state as the absolute referent point for security. It emphasizes basic human needs, distributive justice, human rights, and the promotion of political participation.

The Brahimi Report issued many recommendations to improve UN peacekeeping. It emphasized the rule of law and improving respect for human rights. It advocated quicker demobilization and the disarmament of warring factions. It supported more robust rules of engagement to deal with those who violate their commitments under a peace agreement. It urged the Council to ensure that member states have committed the troop levels and other necessary resources prior to authorization of a sizable mission. It recommended the Council improve coordination with a wide variety of UN human and economic development agencies. It encouraged states to form standby forces ready to deploy within 30 days of a Council resolution authorizing peacekeeping and within 90 days for complex peacekeeping operations. And it advocated an "on call" list of experts who would be available on seven days' notice to develop concrete operational and tactical plans in advance of the deployment of troop contingents.

A 2004 UN High Level Panel Report on global security threats (United Nations 2004) also analyzed peacekeeping operations and issued a series of recommendations. It endorsed the emerging norm of the responsibility to protect and embraced peacekeeping as a valuable tool in ending wars. It reiterated the Brahimi Report's recommendations for standby forces and on-call personnel to enable rapid deployment. It urged states to double the number available peacekeepers. It advocated the creation of a Peace Building Commission to develop lists of best practices for dealing with countries emerging from conflict. It urged a much more structured relationship between the Council and regional organizations to more efficiently allocate existing resources toward the resolution of conflict. And it recommended the democratization of peacekeeping through broader representation on the Security Council and including local, civilian participation in the implementation of peace-building missions.

All of these recommendations are intended to increase the efficiency and legitimacy of peacekeeping, and the UN has implemented many of them. For example, the UN created a Peace Building Commission in 2006 as an advisory body to the Security Council and the General Assembly. But these suggested reforms have varied implications for the amount of hierarchy in future global security arrangements. The veto powers are reluctant to implement the recommendations that reduce their privileged position in the collective security arrangement. The obvious one is increased representation on the Security Council. But the Council is reluctant to pursue others that would reduce hierarchy between the veto powers and all other states.

For example, having quick-response, standby forces would make the UN less dependent on the United States and NATO for the military resources necessary for third-generation peacekeeping. Western powers could no longer withhold their own troops as a strategy to prevent action when the international community wants to act. With the existence of standby forces, the international community could more effectively lobby to use them in situations that might not obviously be in the interests of the great powers. And if the veto powers refuse to authorize their use in such situations, then the legitimacy of the Security Council – and thus the authority of the veto powers – decreases.

In this context the security–hierarchy paradox applies to all five veto powers. Many of these recommendations simultaneously enhance the legitimacy and effectiveness of peacekeeping while reducing the privileged position of the five veto powers. At some point the veto powers' pursuit of hierarchy can undermine the legitimacy and effectiveness of the Security Council. Are they willing to embrace a less hierarchical arrangement – broaden representation on the Council, establish standby forces, and increase coordination with UN agencies – in order to construct more legitimate global security rules and more effectively solve post-cold war security issues? Are they willing to support peacekeeping missions so that the rest of the world does not interpret them to be pursuing only narrow interests at the expense of broader international security goals? Peacekeeping is another example of the security–hierarchy paradox: while achieving security in the post-cold war world requires some hierarchy, too much hierarchy becomes counterproductive.

4   Economic sanctions

The most common enforcement tool used by the Security Council is economic sanctions, which end normal economic relations to pressure a target to comply with international rules. They range from complete economic embargoes to commodity specific boycotts to "smart sanctions" against individual decision-makers in the target state. Sanctions raise issues of hierarchy and the appropriate way to implement collective security rules. Should the Council routinely authorize sanctions? Should sanctions be comprehensive or partial? Should they be imposed immediately or incrementally? Should they remain in place until the target state complies with all demands, or should partial compliance be rewarded with reduced sanctions?

This chapter discusses sanctions as a collective security enforcement tool since the cold war. The first section discusses both the increased use of sanctions by the Council and the limitations of sanctions. The second section discusses "smart sanctions," an innovation the Council developed in response to criticisms about the negative impact of comprehensive economic sanctions. It includes an example of Council sanctions against groups exporting "blood diamonds" to fuel conflicts in Western Africa. The third section uses the examples of sanctions against Libya and Iraq in the 1990s to illustrate the United States and the United Kingdom preferring a more hierarchical approach than the other veto powers.

The uses and limitations of sanctions

The Security Council authorized economic sanctions only twice during the cold war. Both were against white minority regimes in Africa: commodity embargos including oil against Rhodesia in 1966 (SCR 253) and an arms embargo against South Africa in 1977 (SCR 418). In the post-cold war world, however, the Council has imposed numerous sanctions against both states and non-state actors.

- *Iraq*. The Council authorized a full trade embargo in August 1990 after Iraq invaded Kuwait. The sanctions remained in place after the Gulf War until Iraq met multiple conditions in SCR 687. The Council passed 21 more resolutions between 1991 and 2002, extending the sanctions owing to Iraqi noncompliance on weapons inspections, providing humanitarian exemptions, establishing the oil for food program, and later authorizing travel sanctions against members of the Iraqi regime. The Council ended the sanctions after the United States invasion in 2003.

- *Yugoslavia.* The Council authorized an arms embargo in September 1991 and a complete economic embargo in May 1992. The Council ended these sanctions in October 1996 given Yugoslav implementation of the Dayton Peace Accords. The Council targeted Bosnian Serbs with trade, travel, and financial sanctions in September 1994 for their human rights violations against Bosnian Muslims. The Council imposed another arms embargo on Yugoslavia in March 1998 for human rights violations in Kosovo. The Council ended those sanctions in September 2001.
- *Somalia.* The Council authorized an arms embargo in January 1992. These sanctions continue.
- *Libya.* The Council authorized an arms and air embargo in March 1992 for failing to extradite terrorist suspects. It then imposed financial sanctions and banned the sale of oil refining equipment in November 1993. The Council suspended these sanctions in April 1999 and terminated them in September 2003.
- *Liberia.* The Council authorized an arms embargo to minimize the level of hostilities during a civil war in November 1992. It imposed an arms embargo, travel sanctions, and bans on diamond exports in March 2001 for Liberia's support of armed groups throughout the region, including the Revolutionary United Front (RUF) in Sierra Leone. It imposed financial sanctions on members of the Charles Taylor regime in March 2004. These sanctions continue.
- *Angola.* The Council authorized an oil and arms embargo on the National Union for the Total Independence of Angola (UNITA) in 1993 for repeated violations of a ceasefire agreement. These were the first sanctions imposed on a non-state entity. The Council subsequently authorized travel sanctions, financial sanctions, and a ban on diamond exports from Angola. The Council ended the sanctions in December 2002.
- *Haiti.* The Council authorized an arms embargo, an oil embargo, and financial sanctions in June 1993 against a military regime that toppled a democratically elected government. These sanctions were suspended in August and then reimposed in October. In May 1994 they were expanded to a complete trade embargo with the exception of food and medicine. The Council ended these sanctions in October 1994 when President Aristide returned to power.
- *Rwanda.* The Council authorized an arms embargo in May 1994. These sanctions continue against all nongovernment forces in Rwanda.
- *Sudan.* The Council authorized travel sanctions in April 1996 for failing to extradite suspected terrorists and other support of terrorist activities. The Council ended these sanctions in September 2001. The Council authorized an arms embargo in July 2004 regarding the crisis in Darfur. It imposed travel and financial sanctions in March 2005 on individuals suspected of war crimes

and other human rights violations in Darfur. These sanctions continue.

- *Sierra Leone*. The Council authorized an oil embargo, an arms embargo, and travel sanctions in October 1997 when a military junta toppled a democratically elected regime. It ended the oil embargo in March 1998 and replaced the remaining prohibitions with travel sanctions in June 1998. In July 2000 it banned diamond exports that funded the RUF. The diamond ban continues.
- *Afghanistan*. The Council authorized travel and financial sanctions against the Taliban in November 1999 for refusing to extradite Osama bin Laden to the United States. It imposed an arms embargo and a complete prohibition on air travel in December 2000 for continued noncompliance, as well as financial sanctions against Al Qaeda members. The sanctions against Taliban and Al Quaeda members continue.
- *Ethiopia and Eritrea*. The Council authorized an arms embargo from May 2000 to May 2001.
- *The Congo*. The Council authorized an arms embargo against all armed groups, foreign and domestic, in the Congo in July 2003. It authorized travel and financial sanctions against political and military leaders preventing the disarmament of warring factions in April 2005 and December 2005. It expanded those sanctions against individuals charged with using child soldiers in July 2006. These sanctions continue.
- *Ivory Coast*. The Council authorized an arms embargo, travel sanctions, and financial sanctions in November 2004 for government violations of a ceasefire agreement with northern rebels. These sanctions continue.
- *North Korea*. The Council authorized an arms embargo, financial sanctions, and sanctions on luxury goods in October 2006 after North Korea conducted an underground nuclear test. These sanctions continue.

There are many limitations to the use of economic sanctions. First, they do not always bring about the desired policy changes (Chesterman and Pouligny 2003, Cortright and Lopez 1999). Many regimes continue violating community rules. Analyses of success vary widely because there is no accepted way to evaluate the success of sanctions. Most agree that sanctions were relatively successful in coercing Iraq, Yugoslavia (regarding Bosnia), Libya, Serbia, Cambodia, and Sierra Leone. However, they had little effect on Haiti, UNITA, Somalia, Sudan, Liberia, Rwanda, Yugoslavia (regarding Kosovo), and Afghanistan (Cortright and Lopez 2004).

Sanctions can also be counterproductive and strengthen the regime they intend to coerce. The target can blame the international community for the hardships imposed by the sanctions and create a "rally-round-the-flag" effect. The sanctions are often more devastating to the civil society than to the regime, undermining the chances of effective domestic pressure on the regime. It is impossible to know what internal dynamics sanctions will initiate. What complicates the effectiveness of sanctions is that the targets most susceptible to economic coercion and domestic political pressure – democracies with high levels of trade – are the least likely targets of economic sanctions. The most likely targets are authoritarian systems with lower levels of trade, the type of state most likely to resist economic coercion and domestic pressure.

Sanctions are also difficult to implement, monitor, and enforce. Sanctions are effective only if all states comply and end the prohibited economic activities with the target. This inevitably requires some states to forgo trade with important economic partners. Other noncompliance exists from black markets and corrupt economic actors. Ensuring compliance requires monitoring the entire border of a target, particularly port cities. While the Council now routinely establishes sanctions committees to monitor implementation, it is extremely difficult to enforce every sanctions regime. Effective sanctions require states to use their own military as enforcement agents, to compensate third parties who harm their own economy through compliance, and to prosecute multinational companies who violate the sanctions.

Comprehensive economic sanctions also can have disastrous humanitarian consequences (Al-Anbari 2001). The horrific impact of the sanctions after the Gulf War on the Iraqi population convinced many that comprehensive sanctions cannot be a legitimate policy tool. Minimizing humanitarian consequences is complicated when the target state does not cooperate with relief activities. This occurs regularly, including Iraq refusing to agree to the oil-for-food program for over four years, Serbs not allowing international aid to Bosnian Muslims, Somali clans not allowing aid to other clans, or the Sudanese government not allowing aid into Darfur. The Council has undertaken many reforms to minimize the humanitarian consequences of economic sanctions, including generating humanitarian assessment reports prior to the imposition of sanctions, establishing criteria for humanitarian exemptions, and monitoring the ongoing humanitarian impact of sanctions.

Smart sanctions

The most important Security Council reform to improve the effectiveness of sanctions is the use of "smart sanctions" (Tostensen and Bull 2002). The Security Council has not authorized comprehensive trade sanctions since those against Iraq, Yugoslavia, and Haiti. Instead, the Council has used targeted "smart sanctions." The intent of smart sanctions is to deal with many of the limitations discussed above: to target the regime rather than the people, to minimize humanitarian impact, to minimize the rally-round-the-flag effect, to minimize costs to third-party states and thus incentives to cheat, and to reduce the perverse incentives for elites to benefit from sanctions. Smart sanctions, however, do not necessarily deal with the other two criticisms of sanctions: overall effectiveness and difficulties with implementation.

There are four types of smart sanctions. One is an arms embargo to reduce the ability of warring parties to pursue the conflict through military means (Knight 2004). The Security Council has imposed arms embargoes twelve times since the cold war. However, most analysts conclude that they rarely work (Cortright and

Lopez 2004); only in Iraq, where the major powers were committed to enforcement, were they clearly effective. They are sometimes too late to stop the conflict, as in Rwanda. They sometimes reinforce an already skewed military balance, as in Bosnia. The Council has tried to improve the effectiveness of arms embargoes by writing more comprehensive resolutions that specify the precise weapons to be prohibited, appointing independent expert panels to monitor the embargoes and issue reports detailing violations, and encouraging multilateral efforts to criminalize violations at the domestic level.

Financial sanctions are a second type of smart sanctions. Financial sanctions target the personal economic assets of political decision makers. They freeze both personal and government funds held abroad, suspend loans and grants from states and international organizations, deny access to international financial markets, and ban investment. Travel sanctions are a third type of smart sanctions. They deny visas to targeted individuals to prohibit them from international travel. The Security Council has authorized financial sanctions seven times and travel sanctions eight times. These sanctions can also be difficult to implement. Financial sanctions require coordination with the global banking industry to trace the assets and private accounts of many individuals and their family members. Travel sanctions require competent air traffic control procedures around the world. Both require a technical capacity to generate an appropriate list of individuals and to constantly update those lists. For example, sanctions against the Taliban and Al Qaeda include 360 individuals and 124 associated entities.

Commodity embargoes are a fourth type of smart sanction in which the Security Council prohibits the export of particular commodities used by warring parties to fund their conflict, usually oil, gold, or diamonds. The Council has authorized commodity embargoes eight times. Commodity embargoes are also difficult to implement. Even when the relevant industry agrees to elevate security concerns over profits, such sanctions require a tremendous amount of cooperation between government and industry to succeed. The attempt to prevent African groups from illegally selling diamonds to fund their insurgencies is a good example. Sanctions on "conflict diamonds" contributed to a historic process in which states, industry and civil society collaborated to prevent the smuggling of illicit diamonds to fund civil wars.

Conflict diamonds

Security Council sanctions prohibiting the illegal sale of diamonds from Angola, Liberia, and Sierra Leone are unique attempts to invoke collective security rules and engage in conflict resolution (Wright 2004; Angell 2004; Hirsch 2004; Sherman 2000). In all of these conflicts warring parties captured territory that included diamond mines, illegally extracted and smuggled the diamonds, and used the proceeds to buy weapons. Sanctions required the cooperation of the diamond industry and all diamond exporting countries, leading to a unique set of rules that can possibly be extended to other commodities in the future.

The Security Council first established diamond sanctions in Angola. After independence from Portugal in 1975, Angola became engulfed in civil war. The government was run by the Popular Movement for the Liberation of Angola, which was politically supported by the Soviet Union and backed by Cuban troops. With cold war politics prevailing, the United States and South Africa tried to destabilize the new regime. They supported two other groups, the National Front for the Liberation of Angola and UNITA.

Angola has one of the largest amounts of diamond reserves in the world, and UNITA used illicit diamond trade and money laundering for over two decades to finance their war. By the 1990s UNITA ran the largest illegal diamond-trafficking operation in the world, earning over $3 billion. They smuggled the diamonds and bought weapons with the proceeds primarily in the Democratic Republic of the Congo (DRC) and Zambia. The diamond industry itself was complicit in the "blood diamond" trade – NGOs charged that security companies affiliated with the giant diamond company DeBeers protected UNITA-controlled mines.

The end of the cold war ushered in a peace process, but UNITA consistently resisted. It contested the legitimacy of UN-monitored elections in September 1992 and restarted the civil war. A November 1994 peace agreement bogged down when UNITA refused to disarm and join a national unity government. The Security Council responded with a variety of sanctions: an arms embargo and an oil embargo in 1993 (SCR 864) – the first time the Council imposed sanctions on a non-state actor – travel sanctions in 1997 (SCR 1127), and finally a diamond embargo in 1998 (SCR 1173). The Council prohibited diamond sales from Angola unless they had been certified by the government of Angola as having come from mines under its control. The diamond sanctions initially were an abysmal failure. Regional states, UNITA, and the diamond industry willfully ignored them, undermining the authority of the Council and the credibility of sanctions as a collective security enforcement tool.

When the Security Council authorizes sanctions, it creates a sanctions committee to monitor those sanctions and make recommendations to the Council about improving their effectiveness. When Canada became the chair of the Angola sanctions committee, it attempted to reinvigorate the sanctions. The committee cooperated with NGOs like Global Witness and Human Rights Watch to "name and shame" sanctions violators, including regional government officials and many in the diamond industry. It encouraged states and the diamond industry to develop a certificate of origin system. It urged media reports to increase awareness of "conflict diamonds" or "blood diamonds." Their work was so thorough that in April 2000 the Council for the first time explicitly threatened to take enforcement action against those who violated sanctions it had imposed (SCR 1295).

The second time the Security Council established a diamonds embargo was on Sierra Leone in 2000 (SCR 1306), prohibiting the sale of all diamonds except those certified by the government of Sierra Leone. The purpose of the sanctions was again to prevent rebel groups from gaining access to weapons and further fuel a civil war, which in Sierra Leone had killed over 60,000 people and displaced over two million people. This conflict was particularly brutal, including the widespread use of child soldiers, rape and sexual slavery, and deliberate amputations.

When the war was over, Sierra Leone was literally the worst place in the world to live, ranking last out of 173 countries on the 2002 UN Human Development Index.

Sierra Leone became independent in 1961 and was governed by a military dictatorship that financed its corrupt rule through the illicit smuggling of diamonds. Civil war broke out in 1991 between the government and the Revolutionary United Front (RUF) led by Foday Sankoh, who was close friends with Charles Taylor, the leader of the National Patriotic Front in Liberia (NPFL). Each supported the other's war efforts: Taylor provided arms and troops in return for diamonds extracted by the RUF. Both also used brutal tactics – amputation, rape, human trafficking, forced labor, child soldiers, etc. – to fight their wars.

The RUF was initially successful, capturing much of eastern Sierra Leone. Many Sierra Leone soldiers even colluded with the RUF and helped exploit eastern diamond resources. The government turned both to civilian militias who also committed human rights atrocities and to a South African mercenary force called Executive Outcomes. The private security forces were pivotal, preventing the RUF from capturing the capital city of Freetown in 1995. In a strange twist, Sierra Leone then held democratic elections in the middle of its civil war in an attempt to woo international donors. The RUF boycotted the elections, and the winner was Ahmad Tejan Kabbah, who ran on a peace platform. The Kabbah government and the RUF signed a peace agreement in November 1996. The agreement called for the withdrawal of foreign forces, but after Kabbah sent the South African mercenaries home in January 1997 the RUF reneged on the deal and restarted the war. In May 1997 junior soldiers affiliated with the RUF carried out a coup, formed a military dictatorship, and committed massive amounts of violence against civilians in Freetown.

The Security Council authorized an arms embargo and an oil embargo on the military regime on 7 October (SCR 1132). The Economic Community of West Africa States (ECOWAS) went further, authorizing its military arm (ECOMOG) to use force to unseat the coup leaders. This was the second time ECOWAS authorized a collective security operation without consulting the Security Council (the first was in Liberia). ECOMOG forces under Nigerian command ousted the junta in February 1998 and restored the Kabbah government to power. The Security Council subsequently lifted the arms and oil embargoes on the Sierra Leone government but retained them on the RUF. The RUF launched another attack on Freetown in January 1999, but after some fierce fighting the ECOMOG troops were able to recapture the capital. Given the continued military stalemate and mounting pressure from the international community, the two sides signed another peace agreement in July 1999. The Council established a peacekeeping force to monitor implementation of the agreement. But the RUF again sabotaged the peace process, ambushing UN troops and confiscating their weapons. In May 2000 the RUF killed four UN peacekeepers and kidnapped 500 more.

The Security Council responded to the hostage crisis with a more assertive collective security approach. It expanded the mission to 17,500 troops with the mandate to militarily coerce the RUF into meaningful negotiations, it established the Sierra Leone Special Court with jurisdiction over war crimes and crimes against humanity committed during the conflict, it imposed sanctions on Liberia for its support of the RUF, and it adopted sanctions against illegal diamond exports in an attempt to thwart RUF access to weapons. The second time the Security Council imposed diamond sanctions, then, it was part of a more comprehensive approach to impose peace in Sierra Leone. The third time the Council imposed diamond sanctions – against Liberia in 2002 – they were also linked to Taylor's support for the RUF in Sierra Leone.

The Sierra Leone and Liberia diamonds sanctions were relatively effective because the work of the Angola sanctions committee had created momentum for a global certification process. NGOs engaged in a successful advertising campaign, including pictures of amputated children and a slogan: "Has the ring on your finger cost the arm of this child?" Suddenly everyone was aware of "blood diamonds." Since there was no way to distinguish legal from illegal diamonds, consumers around the world became concerned that their jewelry indirectly fueled African civil wars.

Negotiations to construct a global certification scheme began in May 2000 in Kimberley, South Africa. The talks slowly incorporated more groups, culminating with an agreement in November 2002 between forty-five states, the European Union, the global diamond industry and NGOs representing over 100 civil society groups. The Kimberley Process Certification Scheme (KPCS) obligated all participants to trade only those diamonds that earn a Kimberley Process certificate issued by the exporting government. They also agreed not to trade diamonds with countries who failed to use the certification scheme.

The KPCS was enacted by each state through national (or EU) legislation. Since it was not a legally binding treaty nor mandated by a Chapter VII Security Council resolution, there was no global monitoring or enforcement mechanism. NGOs lobbied to strengthen the agreement, and throughout 2003 the Kimberley Process established audits of each country's legislation and voluntary "review visits" to examine implementation. Despite the lack of sanctions for those who did not meet the standards, the KPCS was a historic agreement. It was the first attempt by the international community to address the problem of the illegal exploitation of natural resources. It was also the first time that an international agreement had been negotiated and adopted on the basis of consensus between governments, industry and civil society acting as equal partners. It contributed to the political progress that ended the civil wars in Angola, Sierra Leone, and Liberia. And it could become a model for dealing with other natural resources illegally exploited to fuel conflicts, including timber, oil, coltan and gold.

Sanctions and hierarchy

Sanctions illustrate the post-cold war pattern of the United States preferring more hierarchy in world politics. First, the United States has advocated the use of sanctions more often than the other veto powers. In cases such as Yugoslavia, Libya, Haiti, and Afghanistan, the United States pushed for sanctions whereas others resisted or delayed. Current examples include American support for sanctions on Sudan regarding the genocide in Darfur and on Iran regarding its nuclear weapons program. Russia and China usually resist the most, and their position is based partially on principle (they prefer a world of low hierarchy based on state sovereignty) and self-interest (they have significant commercial ties to the proposed targets).

The United States has imposed far more bilateral sanctions than any other country, and it has attempted to coerce others into supporting those sanctions. Twice the United States has passed legislation authorizing sanctions against any state or company that violated its own bilateral sanctions policy and traded with the target state. Both the Helms Burton Act regarding Cuba and the Iran–Libya Sanctions Act threatened to retaliate against any state or company that defied United States sanctions and traded with Cuba, Iran, or Libya. The United States attempted to use the power of its own market to dictate trade policy to other countries. While impossible to implement, such legislation illustrates the hierarchical tendencies in American foreign policy. The United States would criticize any other state acting in the same way.

This hierarchy pattern is also illustrated by veto power disputes over how to implement sanctions. Should they increase sanctions incrementally over time, or should they immediately impose sanctions at comprehensive levels? Should sanctions have time limits and expire unless the Council takes action to extend them, or should they remain in force until the Council takes action to end them? The former enables one veto power to end sanctions when the other four want them to continue, and the latter enables one veto power to continue them when the other four want them to end. Should sanctions continue until the target complies with all Council demands, or should the Council recognize progress made toward full compliance and reciprocate by reducing some of the sanctions? Are sanctions primarily about punishment or about persuasion and bargaining?

The United States (with the United Kingdom) is more likely to prefer the comprehensive, punishment model of sanctions with no time limits. Russia, China, and France are more likely to prefer an incremental, bargaining model of sanctions with time limits. The United States generally wants a punitive process that maintains harsh sanctions until it agrees that the target has complied in full. The others generally want a bargaining process in which the Council can flexibly alter the sanctions depending on the amount of compliance at a particular time. Using sanctions as punishment invokes more hierarchy than using sanctions as a negotiation. Sanctions against Iraq in the 1990s and Libya provide good examples of this veto power conflict.

Iraq

The Security Council imposed a comprehensive trade embargo on Iraq four days after it invaded Kuwait in August 1990. The invasion generated consensus among the veto powers about the need to enforce the traditional rules of sovereignty and territorial integrity (Rose 2005; Van Walsum 2004; Loehr and Wong 1995). The

United States jumped ahead of the other veto powers, however, by beginning a naval blockade to enforce the embargo on 16 August, nine days before the Council authorized such enforcement. When Iraq refused to withdraw from Kuwait, the Council authorized the use of force and United States-led forces repelled the Iraqi military from Kuwait (see Chapter 5).

After the war the Security Council passed SCR 687, known as the "mother of all resolutions." It authorized the comprehensive economic embargo until Iraq complied with the following demands: (1) recognize Kuwait's sovereignty and borders; (2) dismantle its WMD programs, including nuclear weapons, as well as its longer range missile programs; (3) accept international monitoring and verification of the disarmament; (4) pay reparations to Kuwait; and (5) renounce global terrorism. Note that the rules enforced by this resolution went beyond the territorial integrity of Kuwait to include weapons proliferation and terrorism. The Council reached the extraordinary conclusion that international security required the virtual disarmament of a sovereign state.

United States policy, however, consistently added two other conditions not included in SCR 687: human rights and "regime change." No Council resolution ever stated that Saddam Hussein had to step down or to respect the human rights of Iraqi citizens to end the economic sanctions. But in May 1991 the United States asserted that it would oppose lifting the sanctions until Saddam Hussein was out of power. The United States thus had a regime change policy that went beyond the cease-fire conditions in SCR 687. The United States also called for a UN police force to protect the Kurds in northern Iraq and the Shia in southern Iraq. While the United Kingdom and France agreed, Russia and China opposed it (see Chapter 5).

Another dispute arose when Iraq blocked UN inspectors attempting to visit suspected weapons sites in June 1991. The United States asserted that it would use force to make Iraq cooperate with weapons inspectors. President Bush said that existing Council resolutions provided legal justification for the use of force, a position challenged by Russia, China, and France. To avoid an American use of force, the Council authorized the most powerful disarmament regime in history, including monitoring, verification, and export–import controls after the lifting of sanctions to ensure that Iraq would not resume its WMD and missile programs (SCR 715). In effect, the Council changed the burden of proof; instead of the UN having to prove Iraqi guilt, Iraq had to prove its innocence (Chellaney 1999).

Iraq initially did not accept any of the cease-fire terms in SCR 687 or the weapons inspections regime in SCR 715. Throughout the spring and summer of 1992, the United States periodically threatened to use force to compel compliance. The United States, in an argument to be repeated eleven years later, argued that Iraqi noncompliance with SCR 687 nullified the ceasefire called for in that resolution, and the parties had reverted to a state of war. Only the United Kingdom supported this interpretation. This round of standoffs ended in July 1992, when Iraq refused to allow weapons inspectors inside the Iraqi Ministry of Agriculture for three weeks. The United States again threatened to use force to gain entry, but other veto power members did not. Eventually the UN brokered a deal with Iraq to allow weapons inspectors into the suspected sites, but none was British, French, or American.

Iraq finally agreed to full weapons inspections, including the installation of monitoring cameras, in November 1993. This partial level of compliance, together with the overwhelming evidence of a humanitarian crisis brought about by the sanctions, created tensions on the Council. Russia, China, and France advocated the bargaining approach, in which the Council would respond to partial compliance by Iraq with a partial lifting of sanctions, in order to both ease the humanitarian crisis and encourage further Iraqi compliance. Britain and the United States preferred the punishment approach, demanding that Iraq comply with all conditions in Resolution 687 before any of the sanctions were eased. Indeed, the United States continued to go further than SCR 687, adding human rights and regime change to its list of conditions.

Iraq tried to take advantage of this dispute, stating that it would cease cooperation with weapons inspectors if the Security Council did not end the sanctions by 10 October 1994. Iraq then deployed military forces toward Kuwait, a provocative move because it had not recognized the sovereignty of Kuwait, one of the conditions in SCR 687 to end the sanctions. The United States pressed for a resolution demanding that Iraq should withdraw its forces and fully cooperate with weapons inspectors. Invoking hegemonic collective security, the United States warned that it would act with or without the Council's support. Despite Russian and Chinese displeasure with the American position, the Council unanimously demanded that Iraq withdraw its forces and fully cooperate with weapons inspectors (SCR 949). The Iraqi ploy failed: it withdrew its forces, and both the weapons inspections and sanctions continued.

In November 1994 Iraq recognized the sovereignty of Kuwait, fulfilling one Council demand. Given this concession, the humanitarian crisis, and ongoing Iraqi compliance with weapons inspectors, China, France, and Russia continued to advocate easing the sanctions. They argued that it would ease the humanitarian crisis and encourage further Iraqi compliance. While China's position was relatively principled, Russia and France had economic motives because they were Iraq's biggest business partners prior to the Gulf War. Iraq owed France an estimated $5 billion and Russia an estimated $7 billion; both wanted to take part in Iraqi reconstruction efforts after the Gulf War. However, the United States (and Britain) threatened to veto any resolution that eased the sanctions.

The only available compromise was an April 1995 resolution establishing an "oil-for-food" program to minimize the humanitarian implications of the sanctions (SCR 986). The Council had earlier authorized the use of oil revenues to finance humanitarian relief in August 1991. Under the original plan, the UN would supervise the sale and distribution of oil to pay for food, medicine, and other humanitarian supplies. Iraq, however, rejected the program as a violation of its sovereignty. In April 1995 the Council agreed to give Iraq primary responsibility for the distribution of the humanitarian goods. (This, of course, contributed to the corruption in the ensuing program.) Iraq finally accepted the program in May 1996, but its implementation was delayed when Iraqi forces marched into Kurdish areas in August. The delivery of aid finally began in January 1997, five and half years after the imposition of the most comprehensive sanctions in history.

In November 1997 the United States again declared a regime change policy: it intended to isolate Hussein, support opposition groups, and move quickly to develop normal relations with a successor. The United States would keep sanctions in place until Saddam Hussein no longer ruled Iraq. Clinton administration officials, again foreshadowing later arguments, routinely said that Hussein had no intention of disarming and that only his removal could bring about the necessary compliance to end the sanctions. This policy invoked an extremely high level of hierarchy: removing a regime from power goes beyond the usual collective security attempts to punish states for violating community rules. But the United States position was that the mere existence of the Hussein regime threatened international peace and security.

While the American position hardened throughout 1997, France, Russia and China called for the end of sanctions. They cited humanitarian implications and criticized the weapons inspectors for their consistently negative reports about Iraqi progress toward meeting Council demands. Dealing with the humanitarian crisis was more important than maintaining the sanctions, let alone policies to bring about regime change. Consistent with the sanctions-as-negotiations approach, one French official said: "Life is constantly moving, time passes, and circumstances change. And we are building oceans of hatred in Iraq among ordinary people who are suffering that will outlast Saddam" (Erlanger 1997a).

While Russia, China, and France wanted to recognize and reward progressive compliance with an incremental easing of sanctions; the United States wanted full sanctions until Saddam was no longer in power. In October 1997 the United States proposed, but failed to get, additional sanctions to restrict international travel of high Iraqi officials. Russia, China, and France all abstained on a 23 October 1997 resolution condemning Iraq for its obstruction of weapons inspectors (SCR 1134). French Foreign Minister Hubert Védrine criticized American policy, arguing that it could only give Hussein the impression that "there would never be a way out of the tunnel" even if he got rid of all his weapons programs (Clines 1997).

In November 1997 the UN weapons inspectors certified that Iraq no longer had a nuclear weapons program. Despite Iraqi compliance with another Council demand, however, Clinton remarked that "sanctions will be there until the end of time, or as long as [Hussein] lasts." When the weapons inspectors' report brought no change to the American position, Iraq began to refuse access to the inspectors. The Council responded by unanimously passing the travel restrictions it had eschewed a month earlier and warning the "severest consequences" for noncompliance. Iraq, however, continued to hinder weapons inspectors throughout 1998.

In an argument that would recur five years later, the United States and Britain argued that existing resolutions authorized the use of force to punish Iraq for noncompliance, and Russia, France, and China argued that any use of force would require Council authorization. Russia, China, and France continued to argue that sanctions were causing too much suffering and should be lessened to offer Iraq incentives to cooperate with weapons inspections. They argued that the United

States kept "moving the goalposts" on Iraq (Malone 1999). Why should Iraq comply if nothing short of regime change would satisfy the United States? Russia, China, and France again abstained on another resolution condemning Iraq for its noncompliance with weapons inspections (SCR 1284).

Iraq ended all weapons inspections on 31 October 1998. The United States responded – without consulting the Security Council – with Operation Desert Fox, a four-day bombing campaign of Iraq beginning on 16 December. France, Russia, and China harshly criticized the American use of force (see Chapter 7). They argued that the United States approach to sanctions exacerbated the humanitarian crisis and squandered opportunities for additional Iraqi cooperation. The results were clear: the hierarchical American approach brought about continued sanctions, a split on the Security Council, an unauthorized American use of force, no regime change, and no weapons inspections.

We cannot know whether a bargaining approach would have convinced Hussein to comply in a more transparent way. But the United States assertion of hierarchy in this case was counterproductive. Iraq ended the weapons inspections because the United States made it clear that disarmament would not be enough to end the sanctions. The lack of inspections between 1998 and 2003 created an uncertainty about Iraq's weapons programs that played a tremendous role in the later United States rationale to invade Iraq. And the United States found no WMD in Iraq after its invasion. This is a curious and tragic chain of events. The sanctions did pressure Iraq into disarming its weapons programs – but without the inspections, the international community was unaware of its success until the United States invaded Iraq in 2003 and found no weapons. It is possible that an alternative approach to sanctions could have persuaded Iraq to continue the weapons inspections, the UN could have verified that Iraq had disarmed, and there would have been no rationale for the disastrous American invasion of Iraq.

Libya

The Security Council authorized sanctions against Libya for failing to extradite suspected terrorists in the bombing of a Pan Am flight over Lockerbie, Scotland (Jentleson and Whytock 2005). As with Iraq, the United States added its own conditions beyond Council resolutions before it would agree to end the sanctions. But this example raised other issues as well. Can the Council abuse its authority and pass "illegal" resolutions? Can the Security Council require states to violate their own treaty rights and obligations? Libya argued that the Montreal Convention to Suppress Acts of Violence against Civil Aviation gave it the right to try its own nationals. The Organization of African Unity concluded that the United States and the United Kingdom did not act in good faith toward Libya and the sanctions were so illegitimate that it formally voted not to comply. This is a clear example of how the pursuit of hierarchy can be counterproductive. Sanctions can only work if the international community accepts the legitimacy of Council actions and agrees to enforce them.

The United States had long considered Libya a "rogue state." Libya supported many revolutionary movements around the world, including Mandela's Pan African Congress in South Africa and the Black Power movement in the United States. Libya was extremely anti-Israeli and opposed the moderate Arab regimes in Egypt and Jordan. During the 1980s the United States routinely violated international law – exercising naval war games in Libyan territorial waters, shooting down two Libyan Air Force planes, attacking Libyan ships, raiding a radar site, etc. – to provoke Libya into responding and provide a pretext for war (Boyd-Judson 2005).

The United States charged Libya was a state sponsor of terrorism. It blamed Libya for bombing the Vienna and Rome airports on 27 December 1985. The United States had little conclusive evidence, and most intelligence agencies around the world accused Iran, Syria, or the Palestinian group led by Abu Nidal. The United States, again without conclusive evidence, blamed Libya for bombing a West Berlin disco on 5 April 1986. The bomb killed three people, including two American soldiers, and wounded 229, including 79 Americans. Nine days later, the United States bombed Libya, targeting Qadaffi's home in the raids and killing one of his daughters. When a bomb exploded on Pan Am flight 103 over Lockerbie, Scotland and killed 270 people on 21 December 1988, the United States again blamed Libya. Iran was a more obvious suspect – earlier that year the Ayatollah Khomeini pledged to target an American civil aircraft after the United States blew up an Iranian airbus killing 290 passengers four days before a Muslim holiday. The Lockerbie explosion was four days before Christmas.

The United States and the United Kingdom nevertheless pursued Libya. In November 1991 Scotland charged two Libyan intelligence officers with the bombings. The United States and the United Kingdom demanded that Libya surrender them for trial in Scotland. Libya, in accord with the 1971 Montreal Convention to Suppress Acts of Violence against Civil Aviation, arrested the officers and said that they would be tried under Libyan law. All three countries had ratified this treaty, which allowed host countries to prosecute its own nationals and did not require extradition. Libya also had no extradition agreement with either the United States or the United Kingdom. There was little legal basis for the American and British demands. When Libya offered to use binding arbitration, the United States and the United Kingdom refused.

They instead went to the Security Council to advocate economic sanctions against Libya for its refusal to extradite the suspected terrorists. The Council resisted sanctions at first, only calling on Libya to turn over the suspects (SCR 731). Libya refused and demanded that the United Kingdom adhere to its treaty commitments and hand over forensic evidence and the airliner's black box to enable Libya to try its nationals. The United Kingdom refused. Libya compromised by suggesting that a trial be held under Scottish law in a neutral country. But the impasse continued. Neither side believed a fair trial was possible under conditions agreed to by the other.

Libya then went to the International Court of Justice (ICJ) in March 1992, asking the ICJ to find that it had complied with all of its obligations under the Montreal Convention, and that the United States and the United Kingdom were not in compliance with the treaty. Libya also requested provisional measures to stop the United States and the United Kingdom from taking any action against Libya intended to coerce it to extradite the suspects. As the ICJ began its deliberations, the United States and the United Kingdom prevailed in the Security Council, which authorized an air and arms embargo because Libya's failure to extradite the suspected terrorists constituted a threat to international peace and security (SCR 748).

The Security Council sanctions complicated the ICJ proceedings. It now had to decide whether the Montreal Convention or the Council resolution took precedence. The United States and the United Kingdom went to the ICJ and argued that it had no jurisdiction in this case. They argued that the Security Council resolution took precedence over the Montreal Convention, that their extradition demand was based on the Council resolution, and that the Montreal Convention was irrelevant. In November 1992 the Council froze overseas Libyan assets and banned the provision of oil equipment to Libya (SCR 883). This is a clear example that the Security Council is a political entity protecting the interests of the veto powers rather than a legal entity enforcing international law. The Council required Libya to violate a treaty in order to end the sanctions.

Libya continued to refuse to hand over the suspects, saying that it would abide by the ICJ decision. The United States and the United Kingdom said that they would not be bound by any future ICJ ruling. The impasse was now bogged down by the tremendously slow pace of the ICJ, and the economic sanctions on Libya continued. Finally, in February 1998 – six years after Libya filed the case – the ICJ made a ruling, but only on the question of jurisdiction. The ICJ ruled against the United States and the United Kingdom, saying that it had the authority to hear the case. The ICJ ruled that it had jurisdiction when Libya made its claim, and it still had jurisdiction even after the Council passed its resolution. Without yet ruling on the merits of Libya's claims, the ICJ ruled that the Security Council could not thwart its legitimate role of resolving legal disputes that arise from treaty obligations.

This ICJ ruling was a political blow to the United States and the United Kingdom, and it emboldened many countries in the developing world to criticize the sanctions against Libya. In July 1998 seven Arab countries wrote to the Security Council stating the sanctions had no legal basis. The Organization of African Unity voted to ignore the sanctions after December unless the West agreed to a solution to the Lockerbie stalemate. The legitimacy of the economic sanctions was crumbling. Diplomatic efforts by South Africa – now led by Nelson Mandela – and Saudi Arabia convinced the United States and the United Kingdom to agree to a trial in The Hague with Scottish judges, laws, and rules of evidence. In August 1998 the Security Council authorized a suspension of the sanctions (not a complete termination) when Libya delivered the suspects to The Hague (SCR 1192).

Mandela continued to mediate the dispute. When the Libyans balked about a provision that the suspects would be imprisoned in the United Kingdom if convicted, Mandela got the British to agree to UN supervision of the Scottish prison. When the Libyans complained that a provision requiring all Libyan witnesses to testify at The Hague was just a ruse to arrest more Libyan officials, Mandela got the United Kingdom to agree to a smaller list of witnesses. Mandela gave Qaddafi his personal assurance that the trial would be fair. After one more act of defiance – Qadaffi asked the Security Council to force the United States to hand over nine soldiers who participated in the 1986 Tripoli bombings that killed his daughter – Libya eventually handed over the two suspects in April 1999. The long-awaited trial ended in January 2001 with an unusual outcome: with the same set of evidence regarding the same act, one suspect was found guilty and sentenced to life in prison, and one suspect was acquitted.

And still the United States and the United Kingdom refused to lift the sanctions. In February 2001 they made new demands on Libya, saying that Qaddafi must take responsibility for the Lockerbie bombing and pay compensation. These conditions were never included in any Security Council resolution. For seven years the United States refused to accept that a trial in a neutral country was sufficient to end the sanctions against Libya. Then, after it agreed to such a trial, it again refused to end the sanctions. Mandela angrily said that the Western countries had reneged on their promises to him. The sanctions continued into 2003, fourteen years after the Lockerbie incident. Qadaffi eventually agreed to the extra two Western conditions, accepting responsibility for the bombing and paying $2.7 billion in compensation for the families. He then agreed to a third demand: withdrawing Libya's case in front of the ICJ, who had still not ruled on the case more than eleven years after it was filed. On 12 September 2003, the Security Council formally lifted the sanctions on Libya. The United States abstained.

Conclusions

The Iraq and Libya examples illustrate the security–hierarchy paradox. Sanctions are a coercive, hierarchical collective security mechanism. They are appropriate enforcement measures that can be effective in certain circumstances. But sanctions that are too "tough" are counterproductive. Sanctions for the explicit purpose of regime change never work and almost always make things worse. The list of failure is quite long, including Cuba, Libya, Iraq, Iran, and North Korea. Either the target is strengthened domestically or it fights back with even more rules violations. The Libya case shows that the Council can undermine its own authority when it ignores basic principles of international law such as good faith and the peaceful resolution of disputes. The United States abused its authority on the Council by requiring Libya to violate a treaty in order to end sanctions. Member states concluded that the United States acted in an inappropriate way, and they willfully failed to enforce the sanctions.

While sanctions with too much hierarchy can be counterproductive, sanctions that include carrots are demonstrably more effective. But they require the United States to negotiate with target states rather than make demands. They require engagement rather than isolation. They require a more legitimate and consensual process of rule construction and enforcement. The United States would have to avoid its urge to treat others as evil, irrational, or untrustworthy. It would have to recognize that even "rogues" have legitimate grievances. It would have to compromise. It would have to consider the possibility that it can increase its own security by reducing the amount of hierarchy in world politics.

5   The use of force

The use of force is the ultimate collective security enforcement mechanism. Coercive operations do not follow peacekeeping norms of consent, neutrality, and self-defense. They are not engaged in peace-building functions in post-conflict situations. When the Council authorizes the use of force, it explicitly becomes a combatant in conflicts in order to punish those who threaten international peace and security (Roberts 2004). Whether to authorize the use of force is thus the most difficult decision the Council can make. The veto powers often disagree about which circumstances merit the use of force. These disputes again generally follow the pattern of the United States favoring more hierarchical arrangements than the other veto powers.

This chapter analyzes the use of force to enforce collective security rules. The first section discusses uses of force authorized by the Security Council. Two examples in this section are the Gulf War after the Iraqi invasion of Kuwait and the authorization to use force in Haiti after a military junta toppled a democratically elected regime. The second section analyzes unilateral uses of force by the United States since the cold war. It discusses the variety of American justifications for those uses of force, including self-defense, humanitarian intervention, and the necessity to enforce Security Council resolutions. It includes the example of enforcing no-fly zones in Iraq. Such uses of force assert a hierarchical security arrangement, and debates about whether they invoke legitimate hegemonic collective security rules or illegitimate rules of empire or preventive war are central to post-cold war world politics.

The uses of force authorized by the Security Council

The cold war rivalry between the United States and the Soviet Union prevented the Security Council from authorizing force to maintain international peace and security. The Council authorized force only once during the cold war, and that resulted from a peculiar set of circumstances. With the Soviet Union boycotting the Council over its recognition of nationalist China over Mao's communist regime, North Korea invaded South Korea. With neither the Soviet Union nor communist China to block action, the Council "recommended" that member states support a

United States-led military force to defend South Korea against invasion from the North. This was not a pure collective security operation; no country pledged their troops to the United Nations. The Council essentially approved United States foreign policy, and the United States commanded the multinational forces in Korea.

The end of the cold war created conditions for the great powers to construct a collective security arrangement. In addition to the increased use of economic sanctions and peacekeeping missions, the Council has also authorized the use of force seven times since the cold war:

- *Iraq/Kuwait (1990)*. The Council authorized a United States-led military force to defend Kuwait against invasion by Iraq. It later authorized a blockade to enforce sanctions on Iraq for failure to disarm its WMD programs.
- *Somalia (1992)*. The Council authorized a United States-led military force to ensure the delivery of humanitarian aid and later to capture tribal leaders responsible for blocking the delivery of humanitarian aid.
- *Yugoslavia (1993)*. The Council authorized NATO to provide safe havens and weapons exclusions zones around Bosnian cities. It also authorized a NATO blockade to enforce sanctions on Yugoslavia for their support of the Bosnian Serbs.
- *Haiti (1994)*. The Council authorized a blockade to enforce sanctions against Haiti for toppling the democratically elected President Aristide. It later authorized a United States-led military force to restore Aristide to power.
- *Rwanda (1994)*. The Council authorized France to provide humanitarian support for mostly Hutu refugees fleeing the country after their defeat in a civil war.
- *Afghanistan (2002)*. The Council authorized an International Security Assistance Force (ISAF) to provide a secure environment for the political and economic reconstruction of Afghanistan. Currently led by NATO forces, the ISAF continues to fight Taliban forces.
- *Congo (2003)*. The Council authorized European Union forces to end violence in eastern regions of the Democratic Republic of the Congo.

Through these uses of force the Security Council has enforced a variety of collective security rules. It has protected state sovereignty, prevented the proliferation of WMD, ensured the delivery of humanitarian aid, protected human rights, restored a democratically elected regime, enforced economic sanctions, and enforced peace settlements. The rationale for collective security now goes beyond preventing countries from invading each other. The Council has authorized the use of force to pursue a human security as well as a traditional state security agenda. This is a significant development in world politics.

However, these seven cases do not necessarily constitute the establishment of a successful collective security arrangement. The Security Council has never required states to place their forces under the command of the UN for collective action. In all cases the Council delegated its authority to regional organizations, alliances, or "coalitions of the willing." The UN has no "rapid response" forces ready to deploy. The Council authorizes force when the veto powers agree that it is necessary and when member states are willing to provide military forces.

It is also debatable whether these uses of force have had a significant and positive influence on international security. While the operation in Somalia prevented a massive famine, the United States pullout after taking casualties weakened the Council's later willingness to act (see Chapter 3). The Council was very slow to act in Bosnia, and the operation in Rwanda came after the genocide was over (see Chapter 8). The more recent operations are still in progress: the war in Afghanistan against the Taliban continues (see Chapter 9), as does the post-conflict reconciliation process in the Democratic Republic of the Congo (see Chapter 3). The only successful operations were Iraq and Haiti. Both immediate goals – removing Iraqi forces from Kuwait and removing the military dictatorship in Haiti – were achieved. But even in these cases, longer term goals were more elusive. Iraq continued to defy the Security Council, and Haiti's fledgling democracy continued to struggle. This section will examine these two cases.

The Gulf War

Nothing created more optimism for the possibilities of collective security than the Security Council response to the 1990 Iraqi invasion of Kuwait (Yetiv 1997). The enforcement action was primarily about state security rather than human security, avoiding controversial issues about the proper scope of Council jurisdiction. The Council imposed comprehensive economic sanctions for the first time. And it authorized the use of force for only the second time – and with all five veto powers acting in concert. After the war, the Council continued the sanctions and expanded the rules it was willing to enforce by including non-proliferation and terrorism demands as conditions for lifting those sanctions. The Gulf War more closely resembles a textbook case of collective security than any other Council action.

There are no other examples like this, though, because the combination of factors that led to the Gulf War has rarely occurred in the post-cold war world (Hurrell 1992, Bennett and Lepgold 1993). Those factors include an obvious act of aggression by one member state against another member state; significant implications for global security and economic stability; an overwhelming atmosphere of multilateral cooperation among the great powers; and the willingness of the United States to commit a great amount of resources. Most post-cold war global security issues have been messier and more complicated than the Iraqi invasion of Kuwait. The Council subsequently found it difficult to replicate the political will necessary to support such forceful measures in later conflicts. Still, the Gulf War is an historic example of post-cold war collective security.

The Iraqi invasion of Kuwait had its roots in the Iran–Iraq war of the 1980s. Iran's 1979 Islamic revolution brought a radical theocratic regime to power, challenging Iraq's secular Arab nationalism as a social force capable of uniting the Middle East. Iran's Shia government also threatened to destabilize Iraq, which had a Sunni-dominated government in a country whose population was two-thirds Shiite. Hussein feared that Khomeini's fundamentalist Islam would threaten his interests both at home and throughout the region. The resulting war (in which the United States armed Iraq to prevent Iran from dominating the region) led to the deaths of over one million people and was largely a stalemate. The two agreed to a ceasefire in August 1988 with the mediation of Secretary General Perez de Cuellar.

The Iran–Iraq war left Saddam Hussein with a militarily weakened Iraq, a devastated economy, and large debts to Kuwait and Saudi Arabia. Iraq needed an increase in global oil prices to get back on its feet. Iraq demanded that Kuwait forgive the Iraqi debt and agree to OPEC oil quotas. When Kuwait refused both demands, Iraq threatened military action, putting 35,000 troops on the Kuwaiti border in July 1990. Hussein felt that Arab states owed Iraq for its war against the fundamentalist Islamic threat in Iran. He resurrected claims that Kuwait was part of Iraq, as it was during the Ottoman Empire. On 25 July Saddam Hussein met United States ambassador April Glaspie. While the nature of the exchange at this meeting is disputed, Hussein left the meeting discounting the possibility of an American response to his plans for Kuwait.

Iraq invaded Kuwait on 2 August 1990 with around 140,000 troops and 1,800 tanks. On that same day the Security Council condemned the invasion and called for the withdrawal of Iraqi troops, with only Yemen abstaining (SCR 660). The Iraqi invasion of Kuwait threatened global security in a number of ways. It challenged the emerging collective security rules following the end of the cold war. It created the possibility that Iraq would continue to threaten or even invade other states, including Saudi Arabia. And it made significantly higher oil prices and global recession more likely. On 6 August the Council authorized comprehensive economic sanctions (SCR 661). President Bush justified Council action:

> This is the first assault on the new world that we seek, the first test of our mettle. Had we not responded to this first provocation with clarity of purpose, if we do not continue to demonstrate our determination, it would be a signal to actual and potential despots around the world. America and the world must defend common vital interests – and we will. America and the world must support the rule of law – and we will. America and the world must stand up to aggression – and we will. And one thing more: In the pursuit of these goals America will not be intimidated.
>
> (Bush and Scowcroft 1998: 379)

This was a crucial test of Security Council legitimacy at the beginning of the post-cold war world. Would Arab and Muslim states in the region comply with the sanctions and/or support an American-led military coalition? The Arab League held an emergency meeting on 10 August and, despite Iraqi pleas for unity, twelve out of twenty states voted to enforce the sanctions and provide troops to the emerging UN coalition. Hussein desperately tried to unite the Arab and Muslim world around his challenge to the UN system. On 12 August he offered to withdraw from Kuwait when Israel withdrew from the occupied territories. On 15 August he agreed to all Iranian demands to end the Iran–Iraq war. But his efforts failed. Very few Middle East leaders – with the exception of Palestinian leader Yassir Arafat – publicly criticized the UN operation and supported Iraq. The military coalition eventually included 30,000 soldiers from Arab states.

One controversial aspect of the Gulf War was whether the United States was simply getting multilateral cover for actions it had already decided to do. For example, the United States began a naval blockade of Iraq two weeks before the Council authorized enforcement of the economic sanctions. The United States also began a military buildup in the region – particularly sending troops to Saudi Arabia – months before the Council authorized the use of force. And when the Council did authorize force after a 15 January deadline for Iraqi forces to leave Kuwait (SCR 678), the resolution did not clearly specify whether it was authorizing collective security enforcement or endorsing an ad hoc alliance led by the United States. To what extent was the Gulf War invoking collective security rules? And to what extent was the Gulf War invoking hegemonic war rules?

The debate within the United States focused on whether to use force immediately after the 15 January deadline or to wait and give the economic sanctions more time. Public opinion was evenly divided. In January, Congress gave President Bush the authority to wage war; the Senate vote was 52–47 and the House vote was 250–183. On 17 January the United States launched an air war against Iraqi military targets, including factories suspected of producing WMD. President Bush said that the world was at:

> a historic moment. We have in the past year made great progress in ending the long era of conflict and cold war. We have before us the opportunity to forge for ourselves and for future generations a new world order, a world where the rule of law, not the law of the jungle, governs the conduct of nations. When we are successful, and we will be, we have a real chance at this new world order, an order in which a credible United Nations can use its peacekeeping role to fulfill the promise and vision of the UN's founders.
>
> (Bush 1991)

Both American and global public opinion supported the war after it began. Iraq engaged in many desperate acts: it used Westerners as human shields at strategic sites, attacked Israel with Scud missiles, dumped Kuwaiti oil into the Persian Gulf, and threatened to assassinate President Bush. When further rounds of diplomacy failed, the United States-led military coalition launched a ground war on 24 February. Within one week Iraq announced that it would accept all UN resolutions and withdraw from Kuwait.

President Bush then decided not to send American troops to Baghdad. He had many reasons for this decision – reasons later rejected by his son twelve years later. The elder Bush concluded that invading Iraq went beyond the Security Council mandate and would thus split the multinational coalition. Since there was no legal basis for ending Saddam's regime, Bush did not want American actions to look like imperialism. Bush knew that it would be a more difficult fight – nations fight harder on their own territory than they do protecting foreign spoils. And he also asked the most important question: what would happen after the military victory? Which groups could rule and bring stability to Iraq? The Shia majority would likely have closer relations with Iran. Bush concluded that United States interests required a secular Iraq to balance the forces of fundamentalist Islam in the region.

Preserving democracy in Haiti

One of the more extraordinary Security Council authorizations of force occurred during the crisis in Haiti (Malone 1998, Mobekk 2001). For the first time the Council declared that a coup against a democratically elected government was a threat to international peace and security. Haiti was an unusual choice for the Council to make its first stand regarding democracy. In 200 years of independence Haiti has had 42 heads of state, and 29 were assassinated or overthrown. Haiti was governed by Francois "Papa Doc" Duvalier and then by his son Jean-Claude "Baby Doc" Duvalier from 1957 to 1986. Haiti was one of many United States cold war allies whose anticommunism trumped abysmal human rights records. "Papa Doc" ruled through terror enforced by American-trained counterinsurgency units. The repression eased somewhat when "Baby Doc" took power. The end of the cold war decreased American support, and the spread of democratic and human rights norms all contributed to the end of the regime.

A transitional government led by General Henri Namphy freed all political prisoners, disbanded the regime's terror police, wrote a new constitution and prepared for elections. But the government did little to stop paramilitary groups from intimidating peasant organizations. A strong grassroots movement led by Father Jean-Bertrand Aristide led protests against both the violence and the greed of the economic elite. Elections held in November 1987 were marred by violence and widely condemned by the international community. The transitional government held new elections in January 1988, but they had only a 5 percent turnout.

The winner – a political scientist named Leslie Manigat – did not last long. After Manigat fired a top general, the military ousted him in a June 1988 coup. In September there was another coup, led by General Prosper Avril, an officer close to Baby Doc. Under Avril the Haitian death squads once again became active, and peasant resistance began to grow. Violence increased throughout 1989. The death of an eleven-year-old girl during an antigovernment rally on 5 March 1990 and the ensuing mass demonstrations during her funeral ended the Avril regime. It was now clear that elections could only be held with extensive international monitoring, and yet another transitional Haitian government requested such assistance from the Security Council.

This was a historic request. The only election monitoring done by the UN to that point had been in Nicaragua as part of a regional peace plan agreed to by multiple countries. This was the first time a state had asked the UN to monitor its own elections in a time of internal conflict. Many on the Council resisted, not wanting to intervene into "domestic affairs." What did an election in Haiti have to do with international security? Notions of human security, the relationship between democracy and conflict resolution, and the corresponding expansion of Security Council jurisdiction had not yet taken hold. In a compromise, the General Assembly authorized a monitoring mission in October 1990.

The Haitian military, now led by Raul Cedras, bowed to international pressure and cooperated with the UN monitors. The December 1990 elections had no violence and a large turnout. Aristide won over 67 percent of the vote even though there were multiple candidates. Aristide achieved a landslide victory by appealing to the Haitian masses with populist rhetoric attacking the economic elite and the military. His inaugural speech was in Creole – the language spoken by the poor – rather than French. He replaced top military officers and attempted to institute civilian control of the military. He created a civilian police force separate from the military. He established commissions to investigate previous massacres. He proposed raising the minimum wage to $5 per day. Aristide's policies alarmed the traditional Haitian elite, and they waited for an opportunity to remove him.

What they used against Aristide were his ambiguous statements about whether his own supporters should use violence. Those loyal to him intimidated officials in the parliament and the judiciary, often referring to "necklacing," the Haitian practice of putting a burning tire around someone's neck. After a fiery address to the General Assembly on 25 September 1991, Aristide returned to Haiti and his supporters showed up with tires. Aristide referred to them as "beautiful tools" and "nice instruments." On 29 September the military arrested Aristide, saying that he was inciting popular violence. Cedras, under pressure from the United States and France, allowed Aristide to leave the country rather than execute him.

The Security Council still opposed any action on the grounds that it was an internal matter. The Organization of American States (OAS), however, urged members on 8 October to freeze Haitian assets and impose a trade embargo except for humanitarian aid. On 11 October the General Assembly passed a groundbreaking resolution supporting a Western notion of democracy, demanding the restoration of Aristide and encouraging states to support the OAS embargo. The United States did not initially support OAS efforts to restore Aristide to power. Many in the Bush administration viewed Aristide as a radical socialist. The United States did not comply with the voluntary OAS embargo on Haiti, and it did not want the OAS to go to the Security Council and ask for mandatory sanctions.

Haitian refugees complicated the American position. In 1981 the United States and Haiti agreed to an "interdiction" program allowing the United States to return all Haitian refugees. To comply with its own laws and treaty obligations, the United States conducted cursory interviews to determine their refugee status. But the United States always called the vast majority economic migrants and sent them back to Haiti. The military coup greatly increased the number of Haitian refugees the United States was sending back to Haiti. When a lawsuit challenged the screening process, the Supreme Court upheld the interdiction program, quite possibly in violation of United States treaty obligations regarding refugees. So the United States continued to send Aristide supporters back to Haiti, where human rights organizations documented thousands of deaths and arrests throughout 1992.

By the end of 1992 the OAS concluded that the crisis in Haiti should trigger Security Council jurisdiction because the military coup threatened other fragile democracies in the region and because Haitian refugees threatened regional stability. Although the Security Council had already recognized refugee crises to trigger its jurisdiction in Somalia and Yugoslavia, citing democracy as an enforceable collective security rule was a novel idea. In December 1992 the OAS asked the Security Council to direct all states to comply with its trade embargo on Haiti. The incoming Clinton administration agreed, pledging United States support to restore the Aristide regime and strengthen American observance of the OAS embargo. In June 1993 the Council unanimously prohibited the sale of weapons, oil, and petroleum products to Haiti (SCR 841). Even China voted in favor of the resolution given the OAS request, equating Haiti with its Somalia position in that this was a unique situation.

The sanctions convinced the military regime to negotiate, and the UN sponsored talks between Cedras and Aristide in New York. The ensuing agreement called for an end to UN sanctions once a prime minister nominated by Aristide and confirmed by the parliament took office. The military junta would receive amnesty, Aristide would return to Haiti in October 1993, and the UN would supervise the establishment of a new police force and judiciary. In accordance with the agreement, Aristide nominated Robert Malval to be prime minister on 24 July, the parliament confirmed Malval on 18 August, the Security Council suspended the sanctions on 27 August, and the UN began preparations for a peacekeeping mission. The expected return of Aristide, however, again increased violence in Haiti. The Council warned the military regime that it would reinstitute the sanctions unless it reduced the level of violence in Haiti.

On 11 October the USS Harlan County arrived in Port-au-Prince with 30 soldiers that the United States was contributing to the UN peacekeeping force. It was eight days after the deaths of American soldiers in Somalia. Armed groups allowed into the port area by police threatened the incoming troops. They yelled: "We are going to turn this into another Somalia!" Since the port was not secure and the troops had no coercive mandate, the United States sent the ship back home. Some armed thugs prevented the deployment of a UN peacekeeping mission. The Harlan County incident convinced the Security Council that it would have to use more coercive methods to restore the democratic regime in Haiti. So at exactly the same time the Council was retreating in Somalia and hesitant regarding Bosnia, it ratcheted up the pressure on Haiti. Two days after the Harlan County incident the Council reauthorized economic sanctions (SCR 873). The United States then sent six warships to Haiti to enforce the embargo.

Domestic politics influenced the more forceful American approach. The Clinton administration was heavily criticized for continuing the forced repatriation policy toward Haitian refugees. Six members of the Congressional Black Caucus

chained themselves to the White House fence and were arrested to gain public-
ity over the issue. Randall Robinson, head of the NGO TransAfrica, launched
a hunger strike. In response, Clinton instituted a credible interview process for
the Haitian refugees and advocated comprehensive economic sanctions to the
Security Council. On 6 May 1994 the Council adopted the comprehensive sanctions, including a travel ban on the regime (SCR 917).

The Haitian regime remained defiant, ordering all international monitors out of
Haiti on 11 July. Many Council members preferred a quick resolution to the crisis
and worried about the humanitarian impact of the sanctions. In return for Russian
support for using military force in Haiti, the United States agreed to favorable
World Bank loans and a Russian-dominated peacekeeping mission in Georgia. On
31 July 1994, the Council authorized the deployment of a United States-led military force to remove the military regime and install Aristide (SCR 940). China and
Brazil abstained on this groundbreaking resolution. For the first time the Council
authorized the removal of one regime and the installation of another (consider the
veto power disputes over "regime change" in Iraq). It was also the first time the
United States sought Council authority for the use of force in its own hemisphere
(consider the many unilateral American uses of force in Latin America, the most
recent in Panama in 1989).

Clinton argued on 15 September that the use of military force was necessary:

> [T]he United States must protect our interests, to stop the brutal atrocities that
> threaten tens of thousands of Haitians; to secure our borders and to preserve
> stability and promote democracy in our hemisphere . . . In Haiti we have a
> case in which the right is clear, in which the country in question is nearby,
> in which our own interests are plain, in which the mission is achievable and
> limited and in which the nations of the world stand with us. We must act.
>
> (Clinton 1994)

On the next day – without consulting the Security Council – Clinton sent former President Jimmy Carter, General Colin Powell, and Senator Sam Nunn to
Haiti in a final attempt to end the conflict peacefully. With American warplanes
ready to take off toward Haiti, General Cedras negotiated the terms of his depar-
ture. United States troops began to deploy on 19 September, and Aristide returned
to power on 15 October.

The Security Council authorization of force helped to restore the democratically elected Haitian government. The immediate goal was successful. But the larger
goal of ensuing democracy in Haiti has been more elusive. Elections in 1995 and
1997 did not meet democratic standards. In 1999 Aristide's successor Réne Préval
dissolved the parliament and ran the country by decree. Aristide returned to power
after elections in 2000 – but all opposition parties had boycotted the election. In 2001
Aristide survived two coup attempts. In 2004 a violent uprising against Aristide
forced him (again) into exile, leading to the deployment of another UN peacekeeping mission into a violent situation. Réne Préval was declared the winner of questionable February 2006 elections. The quest for Haitian democracy continues.

Unilateral uses of force by the United States

The use of force authorized by the Security Council invokes procedural collective security. Unilateral uses of force by the United States without Council authorization invoke hegemonic collective security. The United States, sometimes alone and sometimes with others, has used force without Security Council authorization in seven different situations since the cold war.

- *Iraq (1993)*. The United States, the United Kingdom and France sent air strikes over Baghdad to enforce a no-fly zone in northern Iraq to prevent Iraqi attacks against the Kurds and in southern Iraq to prevent Iraqi attacks against the Shia. The United States again used force in 1996 to enforce a no-fly zone in northern Iraq.
- *Iraq (1993)*. The United States bombed sites in Iraq in retaliation for an assassination attempt on former President Bush.
- *Iraq (1998)*. The United States engaged in four days of bombing – known as Operation Desert Fox – because Iraq refused to allow weapons inspectors into suspected sites.
- *Sudan and Afghanistan (1998)*. The United States bombed terrorist camps and other targets in Afghanistan and Sudan in retaliation for their role in the terrorist bombings of American embassies.
- *Yugoslavia (1999)*. The United States, as part of a NATO operation, engaged in ten weeks of bombing Yugoslavia for its treatment of Bosnian Muslims in Kosovo.
- *Afghanistan (2001)*. The United States invaded Afghanistan to take out the Taliban government for their support of the Al Qaeda terrorists who committed the terrorist acts of 11 September 2001.
- *Iraq (2003)*. The United States and a "coalition of the willing" invaded Iraq because of its alleged WMD programs and alleged ties to terrorist groups.

The crux of post-cold war world politics is how to interpret these unilateral uses of force. Which rules of global security do they invoke? Do they invoke hegemonic collective security? Are they legitimate use of force by the militarily dominant state because they attempt to enforce mutually agreed upon rules? Or do they invoke rules of war or rivalry? Are they legitimate exercises of self-defense? Or do they invoke preventive war or empire? Are they illegitimate uses of force because they are solely an attempt to maintain the privileged status of the United States? The United States has justified these uses of force by invoking both hegemonic collective security ("we are enforcing Security Council resolutions" or "we are engaging in humanitarian intervention") and war/rivalry rules ("we are engaging in self-defense"). But others have challenged the legitimacy of those justifications throughout the post-cold war world, arguing that the United States has engaged in preventive war and invoked rules of empire.

A crucial part of this debate is the scope of anticipatory self-defense claims. Customary international law recognizes the right of anticipatory self-defense if the threat of attack is imminent, there is no other way to prevent the attack, and the use of force is proportionate to the threat. But Article 51 of the UN Charter asserts that states have "the inherent right of individual or collective self-defense if an armed attack occurs." This seems to restrict the previous notion of self-defense and limit legitimate uses of force to instances after one has been attacked (Arend and Beck 1993). In its only case regarding Article 51, the International Court of Justice interpreted self-defense rights narrowly, rejecting United States claims that self-defense justified its actions in Nicaragua (supporting the contras, mining harbors, etc.) during the 1980s. It ruled that (1) Nicaragua had not engaged in an armed attack against the United States and (2) no other state had requested a collective self-defense effort against Nicaragua.

Whether Article 51 altered customary international law or not, United States claims of self-defense to justify uses of force since the cold war both go beyond UN Charter language (Hendrickson 2001) and stretch the customary notion of self-defense in international law (Byers 2003). The United States has claimed self-defense to justify four post-cold war unilateral uses of force: (1) bombing Iraq after the assassination attempt on President Bush; (2) the 1998 bombing of Sudan and Afghanistan after the terrorist attacks on American embassies; (3) the 2001 invasion of Afghanistan; and (4) the 2003 invasion of Iraq. In none of these cases was there reason to believe that further plots or attacks were imminent. There was no armed attack against the United States in cases (1) and (4). Cases (2) and (3) followed terrorist incidents, which had never been understood to constitute an "armed attack." For example, United States' claims of self-defense after bombing Libya in 1986 for supporting a terrorist attack were widely criticized.

Yet out of these four cases only the invasion of Iraq brought widespread condemnation on the United States for abusing the concept of self-defense. Few beyond Arab League countries complained about the retaliation against Iraq for the assassination attempt. Criticisms of the 1998 bombings of Sudan and Afghanistan focused on whether the targets were appropriate, not whether the United States had the right to retaliate. The small amount of criticism for the invasion of Afghanistan suggested that states now considered a major terrorist incident to rise to the level of an "armed attack" and thus legitimately trigger an Article 51 response. Perhaps United States uses of force since the cold war have expanded customary notions of self-defense. Or perhaps states interpreted these uses of force as hegemonic war: a legitimate use of force by the dominant power to maintain stability in addition to protecting American national interests.

But the American rationale for the 2003 invasion of Iraq went too far: we think that Iraq has WMD, and we think that Iraq has ties to Al Qaeda, and we think that Iraq might give those weapons to Al Qaeda, and we think that Al Qaeda might use those weapons against us. This does not rise to the level of preempting an imminent threat in self-defense. Consider how the United States would respond if Russia or China made the same argument to justify a use of force. The vast majority of states have accordingly criticized this understanding of self-defense. They interpret it as an attempt to enable the United States to use force outside the constraints of the UN Charter system. They reject a global security arrangement with that much hierarchy. They want traditional notions of self-defense to bind the United States.

A second justification for unilateral uses of force since the cold war has been to enforce Security Council resolutions. The United States used this justification in four cases: (1) the no-fly zones in Iraq (see below); (2) the use of force against Iraq in 1998 (see Chapter 7); (3) bombing Yugoslavia in 1999 over Kosovo (see Chapter 8); and (4) the 2003 invasion of Iraq (see Chapter 9). With this justification the United States invoked hegemonic collective security rules, claiming it had the authority to enforce Council resolutions. The vast majority of states rejected this claim in all four cases. The uses of force against Iraq in 1998 and 2003 were roundly criticized. The no-fly zones and the Kosovo operation were criticized less because they included a humanitarian component, discussed below. There is not one post-cold war example of the United States invoking hegemonic collective security and a majority of states accepting the legitimacy of that act. States reject the hierarchical implications of this security arrangement. They reject the notion that the United States can legitimately bypass the authority of the Security Council (Byers 2003).

A third justification for the unilateral use of force has been humanitarian intervention, or the use of force to protect individuals in another state from widespread human rights violations. These interventions go forward without the consent of the target state and without the authorization of the Security Council. There have been four humanitarian interventions since the cold war: the United States-led "no-fly zones" in Iraq (1991), the NATO intervention into Kosovo (1999), and the ECOWAS interventions into Liberia (1990) and Sierra Leone (1997). This level of state practice has led to a debate about whether humanitarian intervention is now a third legitimate justification for the use of force, in addition to self-defense and Security Council authorization (Macrae 2002, Wheeler 2001, Aview 1998). Many developing countries, however, argue that humanitarian intervention is another form of cultural imperialism. They are suspicious that the emerging Western notion of a "responsibility to protect" is a pretext to violate their sovereignty and enable powerful states to exercise influence over them (Wheeler 2002). Humanitarian intervention will continue to be a contested state practice for the foreseeable future.

No-fly zones in Iraq

A good example of the complicated issues surrounding humanitarian intervention is the Western attempt to establish no-fly zones for Kurds in northern Iraq and Shia in southern Iraq after the Gulf War. While the Security Council did not explicitly authorize this use of force, many in the West believed it was necessary to protect the human rights of Iraqi citizens. Depending on one's interpretation, this use of force was either an egregious violation of state sovereignty or a landmark use of force to protect human security.

After the Gulf War, significant portions of the Iraqi Kurdish and Shiite populations rebelled against Saddam Hussein's regime. The United States encouraged this rebellion, and the Kurds and Shiites expected American support. But no support came, and the Iraqi military began a crackdown against both movements. Given the Iraqi use of chemical weapons against both groups in the 1980s, the crackdown created a massive exodus of nearly two million Iraqis into Turkey, Iran and Kuwait. Iran and Turkey brought the issue to the Security Council, saying that they were unable to cope with the humanitarian crisis.

The Council had to determine if this was within its jurisdiction. Generally, the relevant UN humanitarian agencies, with the consent of local states, dealt with refugee crises. But this time the Council determined that a state's oppression of its own citizens was a threat to international peace and security (SCR 688). It demanded that Iraq end the repression to stem the flow of refugees. SCR 688 was also the first resolution to order a state to receive humanitarian assistance from international agencies. It won only ten votes; China and India abstained, and Cuba, Yemen, and Zimbabwe voted against. The resolution, however, included no enforcement language, to persuade China to abstain rather than veto.

Turkey feared that Kurdish refugees would destabilize its country by agitating Kurds within Turkey to demand independence. Not wanting to establish refugee camps from which Kurdish separatists could attack Turkish targets, Turkey closed its border. Assisting Kurdish refugees now meant that the aid would have to go within Iraq itself. Western countries thus began a humanitarian relief program in northern Kurdish areas – without Iraqi permission. European countries proposed the idea of "safe areas" within northern Iraq in which the refugees would be protected by coalition forces. The United States announced on 16 April 1991 that it would deploy forces in northern Iraq to establish relief camps for Kurdish refugees. To prevent a clash between Iraqi and coalition forces, the United States ordered a "no-fly zone" for the Iraqi military, north of the 36th parallel.

There was huge public support throughout the West for this legally questionable intervention. Western countries offered two reasons why this was not military intervention into Iraqi internal affairs: (1) SCR 688 authorized it and (2) it was a short-term humanitarian intervention, and the UN would eventually take over the operation. The problem with the first argument was that SCR 688 did not invoke any Chapter VII powers. It could not be construed to have authorized the no-fly zones. And none of the postwar resolutions that did invoke Chapter VII powers mentioned Iraq's treatment of its own citizens. Both China and the Soviet Union pledged to veto any resolution authorizing Chapter VII action in northern Iraq to assist the Kurds. They were not ready to enshrine human rights with Security Council protection. The United States, Britain and France were clearly acting without Council authorization.

The problem with the second argument was that the Secretary General criticized the West's efforts and urged them to consult with Iraq before deploying forces to help the Kurds. There was no initial coordination between the Western humanitarian effort and UN humanitarian agencies. There were no immediate prospects that the UN would eventually take over the Western humanitarian efforts. However, in late May Iraq consented to a UN humanitarian operation in the north in an attempt to remove coalition forces. Eventually coalition forces were replaced with UN civilian police. At that point all humanitarian relief efforts in Iraq had the stamp of UN legitimacy.

In the summer of 1992 Iraq began to harass UN officials and deny visas to UN civilian police bound for northern and southern Iraq. In August the United States, Britain, and France reiterated their enforcement of "no-fly zones" to protect the Kurds in the north and the Shia in the south. Iraq often tested Western resolve and sent planes into the no-fly zones. The United States shot down an Iraqi plane in the southern no-fly zone on 27 December 1992. Iraq then moved surface-to-air missiles into the no-fly zones and continued their flights into the south. On 6 January 1993 the Western powers, this time joined by Russia, gave Iraq 48 hours to remove the surface-to-air missiles. When Iraq continued its flights into the south, the United States, Britain and France participated in air strikes against the Baghdad regime on 13/14 January. Iraq did not violate the no-fly zones for several years after this use of force.

The Security Council did not authorize the January 1993 strikes. The United States cited SCR 688 to justify the bombings. Madeleine Albright, then the Ambassador to the United Nations, foreshadowed later arguments by the Bush administration and stated that the United States "recognize[s] [the Persian Gulf] as vital to US national interests, and we will behave with others multilaterally when we can and unilaterally when we must" (Rouleau 1995). Russia and China heavily criticized the bombing. Russian President Boris Yeltsin argued that the use of force violated international law because it was taken without Security Council authorization: "We firmly believe that there should be an adequate reaction to Iraq's actions, which must be based on concerted decisions. The situation obviously needs to be considered by the UN Security Council" (Schmeman 1993).

Division on the Security Council renewed when Iraqi interference in warfare between two Kurdish factions in 1996 initiated another United States use of force. Hussein, despite warnings to stay out of the Kurdish dispute, violated the no-fly zone and sent troops into the north. The United States retaliated against the Iraqi violation of the no-fly zone with missile strikes in the south and extending the southern no-fly zone 60 miles to the north (to within 30 miles of Baghdad). The missile attacks were in the south to prevent any appearance that the United States was taking sides in the Kurdish dispute. The United States again cited SCR 688. Clinton argued that the strikes were necessary "to demonstrate once again that reckless acts have consequences, to reduce Saddam's ability to strike out again at his neighbors and to increase America's ability to prevent future acts of violence and aggression" (Mitchell 1996).

The political support for this United States use of force declined considerably. Britain supported the strike but did not participate. Turkey and Saudi Arabia refused to allow United States planes on their bases. France refused to enforce the extended no-fly zone and did not support the strike, arguing that the use of force without Council authorization was not appropriate. France also argued that Iraqi troops going into the north did not violate any UN resolutions, and that the strikes would strengthen fundamentalist Islamic groups in the region. Russia and China heavily criticized the use of force, suggesting that the real reason for the strikes were the upcoming United States elections. Yeltsin argued that the strikes were "an inappropriate and unacceptable reaction to the latest events in northern Iraq." Despite these tensions on the Council, Hussein removed his troops from the north within a few days after the bombing.

Conclusions

Whether unilateral American uses of force contribute to or hinder international peace and security is a central part of world politics since the cold war. Many scholars from a variety of traditions criticize United State unilateralism. Realists warn that unilateralism encourages the formation of a counterbalancing alliance (Walt 2002) or at least "soft balancing" against the United States (Paul 2005). Neoliberals argue that unilateralism is less efficient because security interdependence requires multilateral cooperation through international organizations (Ikenberry 2003). Constructivists argue that unilateralism undermines the legitimacy of the international order (Cronin 2001).

Other scholars argue that the merits of multilateralism are not intrinsic but depend on the circumstances (Brooks and Wohlforth 2005). Against the realists, they argue that the qualitative nature of United States military dominance makes it extremely difficult to counterbalance. Against the institutionalists, they argue that multilateralism also includes costs for the United States, including reduced constitutional autonomy, impaired popular sovereignty, and limitations on foreign policy options. And against the constructivists, they argue that legitimacy comes from the successful provision of public goods rather than adherence to Charter procedures.

This last point is crucial given the constructivist argument of this book. Advocates of unilateral uses of American force argue that what matters is effectiveness. The United States is the militarily dominant country, and others will see its actions as legitimate because the United States provides order. Order – brought about by military dominance – creates legitimacy. Material realities drive social relations. The rule-oriented constructivist argument, however, is the opposite: legitimacy leads to order. The social world is primary. The material world is interpreted through social rules. How others interpret the United States is more important than the material fact that the United States is militarily dominant. If American military might is to contribute to global order, it must invoke a legitimate set of global security rules and avoid asserting too much hierarchy.

6   International tribunals

An important development since the cold war is the use of international tribunals as a collective security enforcement mechanism. Tribunals are institutionalizing international humanitarian law, the emerging norm of "human security," and the meaning of state sovereignty toward a "responsibility to protect." Like smart sanctions, they hold individual decision-makers accountable for violating community rules. State leaders can no longer claim a sovereign right to pursue national security or maintain domestic order through actions that violate international humanitarian law. Rules prohibiting genocide, crimes against humanity, and war crimes now universally bind even heads of states, and the international community has created a variety of international tribunals to punish those who systematically violate those rules.

This chapter discusses the development of international tribunals since the cold war. The first section analyzes two ad hoc tribunals created by the Security Council to prosecute war criminals in the former Yugoslavia and Rwanda. The second section discusses hybrid courts operating in Sierra Leone and Cambodia. The third section analyzes the creation, development, and early investigations of the International Criminal Court (ICC), a potentially revolutionary new court with jurisdiction over genocide, crimes against humanity, and war crimes.

International tribunals illustrate the security–hierarchy paradox. Tribunals increase hierarchy in world politics by holding state decision-makers accountable for their actions. The United States, consistent with its preference for more hierarchical security arrangements, has strongly supported the use of tribunals to prosecute those who violate international humanitarian law. However, the United States has tried to undermine the ICC because its jurisdiction could theoretically extend to American citizens. The United States wants rules against genocide, crimes against humanity, and war crimes. It just does not want those rules to apply to the United States. This is another example of how the American pursuit of hierarchy can at some point become counterproductive. Only the invasion of Iraq has done more harm to the legitimacy of American hegemony than United States efforts to undermine the ICC.

Ad hoc tribunals for Yugoslavia and Rwanda

The nature of post-cold war conflicts convinced the Security Council that international tribunals were necessary to maintain international security. The typical conflict is an ethnically based civil war in which all sides violate international humanitarian law. Combatants have engaged in an incredible variety of illegal ways to fight: ethnic cleansing, genocide, rape, torture, child soldiers, enslavement, starvation, etc. Peace-building efforts are often fatally damaged when the perpetrators of these acts remain in civil society as post-conflict political leaders. Bringing war criminals to justice and establishing the rule of law are often crucial steps toward political stability. Post-conflict peace processes often require a judicial mechanism to succeed.

International law obligates states to prosecute violations of international humanitarian law in their own territory. But many war-torn states cannot or should not take on this responsibility. Some states (e.g. Sierra Leone, Rwanda) are unable to do so: they do not have the necessary resources, legal framework, trained professionals, administrative capacity, and judicial infrastructure. Some states (e.g. Cambodia, Yugoslavia, or Indonesia) are unwilling: they do not have a legal culture of accountability or judicial independence and will shield war criminals from prosecution. Others (e.g. Iraq?) may be able but will likely mete out a "victor's justice" that does not meet international standards. International tribunals can be necessary components of a peace-building process when a state is in one of these situations.

The Security Council broke legal and political ground on 25 May 1993 when it created the International Criminal Tribunal for Yugoslavia (ICTY) to prosecute those who systematically violated international humanitarian law during the wars in the former Yugoslavia (SCR 827). The ICTY was the first tribunal established with Chapter VII powers; the first to indict an acting head of state (Slobodan Milosevic); the first to convict anyone for the crime of genocide; and the first to prosecute rape as a crime against humanity. The following year the Security Council established the International Criminal Tribunal for Rwanda (ICTR) to prosecute violations of international humanitarian law during that conflict (SCR 955). The ICTR was the first tribunal to convict a former head of state (Rwandan Prime Minister Jean Kambanda) of genocide.

The ICTY and the ICTR have similar structures. Both are subsidiary organs of the Security Council with Chapter VII powers. For example, the ICTY ordered Slobodan Milosevic's assets to be frozen until he was in custody. Both have Chambers and an Office of the Prosecutor. The Prosecutor's office is independent of the Security Council and initiates investigations on its own discretion. It is limited only by the jurisdiction established by the Council and the requirement that a tribunal judge confirm the indictment. Both tribunals had the same prosecutor until 2003, when the Council created a separate prosecutor's office for the ICTR to deal with the burgeoning caseload. The Chambers have also grown over time, currently consisting of sixteen permanent judges plus additional *ad litem* judges who are elected by the General Assembly for a term of four years. They are divided between multiple Trial Chambers and one Appeals Chamber, which presides over both tribunals to ensure the development of a coherent body of international criminal law.

The tribunals have similar rules of procedure. Trials can only begin once the accused is physically present. The trials include elements of both adversarial and inquisitorial procedures. Internationally recognized principles of due process apply: the presumption of innocence, the right to a speedy trial, the right to examine witnesses, the right to appeal, the provision of legal aid, etc. They include an elaborate witness protection system. The accused are held in local detention facilities (The Hague for the ICTY and Arusha for the ICTR). Sentences are served in states who have agreed to accept persons convicted by the tribunals. The maximum sentence is life imprisonment because the death penalty violates international human rights law.

These historic tribunals have established a large number of legal precedents, which are essentially collective security rules that future tribunals will enforce. They:

- extended and clarified the definition of a "protected person" under the Geneva Conventions;
- narrowed the differences between the laws of war regarding the protection of persons in international and internal conflicts;
- established a general prohibition on torture, which cannot be derogated by any treaty or domestic law;
- established sexual violence as a violation of international humanitarian law;
- included slavery as a crime against humanity;
- extended the doctrine of "command responsibility," or the criminal responsibility of superiors, to nonstate actors.

Despite their path-breaking nature, or perhaps because of it, these tribunals consistently struggled to adequately function and endured many criticisms (Snyder and Vinjamuri 2003, Dougherty 2004). Both had to overcome tremendous logistical obstacles: collecting evidence in war zones and testimony from frightened victims; transporting, protecting, and relocating witnesses; getting state commitments to incarcerate those convicted; and creating, literally, from the ground up many principles of international criminal law. The unusual circumstances of these trials have raised some basic due process issues. For example, both tribunals prevented the accused from crossexamining witnesses in some cases by allowing anonymous testimony.

Both tribunals were inefficient and expensive – by 2000 they accounted for over 10 percent of the regular UN budget. The Council mandate for the ICTY had few restrictions, and it later expanded to include the atrocities in Kosovo. The scope of the Rwandan genocide was simply overwhelming – the ICTR could prosecute only a tiny fraction of the over 90,000 persons awaiting trial in Rwandan jails. Both tribunals were extremely slow getting off the ground. It took each tribunal over two and a half years to begin its first trial. The tribunals have spent over $1 billion to prosecute 250 persons. In 2003 the Council required both tribunals to complete their activities by the end of 2008.

Both tribunals had trouble getting states to arrest and extradite the accused (Barria and Roper 2005a). The Council did not give the tribunals any law enforcement personnel; it instead required all states to assist the tribunals. Cooperation was initially slow but eventually gained momentum. Over twenty countries have arrested and extradited suspects to each tribunal (NATO forces accounted for one-third of all ICTY arrests). When threatened with economic sanctions, even Serbia extradited six suspects, including Milosevic in June 2001. As of 2006 only 6 out of 161 persons indicted by the ICTY are still at large (although two are Radovan Karadžić and General Ratko Mladić, the political and military leaders of the Bosnian Serbs). After years of reluctance from Kenya and the Democratic Republic of Congo (DRC) to extradite suspects to the ICTR – they accepted Hutu refugees and considered the Tutsi-led government of Rwanda as a rival – both began extraditing suspects in 2002.

Neither tribunal is likely to finish its work by 2008. As of October 2006 the ICTY has completed 98 out of 161 cases (fifty-seven convicted, twenty-five released, eleven deceased, and five acquitted). It is still in the process of trying fifty-seven persons, and six remain at large. Its most famous defendant, Slobodan Milosevic, died during his trial. Milosevic was charged with genocide in Bosnia and with crimes against humanity, grave breaches of the Geneva Convention and war crimes for his actions in Bosnia, Croatia, and Kosovo. The ICTR has indicted ninety persons. It has completed thirty of those cases (twenty-one convicted, seven released, and two deceased). It is still in the process of trying forty-two persons, and eighteen remain at large.

While the tribunals have not completely fulfilled their mandates, the ICTY and the ICTR provided more justice than Yugoslavia was willing to provide and Rwanda was able to provide. They did not issue a "victor's justice" but instead meted out punishment based on the gravity of the crimes committed and the defendant's level of responsibility in the political and military chain of command (Meernik 2003). They shifted the global political culture from impunity toward accountability and the rule of law, even for those at the highest political levels. They helped establish the historical facts of two brutal conflicts, preventing future attempts at denial or revisionism. They provided a forum for thousands of witnesses to tell their stories and confront their attackers. And they institutionalized the priority of human security over national security.

Hybrid international tribunals

The ICTY and ICTR are international tribunals, staffed by international prosecutors, judges, and defense attorneys. They are hierarchical institutions. Like all collective security enforcement mechanisms, they represent the collective effort of the international community to punish those who violate fundamental rules. The International Criminal Court, discussed in the next section, continued this trend.

When the Council had another opportunity to establish an international tribunal, however, it created a less hierarchical "hybrid" court for Sierra Leone.

On 12 June 2000 Sierra Leone asked the Security Council to help establish a tribunal to try those responsible "for crimes against the people of Sierra Leone" during its civil war. The Council was sympathetic because the Sierra Leone rebel group called the Revolutionary United Front (RUF) had kidnapped and killed UN peacekeepers. But the Council did not want to repeat the model of the ICTR and ICTY, which was on its way to spending over $1 billion and operating for over fifteen years. So it instead authorized the Secretary General to negotiate an agreement with Sierra Leone to create a "hybrid" tribunal (SCR 1315), and the UN and Sierra Leone subsequently signed a treaty establishing the Special Court for Sierra Leone (SCSL).

The SCSL was less hierarchical than the earlier tribunals (Pack 2005, Barria and Roper 2005b). It was not established as an organ of the Security Council with Chapter VII powers. The SCSL is a true hybrid court, combining domestic and international law in its proceedings and including both national and international judges, prosecutors, and defense attorneys. But without Chapter VII powers, states were under no obligation to cooperate with the tribunal by arresting and extraditing suspects. Liberian President Charles Taylor was in Ghana in June 2003 when the SCSL indicted him, but Ghana did not arrest him. Taylor later went into exile in Nigeria – which had no extradition agreement with Sierra Leone. In March 2006 the Liberian government asked Nigeria to transfer Taylor to the SCSL, and Nigeria immediately arrested the fleeing Taylor on the Cameroon border and extradited him to Sierra Leone. Bringing Taylor to justice was an African political issue rather than an obligation imposed by the Security Council.

Two other indications of the decreased hierarchy of the SCSL are funding and jurisdiction. Funding for the SCSL is based on voluntary donations rather than from the regular UN budget. Disputes over funding the tribunal delayed the trials until February 2004. When the Council established the court through volunteer contributions, the Secretary General insisted that the tribunal should not begin until it had received pledges for two years of operation. Also, its jurisdiction was limited to a small number of individuals "who bear the greatest responsibility" for war crimes and crimes against humanity in Sierra Leone since November 1996. The SCSL is thus an intentionally scaled-down version of the ICTY and the ICTR.

A controversial aspect of the SCSL was its jurisdiction over children. Sierra Leone wanted to prosecute child soldiers for their crimes. Children aged 8 to 14 years accounted for nearly one-half of all RUF fighters. However, the International Criminal Court cannot prosecute children, and the statutes creating the ICTR and the ICTY never mentioned children. UNICEF and many NGOs campaigned vigorously against prosecuting children. The Security Council compromised with Sierra Leone by allowing the prosecutor to indict those at the age of 15 and over, but imprisonment would not be a possible punishment for those between ages 15 and 18. Although the prosecutor has not indicted anyone under 18, this issue illustrates the difficulty of applying one set of global rules to every conflict around the world.

As of 2006 the SCSL has indicted thirteen persons. Twelve of the accused are currently on trial in Arusha, bundled in three trials of four persons each. The final person, Charles Taylor, is charged with eleven counts of crimes against humanity and war crimes, including murder, rape, terrorism, sexual slavery, the use of child soldiers, abductions, slavery, and forced labor. On 16 June 2006 the Security Council ordered that for security reasons the SCSL try Taylor at The Hague. When Taylor argued that as a head of state he was immune from prosecution, the SCSL followed the precedent set by the ICTY and ICTR and ruled that such immunity does not extend to prosecutions for crimes against humanity and war crimes by an international tribunal. Taylor's trial is scheduled to begin in April 2007.

While the SCSL demonstrates that hybrid tribunals can be effective instruments of justice and reconciliation, the UN experience with Cambodia shows the difficulties of creating hybrid tribunals in countries without judicial independence (Barria and Roper 2005b). In June 1997 a national unity government in Cambodia requested assistance from the UN to prosecute persons responsible for genocide and crimes against humanity during the Khmer Rouge regime from 1975 to 1979. When the Security Council did not act due to fears of a Chinese veto, the General Assembly endorsed the request. The Secretary General convened a panel of experts, who recommended an international tribunal modeled after the ICTY and the ICTR to avoid the lack of independence and transparency in the Cambodian justice system. Cambodia, now governed by Hun Sen after a coup, rejected this recommendation and demanded that the court not violate Cambodian sovereignty. The Hun Sen government included some former members of the Khmer Rouge who had defected to Vietnam in 1977–8. Under heavy international pressure, however, Hun Sen agreed to negotiate with the UN over the establishment of a hybrid tribunal.

The UN and Cambodia differed over issues like the relative domestic and international composition of the prosecutors and judges, the minimum level of international due process standards, and whether the tribunal could issue death sentences. After three years of talks the UN and Cambodia finalized the details, but Hun Sen did not send that agreement to the Cambodian parliament in January 2001. The UN abruptly ended the negotiations, and no progress was made for two more years. The talks resumed in January 2003, and a new agreement reached in March to establish the Extraordinary Chamber for Cambodia (ECC) was approved by both the Cambodian government and the UN General Assembly.

The ECC may be a hybrid court, but it is tilted toward a Cambodian court more than an international court. At the insistence of Cambodia, each chamber will have a majority of Cambodian judges. At the insistence of the UN, each chamber requires a super majority vote beyond the number of Cambodian judges. The ECC will have two prosecutors, one Cambodian and one international. The international judges and international prosecutor are selected by the Cambodian judiciary from a list supplied by the Secretary General. ECC procedures will be based on Cambodian law, but international standards will also be used where inconsistencies prevail or Cambodian law is silent. Even the financing of the tribunal was shared, with Cambodia paying for the buildings and the Cambodian personnel and the UN paying for the international personnel, witness and defense expenses, and security.

The reluctance of the Cambodian government and the tilt toward a traditional notion of Cambodian sovereignty in the structure of the tribunal lead many to doubt its effectiveness. The ECC has barely begun its work. Haggling over finances has led to a global fund raiser to get the tribunal off the ground. The trials are expected to begin in the middle of 2007. The ECC will have to decide whether it can abrogate earlier amnesty deals given to Khmer Rouge leaders by the Cambodian government. The ECC may not declare itself "above" Cambodian law and order arrest warrants. And even if it does, then it may not be able to get neighboring countries like Thailand to extradite the suspects. Without a more hierarchical security arrangement, no Khmer Rouge leader may ever be tried.

Hybrid tribunals like the SCSL and the ECC try to reconcile limited finances and the protection of state sovereignty with the need to prosecute war criminals. The experiences of these tribunals suggest that legitimate prosecutions of individuals for violating international humanitarian law require truly international courts. For example, a tribunal set up by the UN in Indonesian courts to prosecute war crimes and crimes against humanity by pro-Indonesia militias in East Timor have been widely criticized as corrupt and biased. The most recent tribunal authorized by the Security Council – to investigate Syrian involvement in the assassination of fifteen Lebanese politicians, including Prime Minister Rafik Hariri, in February 2005 – would have an international prosecutor and a majority of international judges to increase its legitimacy. This tribunal, which Lebanon had yet to endorse as of November 2006, could also be significant because it targets destabilization policies that many states considered routine during the cold war.

But if maintaining international security through tribunals requires truly international courts, then how hierarchical should these courts be? Should tribunals perpetuate the current arrangement privileging the veto powers? Should the Council be able to direct prosecutors to indict, or not to indict, particular individuals? Or should tribunals reduce the level of hierarchy, invoke pure collective security rules, and hold everyone accountable? Should prosecutors be independent of political influence? Should we have a collective security mechanism beyond the political control of the Security Council? These debates are at the heart of the dispute over the International Criminal Court.

The International Criminal Court

The success of the ad hoc judicial tribunals for Yugoslavia and Rwanda led to global negotiations for an International Criminal Court (ICC). The United States was a strong proponent of the ad hoc judicial tribunals, primarily because the Security Council established their authority to prosecute individuals within a circumscribed jurisdiction. The veto powers themselves were not held accountable to these tribunals. But an ICC could possibly have jurisdiction over all instances of genocide, crimes against humanity, and war crimes. Such a court would reduce the hierarchy in world politics by holding the veto powers responsible for their actions as well. The ICC was the next logical step in the development of international humanitarian law, but it threatened the privileged status of the veto powers, particularly the United States.

Delegates from over 140 states met in Rome in the summer of 1998 to create the ICC (Krisch 2003). The United States argued that: (1) the ICC should prosecute individuals only with the consent of the state of the accused nationals; and (2) the ICC should prosecute the citizens of nonparty states only through Security Council authorization. This approach was consistent with current collective security rules: state sovereignty holds sway until the Security Council determines that action is necessary to maintain international security. The ICC prosecutor would act only at the behest of the Security Council or with the consent of the relevant state.

Most states argued that the American approach undermined international law and allowed governments to opt out of ICC jurisdiction. International law recognizes universal jurisdiction: any state can act as an agent of the international community and prosecute violators of *jus cogens* rules, or rules that bind all states (Weller 2002). Historically, these rules were used against slavery and piracy, and the Genocide Convention established genocide as a *jus cogens* rule. Most states argued that customary international law also included crimes against humanity and war crimes as crimes with universal jurisdiction. The ICC, acting as an agent of the international community, would exercise universal jurisdiction over these crimes. They argued that the prosecutor should be independent of the Security Council to ensure that political influence would not lead to selective prosecutions. This approach would bypass the Security Council and transform the rules regarding genocide, crimes against humanity, and war crimes into a pure collective security arrangement. The amount of hierarchy in world politics would be reduced. All states would be subject to punishment.

The United States would not agree to such an arrangement. So the international community compromised. They agreed not to universal jurisdiction but "complementary jurisdiction." The ICC would have jurisdiction only if the accused is a national of a party to the statute or the alleged activities took place on the territory of a party to the statute. If Country A and Country B do not ratify the Rome Statute, and a citizen of Country A commits a war crime in Country B, the ICC does not have jurisdiction – unless the Security Council authorizes it. Complementary jurisdiction emphasizes that states have a prior right to prosecute and investigate its own nationals. The ICC has jurisdiction only if no state is willing and able to prosecute the case in good faith. Also, American concerns about politicized indictments led to two changes: prosecutors must obtain the authorization of ICC judges before initiating investigations, and a majority of state parties can impeach a prosecutor. The Statute also limits jurisdiction to the most serious crimes committed on a widespread basis. And most importantly, it enables the Security Council to (renewably) delay an ICC investigation for twelve months.

These concessions both recognized the authority of the Security Council and weakened international humanitarian law. They endorsed a more hierarchical arrangement which privileges the veto powers. The ICC does not have universal jurisdiction for genocide, crimes against humanity, and war crimes. The Council has the authority both to refer cases to the ICC and to order the Court to delay investigations. The only possibility of ICC jurisdiction over American citizens would be if those citizens commit war crimes on the territory of a state party to the Rome Statute and the United States failed to legitimately investigate and prosecute those individuals. But, even with these concessions, the United States did not budge. It refused to accept a situation in which an international court could pass judgment on its own courts. It wanted complete immunity for its citizens. Clinton repeatedly said that he was in favor of the ICC "in principle." But the principle was this: those on the lower end of the hierarchy are bound by these rules, but the United States is not. The unique responsibilities of the hegemon afforded it special privileges.

The international community created the ICC without American support. The Rome Statute was adopted on 17 July 1998 by a vote of 120 to 7, with twenty-one abstentions. Those voting against were China, Iraq, Libya, Yemen, Qatar, Israel and the United States. It became operational four years later on 1 July 2002. This is a stunning example of the limits of United States hegemony and an indication that the post-cold war world is not an American empire. The international community created a collective security mechanism outside the total control of the Security Council. Individual states could refer cases to the ICC prosecutor, and the prosecutor could initiate independent investigations, albeit within a circumscribed jurisdiction. But regardless of these limitations, the principle was established: the Security Council no longer had a monopoly on enforcing all collective security rules.

The United States responded by going to great lengths to seek immunity from the ICC (Johansen 2006, Weller 2002). It took the unprecedented step of "un-signing" the Rome Statute. It passed legislation in 2002 authorizing the military "rescue" of all American citizens held in ICC custody. It urged all countries to sign a bilateral agreement permanently exempting American citizens from ICC jurisdiction. Despite the fact that they violated both the ICC and the Genocide Convention, around 100 countries signed such bilateral agreements, including forty-two who ratified the ICC. When the majority of the ICC parties (58 out of 100) did not sign, the United States cut military assistance and economic development aid, totaling $2.5 billion, to eighteen of those states. (The United States restored their eligibility for military assistance in September 2006.) When the United States tried to make signing the agreement a condition for eligibility into NATO, its Western allies rejected the proposal. No European Union country signed, and they made *not* signing the agreement a condition for membership into the European Union. United States policy was now in the awkward position of simultaneously urging Serbia, Bosnia, and Croatia both to turn over their own citizens to the ICTY and exempt Americans from ICC jurisdiction.

The United States also used the Security Council to undermine the ICC. In May 2002 it tried and failed to exempt United Nations peacekeepers in East Timor from ICC jurisdiction. In June 2002 it vetoed a routine resolution renewing the peacekeeping mission in Bosnia because it did not exempt United States participants from ICC jurisdiction. It then made an outrageous threat to withdraw its contributions to the United Nations peacekeeping budget and veto the renewal of all peacekeeping operations that did not have this exemption. It also demanded a resolution requiring states either to not pass or rescind all national legislation implementing ICC treaty obligations. The United States, like the Libya sanctions case, was trying to use the Security Council to override treaty obligations. It tried to destroy the ICC by holding all United Nations peacekeeping missions hostage.

Criticism of the United States was immediate and near universal. The Security Council convened a highly unusual open session and seventy-two countries condemned the American position. Even Kofi Annan personally protested with Secretary of State Colin Powell. This widespread global support bolstered the Council, which did not give in to American demands. However, since the veto of peacekeeping missions would create havoc in many conflicts around the world, the Council reluctantly agreed to compromise: the ICC would not prosecute any nationals in UN peacekeeping operations from countries that had not ratified the Rome Statute for one year (SCR 1422). In an astounding show of global unity, over 100 states took the floor of the General Assembly to criticize that Council resolution. They argued that it violated the Rome Statute, which does not enable the Council to exempt an entire class of people from future investigation. They questioned the power of the Security Council to essentially amend a widely endorsed, multilateral treaty. And they criticized the United States for coercing others into violating their treaty obligations.

Despite the near unanimous criticisms of this resolution, the Council renewed the exemption for another year on 12 June 2003 (SCR 1487). When the United States asked for another renewal in 2004, however, the Council rejected it. The exemption would have included United States troops in Iraq (the Security Council by then had authorized the United States occupation), and the emerging scandals regarding prisoner abuse, renditions, and torture allegations gave an ominous ring to American demands for immunity from war crimes prosecution. After the United Kingdom persuaded the United States not to veto the renewal of peacekeeping missions, it responded by removing American soldiers from United Nations missions in Kosovo and Ethiopia, states that did not sign the bilateral agreement exempting American soldiers from ICC jurisdiction (even though the ICC had no jurisdiction in these states because neither had ratified the Rome Statute!).

Few examples more clearly show the United States preference for hierarchy. The United States is in favor of holding (other) state leaders accountable for genocide, crimes against humanity, and war crimes. It is even willing to hold (other) state leaders accountable for these crimes when that state has not ratified the Rome Statute. When the Security Council passed a resolution authorizing an ICC prosecution of Sudanese officials for their role in the Darfur genocide (SCR 1593), the United States abstained. After going to great lengths to argue that its citizens should not be subject to the ICC because it had not ratified the Rome Statute, it allowed Sudanese citizens to be prosecuted by the ICC even although Sudan had not ratified the Rome Statute. The United States could not bring itself to veto a resolution to punish war criminals, even though they would be prosecuted by the ICC. The United States does believe that states have a responsibility to stop genocide. But it does not want a collective security arrangement in which it cannot control international criminal jurisdiction. The ICC institutionalizes the rule that no state can shield its citizens from criminal responsibility for genocide, crimes against humanity, or serious war crimes. The ICC reduces hierarchy in world politics. The United States has undermined the ICC because it believes that its own security requires more, not less, hierarchy.

The ICC has not conducted itself in a way that threatens United States interests. The prosecutor – Luis Moreno Ocampo of Argentina – did not investigate the United States for war crimes in Iraq, concluding that there was insufficient evidence for such an investigation. He has not formally investigated Israel or any important American ally. He has initiated no formal investigations on his own. Of the four current cases, state parties referred three (Uganda, the DRC, and the Central African Republic), and the Security Council has referred one (Sudan). The early evidence suggests that the ICC is hardly a legal behemoth run amok.

1   The first situation investigated by the ICC regarded the war in the DRC (see Chapter 3). In March 2004 DRC President Joseph Kabila requested that the ICC investigate crimes committed in his country since July 2001. The DRC had neither an independent judiciary nor the institutional capacity to prosecute such a large number of perpetrators (Katshung 2006). The ICC investigation to date has led to the indictment of only one person – a militia leader in the Ituri province named Thomas Lubanga Dyilo – for the recruitment of child soldiers. Dyilo became the first person to be arrested under a warrant issued by the ICC.

2   The second situation for the ICC concerned Uganda (El Zeidy 2005). Ethnic conflict in Uganda goes back decades, including a 1970s genocidal campaign by Idi Amin against ethnic groups in northern Uganda. His rule ended in 1979 when Tanzania invaded and restored the northern groups to power. In 1981 a southern rebel group called the National Resistance Army led by Yoweri Museveni started a guerrilla war against the northern rulers. Museveni seized the capital city Kampala in January 1986, named himself president, and continued violent policies toward the northern groups. Eventually, antigovernment rebels known as the Lord's Resistance Army (LRA) formed in northern Uganda and southern Sudan. Now the southern groups were in power, and the northern groups were fighting a guerilla war. Although the Ugandan government does not have a spotless human rights record, the LRA was a particularly brutal group. It abducted thousands of children, forcing the boys to fight in the army and the girls into sexual slavery. They either killed the children who did not comply with their demands or sold them as slaves in Sudan in exchange for firearms. They regularly killed noncombatants, tortured civilians, and destroyed entire villages. Their actions clearly violated international humanitarian rules. So in December 2003 Uganda President Museveni requested the ICC investigate the LRA. The ICC began

its investigation in February 2004, eventually issuing indictments and arrest warrants against five LRA leaders for war crimes and crimes against humanity in July 2005.

3   The third situation concerned the Central African Republic. In January 2005 the government requested the ICC prosecute crimes within the jurisdiction of the Court committed on its territory since July 2002. However, nearly two years later the prosecutor has not initiated an investigation.

4   The fourth situation regards the crisis in Darfur, Sudan (see Chapter 8). The Security Council referred the situation to the ICC in March 2005 (SCR 1593), including a sealed list of fifty-one suspects. The ICC has initiated an investigation but there were no indictments as of November 2006. This situation is different because Sudan is not a state party and has no intention of cooperating. Although SCR 1593 requires all states to cooperate with the ICC in its investigation, the president of Sudan has stated that no Sudanese citizen will ever be surrendered to the ICC.

The first three cases raise interesting legal and political issues. In all three the territorial state (where the alleged crimes occurred), the state of nationality (the accused citizens), and the state that referred the case are all the same. All three have essentially waived their prior jurisdiction and deferred to the complementary jurisdiction of the ICC, a situation unanticipated by the drafters of the Rome Statute. Instead of the ICC determining that states have failed to appropriately exercise its jurisdiction, governments engaged in civil wars are asking the ICC to prosecute rebel groups for war crimes. This could be a benign development, with the ICC acting as the appropriate international tribunal when states are unable to do so. But it might indicate that states will use the ICC as a tool to eliminate domestic political enemies.

The litmus test is whether the ICC prosecutes only the leaders of nonstate rebel groups. Sudan thus becomes an extremely important case. Will the ICC also hold state officials responsible for their violations of international humanitarian law? Will it impose hierarchy on a reluctant state? This is another example of how the pursuit of global security – that is, human security – requires hierarchy. Will the world accept an international tribunal that institutionalizes such hierarchy? The ICC also illustrates that the American pursuit of hierarchy can go too far. Will the world accept an international tribunal that can impose itself on countries such as Sudan but not the United States? For a hierarchical collective security arrangement to be legitimate in the long run, can the hegemon continue to be exempted from the rules?

7 The proliferation of weapons of mass destruction

Constructing rules against the proliferation of weapons of mass destruction (WMD) is an excellent example of the security–hierarchy paradox. Dealing with this transnational security threat requires some hierarchy: agreed-upon rules in treaty language and Security Council resolutions; global bureaucrats to monitor, inspect, and verify compliance; and enforcement mechanisms for those who fail to comply. To solve this problem we cannot have a world with too little hierarchy where states assert a sovereign right to accumulate whatever weapons they want. Global security requires states to follow certain rules, and preventing WMD proliferation is one of those rules. The United States supports its own interests and the interests of the global community by pursuing hierarchical proliferation rules.

Rules against weapons proliferation, however, must be fair and legitimate to be effective (Tannenwald 2004). Too much hierarchy also harms both American and global security. The United States has pursued a hierarchical global security arrangement regarding WMD proliferation in four ways: (1) by not ratifying all major weapons treaties and by undermining treaties it has ratified by asserting exceptions to those rules; (2) by accepting nuclear proliferation in Israel, Pakistan and India; (3) by using force numerous times against Iraq for its weapons programs without explicit Security Council authorization; and (4) by advocating a harsh approach toward the "axis of evil" countries, including sanctions, diplomatic isolation, and hostile regime change.

This chapter includes a section on each of these four points. Instead of adhering to the rules in order to increase the legitimacy of the proliferation regime and encourage greater participation in that regime, the United States has argued that its unique role in maintaining international security exempts its policies from those rules. The question is at what point does this pursuit of hierarchy become counterproductive? Can the United States convince the rest of the world that such a hierarchical arrangement is legitimate? Or will it erode the legitimacy of American hegemony to such an extent that many will no longer comply with the rules? To what extent have United States policies encouraged rather than discouraged the nuclear policies of India, Pakistan, North Korea, and Iran, which threaten to unravel the nuclear proliferation rules?

Weapons proliferation treaties

Both Security Council resolutions and treaties generate nonproliferation rules. While Council resolutions tend to increase hierarchy because they cannot target the veto powers, treaties are more likely to reduce hierarchy by establishing equal obligations among all states. There are fifteen major weapons treaties and protocols, and the United States has ratified fewer of them than any of the other veto powers. The United States has failed to ratify the Comprehensive Test Ban Treaty (CTBT), the Convention on Anti-Personnel Landmines, and two protocols to a conventional weapons treaty banning the use of blinding lasers and other weapons in civil wars. Even Russia and China have ratified more weapons treaties than the United States. France and the United Kingdom have ratified all fifteen agreements.

While this chapter focuses on WMD rules, many global proliferation rules target conventional weapons. Combatants in most conflicts since the cold war have used small arms. The proliferation of these weapons has fueled wars all over the world. The UN has prioritized efforts to regulate transnational arms sales in an attempt to prevent illegal sales into war-torn areas. The United States, however, does not support UN efforts to track and confiscate small arms trade to nonstate groups. In October 2006 the General Assembly passed a resolution to begin work on a treaty establishing global standards for arms sales, and the United States was the only country to vote against the resolution. This position contradicts a universally recognized principle of conflict resolution, one that the United States is also attempting to follow in Iraq – the first task of post-conflict peace-building is to provide security by disarming militias.

Nuclear weapons

The United States has undermined some weapons treaties that it has ratified (Bajpai 2003). One example is the 1970 Treaty on the Non-Proliferation of Nuclear Weapons (NPT). The NPT did not establish equal obligations among all states. It instead institutionalized a nuclear hierarchy, establishing different rules for nuclear powers and non-nuclear states. The NPT prohibits non-nuclear states from developing nuclear weapons and obligates them to accept regular inspections by the International Atomic Energy Agency (IAEA) to monitor compliance. The NPT obligates the nuclear powers in three ways: (1) to make good faith efforts to reduce their nuclear stockpiles and make progress toward nuclear disarmament; (2) to provide nuclear technology, with safeguards monitored by the IAEA, to non-nuclear states; and (3) to extend nuclear deterrence policies to any NPT member threatened by nuclear weapons.

The first obligation was the most important: non-nuclear states accepted a nuclear hierarchy only under the condition that it would decrease rather than increase over time. The explicit premise of the nuclear proliferation rules was and continues to be that nuclear disarmament is the ultimate goal. This was the price that nuclear powers had to pay to get others to agree not to build nuclear weapons.

This bargain, though, was not good enough for many states at the time. Both recent nuclear states (China and France) and aspiring nuclear states (South Africa, Argentina, Brazil, Israel, India, Pakistan, and others) refused to ratify the treaty. Regional rivalries dominated the cold war security rules, and states believed that increasing their military capability with nuclear weapons would increase their security.

The end of the cold war created the conditions for a strengthened nuclear proliferation regime. China and France ratified the NPT as nuclear powers. South Africa, Argentina, and Brazil abandoned their nuclear programs and ratified the NPT. Former Soviet republics Kazakhstan, Belarus, and Ukraine ratified the NPT and dismantled the nuclear weapons they inherited from the fragmented Soviet Union. Country after country decided that possessing nuclear weapons would actually harm their security. The diplomatic isolation, political suspicion and economic reprisals associated with possessing nuclear weapons cost more than the benefits of increased military capability. Most countries instead chose the benefits of political goodwill, increased economic relations, and being a "responsible" member of the international community. The relevant holdouts were states in a local rivalry: India, Pakistan, Israel, and North Korea (who ratified the treaty but then opted out in January 2003). Even "rogue states" such as Iran, Iraq, Libya, Syria, and Cuba ratified the NPT.

The NPT rules are institutionalized in the IAEA. The IAEA has three main functions: (1) to inspect member states and verify that nuclear materials are not used for military purposes; (2) to ensure that nuclear industries in member states adhere to nuclear safety standards; and (3) to facilitate the transfer of peaceful nuclear science and technology to developing countries. The IAEA has safeguard agreements to inspect nuclear and related facilities with more than 150 states. Each year the IAEA carries out over 2,000 inspections at over 600 facilities. The IAEA has no independent enforcement authority – it provides annual reports to the General Assembly and notifies the Security Council when states fail to comply with the NPT. Ultimately, the Security Council must enforce the nuclear rules.

The NPT parties meet every five years to review the treaty. The NPT included a twenty-five-year time limit, requiring the parties to decide at the 1995 review whether to permanently extend the treaty or agree to another fixed time limit. The United States and the other nuclear powers wanted a permanent extension of the treaty. To achieve this they agreed to three demands by the non-nuclear states: (1) complete negotiations on the Comprehensive Test Ban Treaty by 1996; (2) seriously discuss nuclear disarmament as mandated by the NPT; and (3) accept strengthened IAEA review processes for nuclear states. At both the 2000 and 2005 reviews the non-nuclear states continued to demand that the nuclear states adhere to the CTBT and begin good faith negotiations toward nuclear disarmament. Many non-nuclear states believe that nuclear states have reneged on their NPT commitment to make progress toward nuclear disarmament (Graham and LaVera 2002).

The United States has received the most criticism, particularly its abandonment of the Anti Ballistic Missile (ABM) Treaty and rejection of the CTBT. The

United States and the Soviet Union signed the ABM Treaty in the 1970s, prohibiting the use of defensive weapons against ballistic missiles. At the time the ABM Treaty cemented nuclear deterrence because both sides would be vulnerable to a nuclear attack. And since each superpower's existing nuclear arsenal would suffice to threaten the other side, the treaty decreased incentives to build more and qualitatively better nuclear weapons. When the cold war rivalry ended, some in the United States began to argue that the greater threat was now a stray ballistic missile from a rogue state, and that missile defenses in the post-cold war world were in American security interests. When the Bush administration opted out of the ABM Treaty to build such missile defenses, the global community heavily criticized the United States. The fear was that this would threaten Russia and China, lead to another nuclear arms race, and propel the nuclear powers into the opposite direction of their NPT commitment to work toward disarmament.

The United States rejection of the CTBT, which bans all nuclear tests, also undermined the NPT rules. States that cannot test nuclear weapons cannot build reliable weapons and develop more advanced weapons. Non-nuclear states that ratify the CTBT strengthen the credibility of their NPT commitment not to build nuclear weapons. Nuclear states that ratify the CTBT strengthen their NPT commitment to make steady progress toward nuclear disarmament. It conveys to others that one does not intend to build newer, more destructive nuclear weapons. Rejecting the CTBT conveys to others that one intends to violate NPT commitments and build the next generation of nuclear weapons.

The international community completed negotiations on the CTBT in 1996. The United States initially supported the treaty – President G.H.W. Bush began a testing moratorium when the cold war ended, and Clinton extended that moratorium. The United States argued for tough inspections provisions during the negotiations. Only India objected to the treaty when the talks were over. Only three countries (India, Libya, and Bhutan) opposed a September 1996 General Assembly resolution endorsing the treaty. Over 130 states have ratified the CTBT. But it does not go into force until a particular set of forty-four states that have nuclear power or nuclear research reactors ratify it. As of 2006, ten out of those forty-four have not done so: China, Columbia, North Korea, Egypt, India, Indonesia, Iran, Israel, Pakistan – and the United States. Most of these ten states have publicly stated that they will ratify the treaty after the United States ratifies it.

The treaty would establish the Comprehensive Test Ban Treaty Organization (CTBTO) to implement the treaty. The CTBTO would monitor seismic activity and levels of radioactivity around the world for evidence of nuclear explosions. It would conduct random inspections and even challenge inspections if authorized by a supermajority of states on the CTBTO Executive Committee. The treaty authorizes the CTBTO to recommend that state parties engage in "collective measures which are in conformity with international law" when states are not compliant with the treaty and to bring the issue to the attention of the United Nations.

The United States rejected the CTBT despite widespread global and domestic support, including from the United States military (Graham and LaVera 2002). Republicans in the Senate doubted the ability of the treaty to verify noncompliance and prevent proliferation. The Clinton administration badly mishandled relations with the Senate during the ratification process. The Senate Foreign Relations Committee chaired by Jesse Helms did not hold a hearing on ratification for over a year. By the time the treaty reached the Senate floor, there were only twelve days left to ratify the treaty so that the United States could be included in initial CTBTO activities. In the midst of the partisan squabbles over Clinton's impeachment, the Senate rejected the treaty with only forty-nine votes in favor.

The nuclear proliferation rules are clearly in United States interests. Of more than fifty countries with the capacity to produce nuclear weapons, only a handful of states have done so. But the bargain of the NPT is nonproliferation in exchange for eventual disarmament. Non-nuclear states considered the CTBT a litmus test for the sincerity of the nuclear powers to keep their part of the nuclear proliferation rules. Asserting the right to test nuclear weapons contradicted a legal and political commitment to make progress toward disarmament. By rejecting the CTBT, the United States potentially undermined the nuclear proliferation rules. The CTBT was the price for non-nuclear states agreeing to an indefinite extension of the NPT. And then the United States reneged. So why should non-nuclear states adhere to the rules? The United States is asking the world to accept a hierarchical arrangement in which certain countries have nuclear weapons but others must not be allowed to have them.

Chemical and biological weapons

The 1997 Chemical Weapons Convention (CWC) established contemporary proliferation rules regarding chemical weapons. The CWC is the first treaty requiring the elimination of an entire category of WMD. The CWC prohibits the development, acquisition, production, transfer, and stockpiling of chemical weapons. It requires states to destroy their chemical weapons, submit declarations of all military and civilian chemical facilities and accept random inspections of those facilities. Under the Reagan and G.H.W. Bush administrations, the United States were staunch supporters of the treaty. At the insistence of the United States, the CWC included unprecedented verification measures. Over 170 states, including all the veto powers, have ratified the CWC. Holdouts include North Korea, Egypt, Iraq, Lebanon, Syria, Israel, the Democratic Republic of Congo, and Myanmar.

The CWC established the Organisation for the Prohibition of Chemical Weapons (OPCW) to implement the treaty, conduct inspections, and monitor state compliance. OPCW inspectors verify that states have destroyed all declared chemical weapons stockpiles and do not divert chemicals toward prohibited uses. The verification process includes reporting requirements, on-site inspections and challenge inspections. Routine inspections are conducted at declared chemical weapons facilities to verify the accuracy of information in state declarations. Challenge inspections "clarify and resolve" questions of possible noncompliance. The OPCW can recommend that state parties engage in "collective measures" when states are not compliant with the treaty and bring the issue to the attention of the United Nations.

Twelve state parties to the CWC declared the possession of chemical weapons to the OPCW, totaling 8.6 million chemical munitions and 70,000 metric tons of chemical agents. The OPCW has inventoried 100 percent of these declared chemical weapons and made them inoperable. It has also verified the destruction of 30 percent of the chemical munitions and 20 percent of the chemical agents. It has either destroyed or helped convert to peaceful purposes fifty-six of the sixty-five declared chemical weapons productions facilities. As of 2006 the OPCW had conducted over 2,500 inspections of nearly 200 military sites and over 700 industrial sites in seventy-six state parties.

Despite this initial success, critics charge that the United States undermined global confidence that state declarations were complete and that the OPCW has inventoried all the chemical weapons of state parties to the CWC (Smithson 1998). The legislation passed by the United States to implement the treaty – in 1999, three years past the deadline – violated many treaty provisions. It allowed the president to refuse a challenge inspection of American facilities; it required the tests on chemical samples gathered by international inspectors to be conducted in the United States; and it reduced the number of facilities obliged to declare their activities. Congressional leaders said they were preserving American sovereignty and preventing the possibility of industrial espionage against American companies.

This legislation damaged the global rules against chemical weapons. The United States opened the door for others to also claim exceptions, and India, Russia, China, Japan, and others have passed similar implementing legislation. If all state parties did this, the treaty would be meaningless. It is important to remember that the United States does not want a weak treaty. It wants rules against chemical weapons, and it wants the institutional ability to investigate states suspected of having chemical weapons. It just does not want a global institution with complete authority to inspect American facilities. The rules are for those at the bottom of the hierarchy. But the United States cannot have it both ways. Given American ambivalence, the OPCW has performed no challenge inspections. There can be no global institution to inspect only "rogue states"; the United States must agree to similar inspections within its own borders.

American reluctance about global inspections also prevented attempts to strengthen rules on biological weapons (Deller and Burroughs 2003). The 1972 Biological Weapons Convention (BWC) prohibited the development, possession and stockpiling of biological weapons. But there were no global rules about monitoring, verification, and sanctions. Given these limitations, there was a relatively high level of noncompliance with the BWC. Experts in the early 1990s believed that twelve countries, including parties to the BWC such as Iraq, Iran, Libya, China, Russia, and North Korea, had active biological warfare programs. After Russia admitted to a massive biological weapons program and UNSCOM verified the existence of an Iraqi program after the Gulf War, the state parties to the BWC began negotiations to add verification measures.

Seven years of talks between 144 states produced verification methods with the following provisions: (1) mandatory declarations of military and civilian biotechnology facilities; (2) random on-site visits to verify the accuracy of the declarations; and (3) short-notice challenge investigations of declared and undeclared facilities suspected of violating the BWC. The Clinton administration was lukewarm toward the protocol, who insisted on limiting the scope and number of facilities to be declared. And the Bush administration flatly rejected it in July 2001, claiming that the inspections would not catch violators and would lead to industrial espionage against American biotechnology companies. It then took the extraordinary step of leaving the multilateral negotiations. The other BWC parties, concluding that they could not proceed without the United States, suspended the negotiations.

In November 2001 – immediately after the post-9/11 anthrax scare killing eight and infecting eighteen Americans – the BWC parties met in Geneva to review the treaty. The United States declared that the draft protocol was dead and advocated an approach in which the Secretary General would authorize inspections of noncompliant BWC members. This proposal went nowhere. On the last day of the conference the United States shocked even its close allies by proposing to terminate the multilateral talks. This threw the conference into such turmoil that it could not agree to any politically binding declarations, and the conference was suspended for a year. The talks resumed in 2002, and another review conference was held in 2006, but there has been no significant progress toward adding verification measures to the BWC.

The growth of the nuclear club

The largest setback to the nuclear proliferation rules was the acquisition of nuclear weapons by Israel, India and Pakistan. The Security Council did little to either prevent these cases of nuclear proliferation or punish these states after they went nuclear. Israel, India, and Pakistan did not violate international law because none had ratified the NPT. But their nuclear programs potentially threatened international security if they encouraged others to build nuclear weapons as well. While the United States tried to discourage all three from acquiring nuclear weapons, it eventually accepted these states as nuclear powers and maintained close security relationship with them. As nuclear powers these three countries entered the upper echelons of the global hierarchy, presumably immune from collective security enforcement.

Israel began its nuclear weapons program in the 1950s. The Kennedy administration urgently discouraged Israel from pursuing its nuclear program, fearing it would lead the Arab world to ask the Soviet Union for nuclear weapons (Cohen 1998). It insisted on international inspections, but Israel refused to allow the IAEA into its facilities and later concealed its nuclear program to American inspectors. United States pressure and the imperative to avoid a regional nuclear arms race forced it to adopt a policy of "nuclear opacity": Israel never declared a nuclear capability and never conducted a nuclear test. While it was understood that Israel had a nuclear weapons capability, it remained intentionally ambiguous whether Israel had operational nuclear weapons. Israel maintained this ambiguity by not ratifying the NPT. Israel became an undeclared nuclear state with no threat of collective enforcement measures against it during the cold war rivalry. The United States in effect extended its privileges in the global hierarchy to Israel.

India and Pakistan, however, are post-cold war cases of nuclear proliferation that faced the Security Council during an era in which proliferation rules were stronger. Both conducted nuclear weapons tests in May 1998 (Nizamani 2001, Sen 1999). Unlike others who had nuclear weapons programs during the cold war and later abandoned them, India and Pakistan's local rivalry continued into the post-cold war world and superseded the global rules regarding nonproliferation (Joeck 1997). Nuclear competition became entrenched into their rivalry, with each country having a psychological and domestic political investment in these weapons. However, both also cited the discriminatory nature of global nonproliferation rules as part of the context for their decision to build nuclear weapons. Neither believed that the veto powers should retain a monopoly on nuclear weapons, particularly when the nuclear powers were not maintaining their NPT commitment to move toward nuclear disarmament.

India believed that nuclear weapons would symbolize major power status and would deter its two regional rivals: China and Pakistan. India and China fought a brief war in 1962, and two years later China conducted its first nuclear tests. India then began its nuclear program in an attempt to catch up with China. But India's rivalry with Pakistan also fueled its nuclear weapons program, particularly the 1947 and 1965 wars over Kashmir, the growing influence of Islam in Pakistani politics, and fears that an alliance between Pakistan, China, and the United States would form after the 1979 Soviet invasion of Afghanistan. But India also believed that going nuclear was a legitimate response to an illegitimate set of global nuclear rules. India did not sign the NPT because it did not include a specific timetable for global disarmament and it required non-nuclear states to rely on nuclear states for security guarantees. India argued that the NPT was discriminatory because it included specific prohibitions on developing countries but only vague disarmament and technology transfer goals for nuclear states.

Pakistan began its nuclear program to catch up with India. Both countries believed that not having nuclear weapons would invite challenges from the other and also invite coercion from a nuclear power. Pakistan did not ratify the NPT because India did not. Pakistani politics justified a nuclear program given India and its position in the NPT, the growing realization of an Israeli nuclear program, and the lack of any meaningful Western disarmament. After the Soviet invasion of Afghanistan and the Islamic revolution in Iran in 1979, Pakistani politics got caught up in a religious identity with a Hindu threat in India and a communist threat in Afghanistan. The nuclear program became enmeshed in its emerging Islamic identity. A Pakistani "Islamic bomb" symbolized resistance everywhere from Kashmir to the Gaza Strip.

When the cold war ended, both India and Pakistan resisted American pressure to abandon their nuclear programs. The United States responded with bilateral sanctions against both countries (it also put Pakistan on its list of states that sponsored terrorism). But the sanctions and global norms against nonproliferation did not work. Both continually cited the unfair nature of the global rules, calling the NPT a "technological apartheid." The permanent extension of the NPT and the conclusion of the CTBT negotiations finally tipped the scales. India saw these treaties as an attempt to keep them out of the nuclear club. It was upset that developing countries did not argue against the double standards of the nuclear rules. India criticized the CTBT because there was no commitment by the nuclear powers to negotiate a time-bound framework for nuclear disarmament. As long as the nuclear powers were unwilling to accept their NPT obligation and make progress toward disarmament, then India would not reduce its strategic flexibility by signing the treaty. And when the United States failed to ratify the CTBT, India concluded that the United States had no intention of pursuing nuclear disarmament. India thus rejected the CTBT to challenge what it considered the unfair nature of the global nuclear hierarchy (Holum 1997).

India conducted nuclear tests on 11 May 1998. Pakistan kept pace, also refusing to ratify the CTBT and conducting its own tests later that month. The Security Council unanimously condemned the tests, urging India and Pakistan to refrain from further testing and begin confidence building measures to ease the situation (SCR 1172). Both Pakistan and India denounced the resolution, the double standard of the nuclear veto powers, and demanded a specific timeframe for nuclear disarmament. But the Council never considered real enforcement measures. The only attempt was some United States bilateral sanctions, and those against India lasted less than a year. There was no political will to punish strategically significant countries. The veto powers accepted selective proliferation (India can have nuclear weapons, North Korea cannot) rather than an absolute proliferation regime.

The United States initially attempted to contain Indian and Pakistani nuclear capabilities, but it could not persuade them to stop producing fissile material or ratify the CTBT (Kampani 2001). The only success was an agreement with India to strengthen controls on the export of nuclear and missile technology. Pakistan, of course, continued to sell ballistic missiles and nuclear technology to North Korea, Libya, and Iran (Braun 2004). But United States pressure on Pakistan to end its proliferation policies waned after the terrorist attacks of 9/11. Pakistan became strategically crucial to American operations in Afghanistan, and United States officials stopped talking publicly about the Pakistani nuclear program or its sales to rogue states. To convince Pakistan – one of the few countries who recognized the Taliban – to support the military operation in Afghanistan, the United States ended its sanctions for the nuclear tests and pledged $1 billion in aid. Terrorism now took precedence over nonproliferation (and human rights).

The Bush administration went further with India, however, and changed decades of United States policy in a March 2006 deal providing nuclear power assistance to India. Under the agreement, the United States provided India with technical expertise, civilian nuclear technology, and nuclear fuel; in return India would subject its civilian (not military) facilities to permanent international inspections. The nuclear fuel that India imported from the United States would enable it to use its own domestic supply to produce fissile material for military uses, even although all five veto powers had agreed to halt the production of this material. There would be no international inspections to insure compliance with IAEA safety regulations in India's military facilities.

The United States nuclear agreement with India harmed global collective security rules in two important ways. First, it openly rewarded rather than punished a country that refused to sign the NPT and then developed nuclear weapons. Even with Israel, the United States had never openly collaborated with a country to violate NPT norms. By encouraging others (such as North Korea and Iran) to believe that possessing nuclear weapons could benefit them as well, the agreement weakened rather than reinforced nuclear proliferation rules. Second, the agreement invoked rivalry rather than collective security rules. Instead of prioritizing global efforts to confront North Korea and Iran over their nuclear programs, the United States prioritized bolstering India as a regional counterweight to China. Instead of isolating India as a violator of nuclear proliferation rules, the United States embraced India as an ally against China. This agreement facilitates the two dynamics that most easily undermine collective security: (1) many states rejecting the double standards of selective enforcement and failing to follow the rules; and (2) the great powers identifying each other as rivals and failing to work together to enforce the rules.

Enforcing proliferation rules against Iraq

During the cold war the Security Council did not deal with proliferation or disarmament issues. It took no action, for example, when Iraq used chemical weapons during its war with Iran and against its own Kurdish citizens. The Council's first enforcement action regarding weapons was its authorization after the Gulf War to destroy Iraq's WMD programs (Krasno and Sutterlin 2003, da Silva 2004). The historic use of collective force after Iraq's invasion of Kuwait, growing concern over WMD, and Iraq's particular record using these weapons all compelled the Council to establish the most extensive disarmament program in history. The Council mandated that Iraq declare the locations, amounts, and types of all its prohibited weapons; destroy them under international supervision; allow inspectors unrestricted access to facilities, records, and officials; and agree not to use, develop, or acquire prohibited items (SCR 687).

This was the first and only time that the Security Council authorized the disarmament of a member state. It clearly established WMD proliferation as a top priority of the post-cold war global security agenda. The Security Council created a subsidiary body called the United Nations Special Commission (UNSCOM) to verify Iraqi compliance with the rules regarding chemical and biological weapons. The Council also charged the IAEA with verifying Iraqi compliance with the rules regarding nuclear weapons. Both UNSCOM and the IAEA verified Iraq's declarations, destroyed or supervised the destruction of prohibited items, established ongoing monitoring systems, and oversaw an import–export control mechanism (Chellaney 1999).

The logic of the initial disarmament program followed NPT rules: Iraq declared its programs and the inspectors verified the declarations. But the inspectors soon realized that they needed a more aggressive approach. Iraq obstructed the program by providing inaccurate declarations, hiding its biological weapons program, preventing accurate inventories by unilaterally destroying prohibited items, moving materials subject to monitoring to undeclared facilities, tampering with monitoring equipment, and refusing to grant full access to inspectors. The lack of Iraqi cooperation forced UNSCOM and the IAEA to intrusively search facilities not declared by the Iraqis so that they could uncover hidden weapons programs.

The Security Council had to decide how to deal with Iraqi noncompliance. It had already imposed the most comprehensive sanctions regime in history. Would the veto powers agree to use force? How much hierarchy was appropriate in enforcing these rules? The tensions among the veto powers about whether SCR 687 authorized force in such situations; the economic interests of Russia, China, and France in Iraq; and the growing recognition of the humanitarian crisis brought about by the sanctions all complicated the Council's efforts to maintain a unified approach to Iraq. In one of the many examples of the cat and mouse game played between Iraq and UNSCOM, Iraq said that it would cease cooperation with weapons inspectors if the Security Council did not end the sanctions by 10 October 1994. The United States pressed the Council to demand that Iraq fully cooperate with weapons inspectors. Again invoking hegemonic collective security, the United States warned that it would act with or without the Council's support. After some Russian and Chinese grumbling, the Council unanimously demanded that Iraq fully cooperate with weapons inspectors (SCR 949). Once again Iraq backed down and allowed inspections to proceed.

By 1997 the tensions between the veto powers had increased dramatically. France, Russia and China all wanted to reduce the sanctions to reward increased Iraqi compliance with weapons inspections and minimize the humanitarian crisis. The United States took the opposite approach, advocating "regime change" – which was never included in any Council resolution – as a condition for ending the sanctions. When Iraq declared that eight "presidential sites" were off limits to the inspectors in October, Russia, China, and France rejected an American proposal to impose travel sanctions on Iraqi leaders and eventually abstained on a resolution condemning Iraq for its obstruction of weapons inspectors (SCR 1134).

When the IAEA declared that Iraq no longer had a nuclear weapons program in November 1997, Russia and China argued that the Council should ease some sanctions given Iraqi compliance with this demand. The United States, though, did not agree. President Clinton remarked that "sanctions will be there until the end of time or as long as [Hussein] lasts" (Crossette 1997). When the IAEA report brought no change to the American position, Iraq again began to refuse access to the inspectors. The Council responded by unanimously passing the travel restrictions favored by the United States a month earlier and again warned of the "severest consequences" for future noncompliance. Once again, the United States and Britain argued that existing resolutions authorized the use of force, and Russia, France, and China argued that any use of force would require further Security Council authorization.

As the United States increased its troop presence during the standoff, Russia brokered a deal with Hussein in which he promised to allow weapons inspections. But on 13 January 1998 Iraq again said that it would not permit UNSCOM to inspect eight "presidential sites." Iraq also said that it would no longer allow Americans on UNSCOM inspection teams because the United States was using it as a spy agency. (These charges were largely true. UNSCOM inspector Scott Ritter admitted that the CIA had worked closely with UNSCOM since 1992. This is another example of United States policies undermining the legitimacy and effectiveness of the global proliferation regime. States will be less likely to allow international inspectors into their countries if they are tied to domestic spy agencies; this was part of United States criticisms of the CWC and the BWC verification systems.)

The United States again threatened to use force and again argued that a series of Security Council resolutions gave it the authority to do so. The United States also argued that a 1991 resolution passed by Congress gave it the authority to use force, invoking a national security rather than an international security rationale for force. The CIA Director told the Senate Select Committee on Intelligence that Iraq continued to hide WMD and retained the ability to make more. The United States was again willing to invoke hegemonic collective security. During the crisis, Secretary of State Albright told reporters prior to a week-long trip to Europe: "I am not going anywhere to seek support. I am going to explain our position" (Myers 1998).

France, Russia and China preferred a diplomatic solution and argued that the United States did not have the authority to use force. The crisis was averted when Kofi Annan brokered an agreement giving UN inspectors "immediate, unconditional and unrestricted access" to suspected sites, including the eight presidential sites. On 2 March the Security Council unanimously endorsed the agreement (SCR 1154). Once again the United States claimed that SCR 1154, which threatened the "severest consequences," authorized the use of force. Eleven Security Council members, including France, China and Russia, explicitly disagreed (Weller 1999). They rejected the assertion that the United States could enforce the "will" of the Security Council without an explicit mandate; that the United States can determine a material breach of a cease-fire; and that the United States can determine the consequences of such a breach. French President Chirac said: "We consider that automatic action is not acceptable. We believe that a military strike is a very serious step and that, because it would be done in the name of the international community, that the Security Council should debate it" (Whitney 1998).

When Iraqi compliance with the new agreement was limited, the tensions between the veto powers erupted again. Russia, China, and France continued to argue that sanctions were causing too much suffering and should be lessened to offer Iraq incentives to cooperate with weapons inspections. They argued that the United States kept "moving the goalposts" on Iraq by citing other reasons for maintaining the embargo (human rights, need for regime change) not specified in Council resolutions (Malone 1999). Why should Iraq comply if there is no real hope for the lessening of sanctions and what the United States really wants is regime change? They convinced the Security Council to agree to a full review of the sanctions regime on 30 October. When the review did not include a promise to lift the oil embargo or other sanctions, Iraq officially ended all weapons inspections the next day on 31 October.

The United States responded – without consulting the Security Council – with Operation Desert Fox, a four-day bombing campaign of Iraq beginning on 16 December 1998. The United States got some international support beyond Britain (Germany and Saudi Arabia allowed the United States to use its air bases). However, the international community heavily criticized the American use of force. Yeltsin argued that the United States violated the UN Charter: "no state can act independently on behalf of the UN as the world's policeman" (Crossette 1998a). Russia recalled its ambassador from Washington, its angriest diplomatic move since the cold war. The Duma shelved the START II nuclear arms agreement ratification vote. The Russian ambassador to the UN said: "Russia wants a very clear statement . . . the Security Council is in charge and the Security Council is in favor of a political settlement of international crises" (Crossette 1998b). China called the attack a "groundless, unprovoked military action." French Prime Minister Jospin said:

> The US often acts in a unilateral way that undermines its ambition of mobilizing the international community. That was clear in the conflict with Iraq. What's the reality after the Anglo-American strikes? We've gone from a situation where the entire international community, with the United Nations, was reminding Iraq of its obligations, to a direct confrontation between the Baghdad regime and our American and British friends. I do not see how that is progress.
>
> (Whitney 1999a)

French Foreign Minister Hubert Védrine said:

> We believe Iraq no longer has any nuclear capability, and large quantities of chemical and biological stocks, we know, have been found and destroyed by the United Nations teams. We do not believe there is any point in going back in and continuing to look for the last test tube, because we'll never find it. What we need is a new system of continuous monitoring that allows us to make sure Iraq does not try to build new facilities to acquire these things again.
>
> (Whitney 1999b)

If these statements are eerily reminiscent of global criticisms of the United States after its invasion of Iraq five years later, consider the following statements by analysts at the time:

With no remaining alternative centers of power, the USA has developed a marked and growing impatience with the constraints of multilateral diplomacy. The give and take required within the UNSC in order to secure support for US policy initiatives is increasingly perceived in Washington as an unnecessary tyranny. There is also a decreasing disposition to convince allies and others of the wisdom of Washington's views: it is deemed sufficient that they be stated. Any disagreement with US policy is seen by many in Washington as driven by irrational anti-American sentiment or posturing.

(Malone 1999: 405)

The United States and its British ally have argued that they were acting to enforce the "will" of the UN Security Council, that they were responding to a "material breach" of the cease-fire that ended the 1991 Gulf War, and also that they were pre-empting Iraq's future potential use of weapons of mass destruction. Neither of the first two arguments stand up to legal scrutiny, while the third suggests a doctrine of preventive war that carries with it extremely dangerous implications for international relations.

(Weller 1999: 81)

Critiques of unilateral United States uses of force clearly predate the Bush administration and the American response to 9/11. The United States has consistently preferred a hierarchical global security arrangement throughout the entire post-cold war period, and much of the world has consistently resisted that hierarchy.

Attempt to enforce proliferation rules after Operation Desert Fox failed. A first attempt was a successor organization to UNSCOM in December 1999 called the UN Monitoring, Verification and Inspection Commission (SCR 1284). This resolution promised to lift the embargo on many goods after Iraq agreed to 120 days of unfettered weapons inspections. But Russia, France, and China abstained because they wanted further reductions in the sanctions. Iraq continued to state that sanctions had to be reduced prior to further arms inspections, and it again refused to admit the inspectors. A second attempt was a smart sanctions proposal by the new Bush administration in 2001. The United States proposed (1) a "goods review list" of dual-use items that would be subject to review by the Security Council before they could be exported to Iraq and (2) border checks to enforce the embargo. This proposal also went nowhere. Jordan, Syria and Turkey would not agree to do the border checks. And Russia argued that the composition of the goods review list would harm its trade and economic interests in Iraq. The Security Council did not even vote on the proposal.

After the subsequent United States invasion of Iraq, we learned, of course, that Iraq had no WMD. The weapons inspections process that the Bush administration so ridiculed – thousands of inspections of more than 300 sites between 1991 and 1998 – had in fact destroyed Iraq's WMD programs. UNSCOM had confirmed that Iraq had no nuclear weapons capability but was unable to make a similar conclusion regarding Iraq's chemical and biological weapons when inspections ended in 1998. The inspections in late 2002 and early 2003 did not last long enough to allow the inspectors to make this conclusion. The United States ended up invading the one member of the axis of evil who had no WMD. The war to enforce proliferation rules had the opposite effect, spurring North Korea and Iran to speed up their nuclear weapons programs in order to deter a United States preemptive invasion of their own countries.

Enforcing proliferation rules against North Korea and Iran

While Iraq has dominated Security Council agendas throughout the post-cold war era, North Korea and Iran have only recently garnered Council attention. China has generally resisted Council interference in its neighborhood, and until recently that included the nuclear crisis in North Korea. And consensual action on Iran is difficult because Russia and China have sold Iran many materials that could be used to enhance Iran's nuclear program. The United States has put sanctions on seven Russian companies and sanctions on Chinese companies three different times for selling nuclear technology to Iran (Ahrari 1999). However, these are clearly issues influencing international peace and security. A nuclear North Korea might sell its weapons, as it has with drugs and missile technology in the past. It could diminish regional stability by triggering further nuclear proliferation in South Korea and Japan. The Iranian nuclear program is worrisome given its ties to terrorist groups, the Holocaust-denying, anti-Israeli rhetoric of its leaders, and its ballistic missiles capability.

The United States has again generally pursued hierarchical policies toward these "rogue states": isolation, sanctions, and regime change more often than engagement. Including Iran and North Korea in the "axis of evil" enabled the United States to treat them as irrational, untrustworthy adversaries rather than negotiating partners with legitimate claims and grievances. But policies such as regime change are also unlikely to work quickly enough to remove the current nuclear threats. The United States would have to be less hierarchical, sincerely negotiate with these "rogues," and address their grievances that America too should follow the rules in order to prevent the proliferation of nuclear weapons.

North Korea

United States policy toward North Korea regarding its pursuit of nuclear weapons also illustrates the security–hierarchy paradox (Kerr 2005, Moon and Bae 2005, Van Ness 2005). North and South Korea have been technically at war since the 1950s. Both Truman and Eisenhower threatened to use nuclear weapons against the North during the Korean War. The United States deployed nuclear missiles in South Korea in 1957. These weapons were targeted toward North Korea until 1991. Throughout the cold war the North embarked on a nuclear program of its own. When the cold war began to thaw and Soviet aid dwindled, North Korea accelerated its nuclear program. When China normalized relations with South Korea in 1992, the North saw it as a betrayal and ended high-level contacts. With few options, the North began to engage the United States. They found that only provocation would get American attention, and they fell into a pattern of bargaining their weapons systems for security assurances and aid.

The crisis of 1992–4 began this pattern. North Korea signed the NPT in 1985 under pressure from Mikhail Gorbachev. However, in 1992 North Korea kicked out IAEA inspectors and threatened to leave the NPT when inspectors found evidence of a nuclear weapons program. In April 1993 the IAEA declared that North Korea had violated its NPT obligations and for the first time asked the Security Council to enforce its provisions. Veto threats from China, however, prevented a strong Security Council reaction. The Council eventually passed a resolution asking North Korea to "reconsider," with China abstaining even on this mild language (SCR 825). The United States took a more forceful approach, imposing bilateral sanctions and negotiating with other Asian countries to pass regional sanctions. In February 1994 North Korea again agreed to inspections but then in March denied the IAEA inspectors complete access to seven nuclear sites.

The Security Council again had to decide how and whether to enforce North Korean compliance with weapons inspectors. China, while not wanting nuclear weapons on the Korean peninsula, also did not support sanctions and did not want to intervene in the north's affairs. The Council settled for a presidential statement – not a resolution – urging North Korea to allow unrestricted access to weapons inspectors. Given North Korean noncompliance and deadlock on the Council, President Clinton came very close to ordering a military strike against North Korea in May 1994. But negotiations continued and, eventually, the United States and North Korea agreed that in return for North Korea freezing its nuclear program, the United States would help the North install light water reactors, supply fuel oil, begin to normalize diplomatic relations, and agree not to use or threaten to use nuclear weapons against North Korea. The North traded its nuclear ambitions for some technology and a security guarantee – very similar to the NPT treaty language itself.

The agreement remained shaky. The United States did not keep its commitment to install light water reactors or normalize diplomatic relations. North Korea did not fully comply with IAEA inspections, and it began selling ballistic missiles to Pakistan and Iran. Still, United States relations with the North improved in the late 1990s, mostly due to a major South Korean engagement policy with the North. By 2000, the two were close to an agreement in which the North would end its nuclear program and stop its missile exports, and in return the United States would normalize diplomatic relations, guarantee the North's security, and (together with Japan) provide billions in economic aid. Secretary of State Albright even visited Pyongyang in October 2000. But the Clinton administration, absorbed by Middle East peace talks, failed to close the deal. The United States missed an opportunity to achieve security through reduced hierarchy: in this case, a mutually negotiated bilateral agreement with a "rogue state."

The incoming Bush administration was more suspicious of the North and contemptuous of the 1994 deal negotiated by Clinton. United States policy toward North Korea drastically changed after the 9/11 terrorist attacks. During the January 2002 State of the Union address, Bush included North Korea in the "axis of evil" with Iran and Iraq. The Bush doctrine of preemption radically changed the nuclear standoff. It gave the United States two options: military invasion or regime change through diplomatic isolation and economic sanctions. The United States was again asserting a hierarchical approach, considering North Korea an illegitimate negotiating partner. Renewed American hostility encouraged the North to build nuclear weapons to deter a United States invasion. The 2003 invasion of Iraq confirmed North Korean beliefs about American intentions.

The United States pressed its harder line throughout 2002. In March it asserted that the North had violated the 1994 agreement because it was not allowing IAEA inspections "in a timely manner." In October it claimed that the North admitted the existence of a highly enriched uranium program. Despite North Korean denials and the lack of verifying evidence, it suspended the supply of heavy oil, part of the American commitment from the 1994 agreement. North Korea responded by saying the 1994 agreement was no longer valid. It reactivated a nuclear facility, removed IAEA monitoring cameras, expelled IAEA inspectors, and announced its intention to withdraw from the NPT. As in Iraq after 1998, the United States advocacy of regime change led to a situation in which there were no weapons inspections to verify compliance with collective security rules. Of course, the irony of United States policy in late 2002 and early 2003 was that Iraq was then allowing inspections, it had no weapons of mass destruction, and the United States was planning for war; while North Korea would not allow inspections, would soon admit to having nuclear weapons, and the United States would not consider the use of force.

In April 2003 China convened negotiations between North Korea and the United States. The North told the United States that it had nuclear weapons. It wanted a bilateral agreement very similar to the 2000 deal almost completed by the Clinton administration: in return for a nonaggression treaty with the United States, normal diplomatic relations, and economic ties, it would agree to abandon its nuclear program, allow inspections, and stop missile exports. For North Korea this was a bilateral issue between it and the United States. It would adhere to the NPT if the United States would guarantee its security – again, demands consistent with NPT treaty language requiring nuclear states to extend nuclear deterrence to non-nuclear states. North Korea simply wanted the United States to follow the NPT rules. The United States rejected this, arguing that North Korea must agree to IAEA inspections without any preconditions. Once again the United States position was that while others must adhere to their NPT obligations, the United States does not necessarily have to.

The April 2003 talks produced no agreement. North Korea demanded bilateral talks to focus on American obligations under the NPT and the 1994 agreement. The United States wanted multilateral talks to minimize its own obligations and bring global pressure on North Korea to rejoin the NPT. China continued to be more aggressive throughout the summer of 2003 (Medeiros 2003). It suspended oil shipments to North Korea, sent high-level envoys, and shifted troops around the Sino-Korean border. China eventually strong-armed North Korea into attending six-way talks in August 2003, February 2004, and July 2004 (also including

Russia, Japan, and South Korea). With the United States in the process of invading Iraq, China saw this as an opportunity to resist American hegemony in the region and avoid a unilateral United States solution to the nuclear crisis. However, these talks were also unsuccessful.

China, Russia, and the United States struggled to maintain a common position. The United States wanted a tough approach, advocating sanctions and the use of military force to cut off exports of nuclear materials and missile components to other countries. China and Russia would not agree to inspect North Korean ships because they did not want to escalate the crisis. Over time China took the lead in the multilateral negotiations. In September 2005 China proposed an agreement offering economic incentives to North Korea if they dismantled their nuclear weapons. The United States initially rejected the deal. But South Korea and Russia supported it, and China would not alter the proposal. Faced with the prospect of isolation and being blamed for the talks breaking down, the United States accepted the Chinese position. North Korea rejected this offer as well. It wanted normal diplomatic relations and an American security guarantee even more than economic assistance.

With diplomatic talks stalled and the use of force not an option, the United States was left with a policy of isolation and regime change. North Korea again fell into its pattern of using provocative actions to get the world's attention. On 9 October 2006 North Korea conducted an underground test of a nuclear weapon, telling the world that it was a nuclear power. Only then did the Security Council become involved, with the United States wanting harsh measures and Russia and China preferring to go more slowly and avoid unnecessary conflicts. On 14 October the Council unanimously authorized financial sanctions and an arms embargo against North Korea for the nuclear test. The resolution prohibited North Korea from conducting further tests or launching ballistic missiles and required it to dismantle its nuclear, chemical, and biological weapons programs under international supervision. The resolution did not authorize the use of force to enforce the sanctions but instead called on nations to inspect cargo "as necessary" going to and from North Korea. It remains to be seen whether this resolution will have any effect on North Korea.

Iran

Similarly to the situation with North Korea, the United States missed diplomatic opportunities with Iran to prevent the theocratic regime from pursuing nuclear weapons. Iran began a nuclear energy program in the 1960s under the Shah. Ayatollah Khomeini continued the program after Iraq ordered chemical attacks on Iranian forces during the Iran–Iraq War. Iran began buying nuclear technology from Pakistan in the late 1980s and concealing its nuclear activities from IAEA inspectors (Iran is a member of the NPT). What put Iran on the global security agenda was a series of IAEA inspections in 2003–4, uncovering hidden nuclear programs. Iran eventually admitted that it had concealed some of its nuclear activities for almost two decades, but claimed that it was pursuing commercial energy rather than military uses. The current crisis began in April 2006 when Iran began enriching uranium, the first step toward building a nuclear weapon, in violation of IAEA rules. It is unclear just how far the program has developed. Most estimates say that Iran is at least five to ten years away from the capacity to build a nuclear weapon.

The United States has also pursued policies of isolation and regime change toward Iran's theocratic rulers. For example, the 2002 Nuclear Posture Review included Iran as one of the states considered a potential target by nuclear war planners. Many Iranian experts argue that harsh American policies toward Iran also missed opportunities for better relations and a negotiated agreement to end Iran's nuclear program (Rajaee 2004, Takeyh 2003, Ramazani 1998, Baghat 2003). Iran is pursuing nuclear weapons because it fears an American invasion and because the radical clerics need the international crisis to legitimize their rule. Not all Iranian Islamists reject modernity or view Islam as something that must dominate all aspects of society. United States policies – particularly including Iran in the "axis of evil" – have undercut arguments for moderation in Iranian policies.

Iran has a complicated structure of government with both traditional and modern elements: it both empowers unelected clerics with ultimate authority while allowing citizens to elect a president, parliament, and local councils. After the death of Khomeini and the end of the war with Iraq, the population began to demand the fulfillment of the promises made during the revolution. By the early 1990s a wide array of society began calling for more public participation in government. The defenders of the regime wanted a strict Islamic orthodoxy, whereas the reformers wanted the Republic to accommodate basic rights and freedoms found in modern societies. Many of the reformers are within the clerical elite, arguing that Islam and democracy are compatible.

In the 1990s, modernist parties began to win national elections. The radicals lost their majority in 1996 parliamentary elections, and in 1997 Iran elected the modernist Mohammad Khatami as president, with 69 percent of the vote with an 85 percent turnout. Khatami encouraged media outlets, civic organization, and political parties. He established elections for local government, and his party won 80 percent of the vote. The number of elected officials in Iran increased from 400 to 200,000, mostly held by modernists. In the February 2000 parliamentary elections, the modernist party won 220 out of 290 seats in a record turnout of 83 percent. In 2001 Khatami won re-election with 77 percent of the vote. On 11 September 2001 Iranians held spontaneous public demonstrations of support and candlelight vigils for the United States.

The United States failed to take advantage of this opportunity. Khatami made courageous overtures for normal relations with the United States. He wanted a foreign policy based on nonviolence and friendly relations. He wanted to reduce international tensions to increase Iranian access to resources and markets. He argued that Iran must become more democratic to become part of the new world order. But President Clinton did little to reciprocate these overtures. Instead, the United States continued its policies of economic sanctions, diplomatic isolation, and regime change. Khatami could point to no foreign policy victories, and the clerics thwarted his modernist domestic legislation. Political support for the modernists ebbed as they could not turn their electoral victories into policy changes.

And then the Bush axis of evil speech elicited a strong nationalist reaction across the Iranian political spectrum. Only the radicals, however, had credibility on this issue. They used the international crisis – the United States was asserting the right to invade Iran – to gain domestic control. The modernist parties lost their majority in July 2002 parliamentary elections. Prior to February 2004 parliamentary elections, the clerics ruled 2,500 candidates "unfit," including eighty sitting members from the modernist party. The elections, with a record low 51 percent turnout, gave the radicals 190 seats to 50 for the modernists. And then the 2005 presidential election, with an even lower turnout, replaced the modernist Khatami with the radical Mahmoud Ahmadinejad.

United States regime-change policies were counterproductive in Iran by harming the reformers and giving credibility to the radicals. Under the pretext of national resistance to external intervention, the clerics have embarked on a new backlash against the reformers. In August 2002 they banned a reform party and shut down two newspapers. They have forced reformers who wanted better relations with the United States to denounce American arrogance. The clerics prefer conflict with the United States to deflect attention from their poor record of governance. The hierarchical policies pursued by the United States have inadvertently helped them continue their rule. And the clerics have used the anti-American atmosphere to bolster their position in the international community: at a 2006 summit of nonaligned states, 118 countries voted for a resolution supporting Iran's right to develop nuclear technology. This resolution was consistent with NPT rules, which enable non-nuclear states to develop a nuclear program for peaceful, commercial purposes. The United States, after the debacle in Iraq, has had difficulty convincing the international community that Iran's nuclear program threatens international peace and security.

Conclusion

The pattern of United States nonproliferation policies since the cold war has been to pursue a hierarchical collective security arrangement. The United States has refused to ratify all major weapons treaties. It has undermined some treaties it has ratified by asserting exceptions to those rules, creating the conditions for countries like India to justify their nuclear program. It has facilitated India's nuclear program with a military assistance agreement. It has used force numerous times against Iraq for its weapons programs without explicit Security Council authorization. It has advocated a harsh approach for the "axis of evil" countries, including sanctions, diplomatic isolation, and hostile regime change. These policies have been counterproductive. It is difficult to conclude that Iraq, Iran, and North Korea present less of a threat to international security today than when Bush made the "axis of evil" speech.

The common thread in these policies is the construction of a hierarchical collective security arrangement. The United States sincerely wants to establish certain proliferation rules that states must follow. And the United States wants to punish the states that violate the rules. These are appropriate goals – nonproliferation rules are in American and global security interests. But the United States wants to be outside the bounds of these global rules. It asserts exceptions to global treaty rules. It works outside the process of Security Council enforcement. It pursues hostile regime change policies toward "rogue" states rather than engagement. It is difficult to solidify the legitimacy of global proliferation rules when the United States is ambivalent about following them or unilaterally tries to enforce them.

This is the security–hierarchy paradox. When the pursuit of hierarchy undermines the legitimacy of global rules, both American and global security is harmed. The United States must recognize this paradox. In a world of security interdependence, the United States can only increase its own security by lowering the amount of hierarchy in world politics. The United States cannot prevent weapons proliferation on its own. It needs China to help deal with North Korea, and it needs Russia to help deal with Iran. This requires the United States, China, and Russia to identify with each other as partners in a collective security arrangement rather than rivals. When the United States' pursuit of hierarchy goes too far, Russia and China are more likely to interpret the United States as a rival. A global rivalry would not be able to deal with the proliferation of weapons of mass destruction; indeed, a global rivalry would exacerbate that security issue. If the nonproliferation regime is to succeed in the long run, the United States must increase the legitimacy of those rules – by following them.

8 Human rights

Human rights have revolutionized state sovereignty and collective security. The UN has embraced the norm of a "responsibility to protect" as part of a human security agenda. A 2004 UN report argued that the international community should act to halt or prevent mass killings when a government will not or cannot do so (United Nations 2004). States no longer have a sovereign right to pursue domestic order or national security without any restrictions. The international community is slowly building rules and institutions to punish individuals who violate the most fundamental human rights by committing genocide, crimes against humanity, and war crimes.

Human rights rules also illustrate the security–hierarchy paradox. Like other post-cold war transnational security threats, protecting human rights requires a hierarchical collective security arrangement: rules prohibiting violations of human rights and humanitarian international law, global monitoring institutions, and enforcement measures such as judicial tribunals for those who violate the rules (see Chapter 6). Too little hierarchy enables states to hide behind a traditional notion of state sovereignty and continue to oppress their citizens without fear of punishment. Too much hierarchy smacks of Western cultural imperialism and undermines the legitimacy and burgeoning universality of human rights rules.

The dominant post-cold war pattern regarding human rights is more complicated than other policy areas. Sometimes the United States follows the major pattern and pursues hierarchical arrangements to such an extent that many criticize its policies. But sometimes the United States – and the Security Council as a whole – pursues too little hierarchy and fails to act when massive human rights violations occur. Since the cold war, the Security Council has struggled to reconcile the traditional notion of state sovereignty and emerging human rights norms, vacillating between inaction, adequate collective security enforcement, and Western countries hierarchically taking matters into their own hands.

The United States has pursued a hierarchical collective security arrangement regarding human rights in two ways: (1) by supporting certain human rights rules but asserting exceptions for itself, particularly regarding the International Criminal Court (see Chapter 6) and the rights of terrorist detainees and (2) by supporting humanitarian intervention without Security Council authorization in

Kosovo and Iraq (see the discussion on no-fly zones in Chapter 5). Both leave the United States open to criticism that it prefers imperial global security rules. But in other ways the United States has also pursued too little hierarchy to adequately enforce human rights rules: (1) it has failed to ratify many human rights treaties, undermining its self-appointed role as a global champion of human rights and (2) it has failed to prevent the worst atrocities, particularly in Bosnia, Rwanda and Sudan. This chapter explores the extremely complicated post-cold war process of constructing human rights collective security rules.

The United States and human rights

Human rights are a fundamental part of the UN system. The Charter mentions human rights more than any other topic except international peace and security. The Universal Declaration of Human Rights remains one of the most important documents of the twentieth century. There are more than twenty-five multilateral human rights treaties. UN agencies and peacekeeping missions routinely incorporate human rights into their mandates. It is widely recognized that protecting human rights helps achieve human, national, and international security. The World Bank recognizes a conceptual link between human rights and economic development. Human rights are increasingly entrenched in the social reality of world politics.

Incorporating human rights norms into collective security rules, however, is challenging. One obstacle, as in every area of collective security, is generating a consensus about which human rights warrant enforcement. To the extent that a consensus exists, it includes the protection of innocent civilians during wartime. Rules against genocide, crimes against humanity and war crimes have "universal jurisdiction": all states are obligated to punish individuals guilty of violating those rules, regardless of nationality or where those crimes occurred. In a practice that continues to blur the traditional meaning of state sovereignty, states are increasingly prosecuting citizens from other countries for atrocities committed in a third country.

These developments require the international community to decide which human rights require collective security enforcement. How far does the responsibility to protect go? There are many kinds of human rights. One category of human rights includes political and civil rights. The exercise of these rights requires limiting the power of states. They include the right to life, speech, religion, press, political participation, property, due process, and personal integrity. The United States generally adheres to such political and civil rights (exceptions include the death penalty and the current treatment of terrorist detainees) and occasionally imposes bilateral sanctions against countries that violate them. But to enshrine such rights with collective security enforcement – for example, if a future Security Council determines that a state torturing its citizens violates international peace and security – would further advance a human security agenda and alter our understanding of state sovereignty.

A different category of human rights are social and economic rights. The exercise of these rights requires states to act and create the conditions for their existence. They include the right to education, clean air, clean water, food, housing, medicine, and employment. The United States generally does not agree that these are fundamental human rights. However, it is not ridiculous to suggest that global poverty, climate change, and AIDS are threats to international security. Could global collective security rules not only prohibit states from violating political and civil rights but also require them to provide social and economic rights? And if poor states cannot provide for basic human needs like schools, food, or clean water, should the Security Council exercise its "responsibility to protect" and require state contributions to UN development agencies so that these rights are provided? Or would that be an illegitimate infringement on state sovereignty?

Given these complexities and profound implications, existing global rules regarding human rights are relatively weak. Human rights treaties require states to pass domestic legislation and issue reports to monitoring committees that investigate these reports and publicize the identity of human rights offenders. Two (on torture and gender discrimination) include processes for states to register complaints about another state party. Two (on race and gender discrimination) enable individual citizens to register complaints about their own state. Only one (on torture) includes random inspections of state facilities. None has a direct mechanism to trigger Security Council action. One major UN human rights organization is the Human Rights Council, newly created in April 2006, which reviews state compliance with human rights obligations and makes recommendations to the General Assembly – not the Security Council – regarding human rights violations.

One major obstacle to stronger human rights rules is that many states prefer to maintain a traditional notion of state sovereignty in this area. This includes China, who does not want an increased institutionalization of human rights norms. China believes that Western countries emphasize human rights to characterize China as a rogue state that should not be considered a legitimate global power. Russia is also increasingly hesitant about human rights enforcement. Under Gorbachev and Yeltsin, Russia was generally supportive, voting for thirty-one out of thirty-two resolutions regarding Somalia, Haiti, Rwanda, and East Timor (Heinze and Borer 2002). But Russia vehemently objected to the NATO intervention in Kosovo and, under Putin, Russia has become more authoritarian, backsliding on many human rights reforms. Neither Russia nor China wants to increase Security Council jurisdiction over an expanded definition of human rights, and both are explicitly against any emerging norm justifying humanitarian intervention.

Another obstacle is that states who champion human rights do not agree on the meaning or the scope of the concept. The United States, for example, does not generally support economic and social rights as fundamental human rights. As a result it has ratified only ten out of twenty major human rights treaties and protocols. As with treaties on weapons proliferation, the United States has ratified fewer human rights treaties than any other veto power, including Russia (who has ratified fifteen) and China (who has ratified thirteen). France has ratified eighteen out of the twenty treaties and the United Kingdom has ratified seventeen. The United States has not ratified the following:

1 Protocol I to the Geneva Conventions, protecting victims of international conflicts.
2 Protocol II to the Geneva Conventions, protecting victims of civil wars.
3 The International Covenant on Economic, Social and Cultural Rights (ICESCR).
4 A protocol to the International Covenant on Civil and Political Rights (ICCPR) enabling citizens to report human rights violations to the Human Rights Committee.
5 A second protocol to the ICCPR, abolishing the death penalty.
6 The Convention on the Elimination of Discrimination against Women (CEDAW).
7 A protocol to CEDAW enabling citizens to report human rights violations to the Committee on the Elimination of Discrimination against Women.
8 The Convention on the Rights of the Child (CRC).
9 The Convention on the Rights of Migrant Workers (CRMW).
10 The Rome Statute creating the International Criminal Court.

The United States has also objected to a protocol to the Convention against Torture including an inspection system for detention facilities. When the General Assembly voted on the protocol in December 2002, the United States was one of only four states to oppose it.

The United States has also ratified other treaties relatively recently, many years after they were open for signature. For example, it ratified the Convention on Genocide in 1988, four decades after the treaty was negotiated. And it ratified the Convention on the Elimination of Racial Discrimination in 1994, nearly three decades after it was negotiated. And when the United States ratifies human rights treaties, it does so in a way that no American citizen can use its provisions in any domestic or international court (Roth 2004).

United States human rights policies are a complicated illustration of the security–hierarchy paradox. While the United States generally prefers increased hierarchy in world politics, its refusal to ratify most of these treaties stems from a preference for minimum hierarchy in particular policy areas. The United States simply does not recognize certain types of human rights as legitimate global rules. Here the United States is not asserting exceptions to rules it supports; it is instead relying on a more traditional notion of state sovereignty and – similar to the American position on climate change and small arms – disputing the need for global rules. By rejecting these treaties the United States blocks the hierarchy necessary to include a more comprehensive understanding of human rights in the global collective security arrangement.

The United States' preference for a particular understanding of market-based economics means that it does not want global rules establishing food, water, and medicine (ICESCR) or labor rights (CRMW) as fundamental human rights. Lingering apprehensions about global governance infringing on United States sovereignty led to rejections of the two protocols enabling citizens to leapfrog their own government and petition the UN with grievances. And two specific domestic policies – abortion and the death penalty – drove the rejection of two other treaties. The CRC would prohibit the United States from using the death penalty against minors, and CEDAW includes references to "reproductive rights." By rejecting these treaties the United States is asserting the right to have certain domestic rules regardless of their status under international law.

This position is perfectly acceptable in a world of sovereign nation states. International law allows states to choose which treaties they ratify. In only a few instances are states obligated to follow rules regardless of their status as treaty signatories. But such a position illustrates why it is difficult to more fully incorporate human rights into a collective security framework. States want the ability to pick and choose from the large menu of human rights which ones they support. They want to recognize human rights from within the context of their own political culture. Rules against the discrimination of women, for example, will be implemented differently in regions across the world. It is difficult to generate global agreement about which human rights rules are so fundamental that they warrant collective security enforcement.

At present, only a few areas approach the status of universally held rules: the Geneva Conventions rules about the treatment of combatants and noncombatants during war; rules against genocide, crimes against humanity, and war crimes; and (perhaps) rules against torture. Rarely do states criticize the appropriateness of these rules. The United States, in particular, supports global rules in these areas. Yet in these few areas in which an international consensus exists, the United States has asserted exceptions to those rules. As discussed in Chapter 6, few United States policies more clearly illustrate a preference for a hierarchical collective security arrangement than its rejection of the International Criminal Court. The United States wants a collective security arrangement to punish those who commit genocide, crimes against humanity, and war crimes, but not one that includes jurisdiction over its own actions.

The United States has similarly asserted exceptions to global rules about the treatment of prisoners in its "war" on terrorism (Alvarez 2006). After the invasion of Afghanistan the United States determined that Geneva Convention rules about interrogation procedures did not apply to its treatment of Al Qaeda and Taliban detainees because they were "enemy combatants." The detainees were neither protected as civilians under American law nor as prisoners of war under the Geneva Conventions. Under Geneva standards, the Taliban soldiers were almost certainly prisoners of war, while the members of Al Qaeda most likely were not. But the United States determined that they were all "enemy combatants" without complying with Geneva Convention requirement that captured combatants be treated as prisoners of war until a competent tribunal determined otherwise.

The United States has also narrowly defined torture to maximize its flexibility in interrogation techniques (Hersh 2004). When the United States began detaining many combatants at Guantanamo Bay, its treatment of those detainees led to widespread international criticism. The Red Cross inspected Guantanamo Bay and reported inhumane treatment (sleep deprivation, exposure to extreme heat and cold, stripping prisoners, and the use of "stress positions") and the lack of a legal system for processing detainees. Human rights groups, the European Union, and Kofi Annan all argued that the United States should shut down Guantanamo Bay and begin a more transparent process either under American domestic law or consistent with the Geneva Conventions. Even the Federal Bureau of Investigation ordered its agents not to interrogate suspected Al Qaeda members to avoid future criminal prosecution. The American proposal to try some detainees in military tribunals did little to stem the global criticism.

After the United States invaded Iraq, it transferred its Guantanamo interrogation policies to Iraqi prisons, including one of Saddam Hussein's torture chambers called Abu Ghraib. The Red Cross and Human Rights Watch constantly complained about physical coercion and sexual humiliation of Iraqi prisoners. When photographs of the abusive practices taken by the soldiers themselves were leaked to the media in April 2004, the world had indisputable evidence of the American use of torture. Global condemnation was immediate and tremendously harmful to United States counterinsurgency efforts. Subsequent United States military investigations discovered widespread prisoner abuses throughout Iraq. The Bush administration was determined to get "actionable intelligence" to defeat the insurgency without regard to global torture rules.

Interrogation policies during the war on terrorism are another example of the United States' pursuit of hierarchy going too far and actually harming American security. Asserting the authority to violate global torture rules undermined the moral legitimacy of the United States, weakened the Geneva Conventions, and exposed American soldiers to retaliation in future wars, all without increasing its ability to get useful information regarding the Iraqi insurgency. The world watched and wondered about the nature of American hegemony as the United States strenuously objected to International Criminal Court jurisdiction over its actions in the middle of these scandals. Compromising on human rights to fight terrorism degrades global human rights rules, is counterproductive to the war on terrorism, and undermines the legitimacy of American hegemony (Weiss *et al.* 2004).

Enforcing human rights rules since the cold war

During the cold war the Security Council rarely authorized enforcement measures regarding human rights violations. The only exceptions were sanctions against white-minority regimes in Rhodesia and South Africa. Not wanting to interfere in the domestic affairs of member states, the Council made only sporadic references to human rights (Hungary in 1956 (SCR 120), Congo in 1961 (SCR 161), and the Dominican Republic in 1965 (SCR 203)). The traditional notion of state sovereignty trumped human rights as a global security rule. When two states engaged in humanitarian intervention to end ongoing genocides – Vietnam into Cambodia in 1978 and Tanzania into Uganda in 1979 – they were widely criticized for violating state sovereignty. How states treated their own citizens was considered a domestic matter.

The global security rules began to change with the campaign against apartheid in South Africa (Klotz 1995). In addition to the ethical issues of a racist regime in a post-colonial world, many began to argue that South African apartheid constituted an international security threat. It created both social tensions and refugee crises that destabilized the entire region. More generally, many began to argue that states who abuse their own citizens are more likely to act aggressively toward other states as well. The Security Council imposed an arms embargo and prohibited nuclear cooperation with South Africa in 1977. Cold war politics prevented a stronger stance; in 1985 both the United States and the United Kingdom vetoed a draft resolution imposing economic sanctions against South Africa.

The end of the cold war elevated human rights to the top of the global security agenda (Bailey 1994). The global reaction to the Chinese massacre in Tiananmen Square, the declining strategic imperative for the West to ally with human rights abusers, and the increase in civil wars elevated human rights to the top of the global security agenda. Human security advocates argued that there was a relationship between justice within states and order among them (Wheeler 2002). The lack of human rights contributed to the outbreak of civil wars and encouraged other states to intervene militarily. Civil wars created tremendous refugee flows, destabilizing other states in the region. Human rights violations were no longer considered to be within the domestic jurisdiction of states; they were now threats to international peace and security.

The Security Council increasingly endorsed the notion that human rights violations constituted a threat to international security. For example, the Council began to comprehensively address human rights issues in peacekeeping missions (Weschler 2004). The Council first said that humanitarian crises constitute a threat to international security on 9 November 1996, regarding the crisis in Zaire (SCR 1078). And a 1999 Council statement unanimously recognized the humanitarian dimension of the maintenance of international security (S/PRST/1999/3). It said that humanitarian crises can be both causes and consequences of conflict. It called on all combatants to ensure the safety of all UN and associated humanitarian personnel. The Council began to receive regular briefings from human rights investigators in 2002.

Support for adopting a human rights agenda also came from Secretary General Kofi Annan and NGOs. Annan consistently advocated elevating human rights over the traditional notion of state sovereignty: "The Charter protects the sovereignty of peoples. It was never meant as a license for governments to trample on human rights and human dignity. Sovereignty means responsibility, not just power" (Annan 1999). Annan called the need to unite and confront massive human rights violations the core challenge of the Security Council and the United Nations. An influential international commission advocated a rethinking of state sovereignty and embracing a responsibility to protect (International Commission on Intervention and State Sovereignty 2001). Successful missions such as the one in East Timor also increased support for strengthened human rights rules.

But the road to collective enforcement of human rights rules has been long and rocky. The Security Council has struggled to deal with the most systematic human rights abuses in the post-cold war world. In none of the following examples – Bosnia, Rwanda, Kosovo, and Sudan – did the Council adopt a hierarchical approach to adequately prevent humanitarian disasters. The Bosnia and Rwanda cases illustrate the ambiguities between a peacekeeping approach and a collective security approach, and how a more hierarchical collective security approach is necessary to prevent human rights violations. The Kosovo case illustrates the competing visions about the appropriate way to implement collective security rules, particularly when the Council is deadlocked. Once again, a more hierarchical approach was necessary to prevent widespread human rights violations. And Sudan is currently providing the same lesson – only a more hierarchical approach can stop the ongoing genocide.

Bosnia

One of the first major post-cold war humanitarian crises the Security Council had to deal with was in Bosnia. The war in Bosnia was part of the fragmentation of Yugoslavia, a federal state with six republics: Serbia, Croatia, Bosnia and Herzegovina, Macedonia, Slovenia, and Montenegro. When the cold war ended, many of these republics wanted to secede, causing conflict with Serbia, who dominated the federal government. Bosnia included three groups: Muslims (44 percent of the population), Serbs (31 percent), and Croats (17 percent). When the Muslim-dominated government of Bosnia declared its independence in April 1992, the Serbs within Bosnia rebelled. With the aid of Serbia and the Serb-dominated federal government of Yugoslavia, they engaged in "ethnic cleansing" of Muslims. Their goal was to live in a "Greater Serbia," and they committed gross violations of human rights to achieve that goal.

The Security Council initially addressed the Bosnian war through neutral peacekeeping measures. It first authorized an arms embargo to prevent the escalation of the war (SCR 713). This ostensibly neutral act, however, harmed the Bosnian Muslims because Serbia was willing to ignore the embargo and arm the Bosnian Serbs. (Indeed, Yugoslavia initially requested the arms embargo!) The Council then authorized a peacekeeping mission to mediate negotiations among the parties and to deliver humanitarian aid (SCR 743). This UN Protection Force (UNPROFOR) was authorized with local consent; the combatants agreed to UN military escorts of humanitarian aid in August 1992.

The Security Council started to authorize enforcement measures as reports increased about concentration camps, ethnic cleansing, and the use of rape as a war tactic by the Bosnian Serbs. On 30 May 1992 the Council authorized comprehensive sanctions on Yugoslavia for its interference in the war and its assistance to the Bosnian Serbs (SCR 757). The sanctions banned air travel, financial transactions, sports and cultural exchanges, and scientific and technical cooperation with Yugoslavia. The Council then authorized NATO to enforce both these sanctions and the earlier arms embargo through maritime inspections in the Adriatic Sea (SCR 787). This was the first time that NATO acted as a collective security entity, using its forces in a Security Council-authorized military operation.

The veto powers, however, did not want to abandon peacekeeping in favor of collective security. The Bosnian Serbs threatened to kidnap UNPROFOR troops if they were not neutral. Britain and France, who contributed troops to UNPROFOR, opposed strengthening the mandate in order to protect their troops. Russia and China refused to provide humanitarian aid, let alone authorize the use of force. The United States said that a Security Council resolution authorizing the use of force would be necessary before it would send any troops to Bosnia. President Bush illustrated the global ambivalence at the time when he said that although the world had a "moral obligation" to relieve the humanitarian crisis, he opposed sending American troops to Bosnia.

Given its reluctance to use force, the Security Council responded to reports of ethnic cleansing, torture, detention, and murder in other ways. In July 1992 it passed its first resolution stating that individuals were responsible for war crimes (SCR 764). It stated that "impeding the delivery of food" violated international humanitarian law (SCR 771). In August 1992 it expanded UNPROFOR's mandate to include escorting humanitarian assistance convoys (SCR 770), albeit with its original peacekeeping rules of engagement and troop levels (SCR 776). When the Serbs interpreted the disproportionate amount of aid going to the Bosnian Muslims to violate impartiality, they often stopped the humanitarian aid from going into Muslim areas. This was a consistent pattern throughout the war. The UN troops, under peacekeeping rules of engagement, could not protect the aid from deliberate and consistent Serb attacks.

The Council next established a no-fly zone (SCR 781), banning all military flights over Bosnia except UNPROFOR flights. The resolution did not include enforcement measures because Britain and France feared Serb retaliation against their peacekeeping troops. When France and Britain finally agreed to enforce the no-fly zone in December 1992, Russia vetoed the resolution. (Thus while the no-fly zones over Iraq were not explicitly authorized but were enforced, the no-fly zones over Bosnia were explicitly authorized but not enforced.) At the same time as the Council squabbled over the no-fly zone, it revolutionized international law by creating an ad hoc judicial tribunal to try individuals guilty of genocide, crimes against humanity, and war crimes in the Yugoslavia wars (SCR 808) (see Chapter 6).

Diplomatic efforts were not succeeding. The veto powers disagreed over the January 1993 Vance–Owen plan calling for a confederation of ten provinces split along ethnic lines. Russia, France and Britain favored the plan, but the United States, now led by the Clinton administration, called it appeasement for rewarding Serb aggression. The Bosnian Serbs also rejected the plan, but for the opposite reason: while by that time they militarily controlled over 70 percent of Bosnia, the plan gave them less than one-half of the country. By May 1993 the United States began to advocate lifting the arms embargo and conducting limited air strikes against the Serbs. But Britain and France feared that lifting the arms embargo would provoke Serb retaliation and end the humanitarian mission, and Russia continued veto threats to any uses of force. The Bosnian Serbs rejected the Vance–Owen in a May referendum.

Serb noncompliance forced the Council to inch toward collective security throughout 1993. When the Serbs violated the no-fly zones and bombed Muslim villages in March, the Council finally authorized NATO to enforce the no-fly zone (SCR 816). It was the first authorization of armed intervention in the former Yugoslavia. However, each use of force had to be explicitly authorized by both the Secretary General and UNPROFOR, who refused to do so throughout 1993 to avoid jeopardizing UN troops on the ground. In April 1993 the Council declared Srebenica a "safe area" (SCR 819) and extended sanctions to territories controlled by Bosnian Serbs (SCR 820). In May the Council extended the safe areas to Sarajevo, Tuzla, Zepa, Gorazde, and Bihac (SCR 824). In June it authorized NATO to use air strikes against Serb forces surrounding the six Muslim safe havens (SCR 836). Russia and China abstained on all of these resolutions.

The Serbs continued to shell Gorazde and Sarajevo throughout June and July. An American-sponsored resolution to end the arms embargo failed with only six votes in favor in late June. At one point in July the Serbs were about to take Sarajevo, and the United States prepared to send in attack planes to defend the city. Prior to the strikes, however, the UNPROFOR commander negotiated an agreement that French peacekeepers would be stationed on the front line between the Serbs and Sarajevo. They were so close to the Serbs that any American strikes would hit them as well. The United States began to openly criticize its European allies for their unwillingness to end the arms embargo and support air strikes. In a familiar post-cold war debate, the United States began to argue that NATO had the authority to carry out air strikes from SCR 770, which authorized states to use "all necessary means" to protect aid shipments to civilians. But NATO members insisted that no bombings could be carried out without the authorization of the Secretary General.

Given British and French reluctance to use military force and American reticence to use force without allied support, the allies negotiated a tortured compromise: NATO threatened on 9 August 1993 to undertake strategic air strikes unless the Serbs stopped their offensive against Sarajevo; but the request for air strikes would come from the UNPROFOR commander, all sixteen NATO ambassadors would have to agree, and the Secretary General would give final approval. Owing to shrewd Serb withdrawals and this complicated bureaucratic formula, there were no strikes throughout the fall of 1993.

Another round of diplomacy again failed. The Owen–Stoltenberg plan divided Bosnia into three ethnic ministates. Reflecting the military reality on the ground, the Serbs would get 52.5 percent of the land, the Croats 17.5 percent, and the Muslims 30 percent. Once again Russia, Britain and France supported the plan, and the United States did not because the proposed borders aligned the Serb part along the Serbian border, implicitly rewarding the campaign for "Greater Serbia." The Serbs and Croats agreed to this plan in August 1993. Although Britain and France wanted to coerce the Muslims to sign, the United States continued to advocate ending the arms embargo and striking the Serbs so that the Muslims could get some of their land back. The Muslims ultimately rejected the plan because their proposed territory was disconnected and had no access to the sea.

In December 1993 the UN reported that the Serbs were close to capturing three safe havens – Srebrenica, Zepa, and Gorazde. Ongoing Serb atrocities, international pressure, and the need to maintain NATO credibility encouraged the Western allies to act more coercively. On 5 February 2004 the Serbs killed 69 civilians in a mortar attack into a Sarajevo market. Four days after the "Market Massacre" NATO said that it would use air strikes in ten days against all heavy weapons within 20 kilometers around Sarajevo. The Serbs withdrew their weapons to outside that perimeter. Later that month NATO forces shot down four Serb warplanes violating the no-fly zone. It was the first use of force in the Bosnian war to enforce Security Council resolutions.

Russia, however, did not want to punish the Bosnian Serbs, and it did not want NATO troops using force in what it considered its own sphere of influence. Yeltsin criticized the NATO ultimatum, saying that military intervention would harm Russia's relationship with the West. To prevent the strikes, Russia sent "peace-keeping" troops to join the Serbs around Sarajevo, knowing that NATO would not use force with Russian troops in the area. When NATO troops bombed Serb tanks and an armored personnel carrier in April to deter a Serb attack on Gorazde – the first NATO ground strikes in the conflict – Yeltsin demanded to be an equal partner in any future military decision. In response, the Western allies agreed to form a "Contact Group" on 25 April 1994 to unify the positions of Britain, France, Germany, Russia, and the United States.

On 24 April NATO issued another ultimatum regarding Gorazde. This time the Serbs did not withdraw and continued shelling the city. To deter a NATO strike, they held over 200 peacekeepers hostage. Security Council resolutions still required the Secretary General to request the NATO strikes. The Secretary General failed to do so when his representative in Bosnia implausibly determined that the Serbs had complied with the NATO ultimatum. The UN bureaucracy wanted to avoid reprisals against UN peacekeepers, to maintain the neutrality of the mission, and to provide humanitarian aid. When the UN and NATO worked out a "dual-key" command procedure, through which strikes could be launched if both the UNPROFOR commander and NATO's Southern Command agreed, the United States complained about UN commanders resisting air strikes.

In July 2004 the Contact Group called for a federal state in which a Croat/Muslim entity would get 51 percent of the land, tougher sanctions on Serbia, stricter enforcement and expansion of weapons exclusion zones, and the eventual lifting of the arms embargo against Bosnia if the Serbs rejected the peace plan. This time the Muslims and Croats grudgingly accepted the plan, but the Bosnian Serbs rejected it in an August plebiscite. In an attempt to end the sanctions against Serbia, Milosevic announced that Serbia was withdrawing its support for the Bosnian Serbs and that it would welcome international monitors on the border to verify this. In response the Security Council on 23 September eased some of the sanctions against Serbia – an example of the bargaining model rather than the punishment model of sanctions (SCR 943).

The failure of the Contact Group peace plan initiated the same debate among the veto powers. The United States wanted to lift the arms embargo and enforce the weapons exclusion zones. But Britain, France, and Russia argued that these actions would pose unacceptable risks to UN troops on the ground and make a peace agreement less likely by fueling more violence. By September the United States began invoking hegemonic collective security, asserting a willingness to undertake unilateral air strikes to enforce Security Council resolutions. In November it announced that it would no longer enforce the arms embargo. This was the first time the United States had unilaterally breached NATO policy. The Bosnian war was now formally splitting the NATO alliance.

The Bosnian Serbs continued to violate Council resolutions with offensives against Sarajevo and Bihac. They attacked French peacekeepers in Sarajevo in September. During the siege on Bihac, Croatian Serbs entered the conflict, using a Croatian airfield in Udbina to launch missiles and air attacks into Bihac. After a unanimous authorization from the Security Council in November, NATO bombed the Croatian airfield. This was NATO's first strategically significant military strike in the conflict, and the Serbs responded by more vigilant ethnic cleansing, setting entire villages on fire, and taking more UN peacekeepers hostage. British and French support for the NATO air strikes waned when the Serbs took more soldiers hostage. The United States chose to maintain NATO unity and did not press for more strikes. A December 1994 American proposal to give UNPROFOR collective security powers failed to receive Council support.

The warring parties concluded that the outside world was not going to intervene and escalated hostilities in 1995. Worried that the fighting might spread throughout the Balkans, the Council on 31 March 1995, authorized its first ever preventive force in Macedonia to ensure that the conflict did not spill over across the border (SCR 983). After another Bosnian Serb attack on Sarajevo in May 1995, NATO launched air strikes, and the Serbs retaliated by taking peacekeepers as hostages and human shields. But this time the Security Council authorized a 12,500-soldier Rapid Reaction Force to enable peacekeeping troops to safely withdraw (SCR 998). The resolution continued peacekeeping rules of engagement because Russia demanded that UN personnel remain neutral.

By August the peacekeepers were in a safer position, and NATO finally embraced collective security rules, warning the Bosnian Serbs that any further attacks on UN safe areas would be met with "disproportionate" and "overwhelming" force. When the Serbs bombed a Sarajevo market place on 30 August and killed thirty-eight people, NATO demanded that the Serbs withdraw their heavy weapons from the Sarajevo exclusion zone, stop shelling Sarajevo and other safe areas, and open the Sarajevo airport and roads into the city. When the Serbs did not comply, NATO began a sustained bombing campaign against Serb positions and facilities throughout Bosnia on 10 September. The Rapid Reaction Force continued shelling Serbian positions beyond the NATO air strikes; the UN and NATO had become participants in the war.

Russia condemned the military action, arguing that NATO exceeded its UN mandate. Yeltsin explicitly complained about the shift from peacekeeping to collective security: "NATO declares its 'peacekeeping mission' but has actually appropriated the role of judge and bailiff . . . How is it when the Muslims attack, no sanctions are applied against them?" (Erlanger 1995b). He interpreted the NATO bombing to invoke rivalry rules. The NATO campaign "means a return to two camps that are at war with one another" and "will mean a conflagration of war throughout Europe" (Erlanger 1995b). He warned that the NATO bombing in Bosnia showed how an expanded NATO would behave on Russia's borders. But when the Russians circulated a draft resolution on 12 September citing "excessive use of force" and calling on NATO to stop the bombing campaign, ten Security Council members explicitly rejected it.

Many things changed during the two-week NATO bombing campaign. The Croats and Muslims stepped up their offensive, taking control of one-half of Bosnia (up from 28 percent). Milosevic and the Bosnian Serbs announced that they would form a joint negotiating team and that the Contact Group plan – which they had earlier rejected – would form the basis for further negotiations. Talks began in Geneva the day after the bombing stopped. This time the Serbs were willing to settle, and the Muslims and Croats were hesitant, wanting to maximize its new-found military advantages on the ground. Milosevic warned that Serbia would intervene in the conflict if the Bosnian Serbs lost too much territory. There was intense international pressure on the Croats and Muslims to make an agreement. The parties agreed to a ceasefire – the Dayton Accords – on 5 October. After more than three years of wavering between peacekeeping and collective security, two weeks of collective security enforcement ended the war in Bosnia.

The war in Bosnia generated a number of "firsts" in the development of post-cold war collective security: (1) the first Council resolution mentioning individual responsibility for war crimes; (2) the first time NATO acted as a United Nations-authorized collective security entity; (3) the first time the Council established an ad hoc tribunal; (4) the first time NATO used force in Europe; (5) the first time American and Russian troops worked together on the same mission; and (6) the first preventive peacekeeping force (sent to Macedonia to prevent the war from spilling over). Despite the overwhelming reluctance on the part of the Council to strongly intervene, Serb belligerence and Western public opinion forced to the Council to take many historic steps.

The war in Bosnia also illustrated the post-cold war pattern of the United States advocating more hierarchical security arrangements than the other veto powers. It took a while – the United States was reluctant for domestic reasons to send troops to Bosnia. But the tensions between (less hierarchical) peacekeeping arrangements and (more hierarchical) collective security arrangements were central to the veto power dispute over Bosnia. When the United States began to advocate more aggressive collective security policies, the other veto powers resisted and preferred a peacekeeping approach. After Britain and France eventually embraced collective security policies and NATO intervened in the war, Russia and China criticized those uses of force. The veto powers could not agree how to implement collective security in this case.

Rwanda

The genocide in Rwanda is a seminal event in the history of post-cold war collective security (Barnett 2002; Dallaire 2003; Des Forges 1999; Gourevitch 1998;

Melvern 2004). When the genocide began, the Security Council responded – by reducing the number of UN forces in the country. When the Council authorized a more robust force, it sent French troops – to protect its allies in the Hutu government that participated in the genocide. While the world watched for ten weeks, Hutu militias and the Rwandan military killed over a million of their fellow citizens, including over 75 percent of the Tutsi population in Rwanda. The Security Council failed to invoke collective security rules and stop the genocide. It adopted a peacekeeping approach and abandoned Rwanda when there was no peace to keep.

Rwanda is a small central African country. The majority of the country is Hutu, and the Tutsi comprise the largest minority group. The Hutu historically were farmers; the Tutsi historically were cattle herders. Both groups have the same language and religion. Rwanda became a League of Nations mandate under the supervision of Belgium in 1923. The Belgians considered the Tutsi more "European" and elevated their status in the colonial regime. The Hutu eventually began to agitate for majority rule and an end to Tutsi supremacy. In 1959 the Rwandan king, a Tutsi installed by the Belgians, died under suspicious circumstances. The Tutsi elite blamed Hutu extremists and removed Hutu leaders from government positions. The Hutu then staged a massive rebellion, and thousands of Tutsi fled to Burundi. Belgium placed Rwanda under military rule but now favored the Hutu over the Tutsi.

A January 1961 referendum established a republic, and Rwanda declared independence in 1962. Over the next decade, the Hutu-dominated government killed or drove out the Tutsi elite, and exiled Tutsis engaged in periodic armed attacks, leading to more massacres and massive refugee flows to Burundi, Zaire, and Uganda. After a failed 1972 coup attempt by Hutus to oust Tutsis from power in neighboring Burundi, Tutsis retaliated by killing over 200,000 Hutus. That violence spilled over into Rwanda, and eventually a 1973 coup brought to power Major Juvenal Habyarimana, a Hutu who created a rigid one-party state. Ethnic tensions flared again in 1986 when the government announced that Rwandan refugees – mostly Tutsi in Uganda – would not be allowed to return. These Tutsi refugees created the Rwandan Patriotic Front (RPF) in Uganda in 1988, and civil war began in 1990 when the RPF invaded Rwanda.

The Rwandan government received military support from France, Belgium, South Africa, and Egypt (whose foreign minister was Boutros Boutros-Ghali). Most support came from France, who trained Rwandan forces. There were close ties between French President Mitterand and Rwandan President Habyarimana. Mitterand's son even owned a plantation in Rwanda and was personally involved in the arms trade (Stanton 2004). When the RPF invaded in October 1990, the French sent 350 troops, ostensibly to protect French expatriates in Rwanda. But the French soldiers engaged in combat against the RPF and manned checkpoints demanding identification cards from civilians. Some human rights organizations charged the French with training the militias that later engaged in the worst atrocities during the genocide (Callamard 1999).

Despite the international support for the Hutu-led Rwandan government, the

Tutsi-led RPF made steady military progress toward capturing the country. Under pressure from its allies, particularly France, the Rwandan government agreed to peace talks in August 1992. France could not convince the Security Council to authorize a peacekeeping force that would monitor the Rwanda/Uganda border and separate the RPF from the Rwandan army. By January 1993 the government and the RPF agreed to a transitional government that excluded the most extreme Hutu groups. During this time the civil war periodically erupted, and each time the RPF would conquer more territory. By February 1993 the RPF reached the outskirts of Kigali. Alienated by these events, extremist Hutu militias grew. The Rwandan government asked the French for help, and France doubled their troops to around 700 and sent $12 million worth of weapons (Callamard 1999).

By this time over one million people were displaced by the fighting. The Red Cross warned of an imminent famine and a major humanitarian catastrophe. With international pressure on both sides to end the fighting, the parties signed a cease-fire in March 1993 and continued peace talks. Intense French lobbying finally succeeded, and in June the Security Council authorized an observer mission to monitor the Rwanda/Uganda border and ensure that Uganda – who supported the Tutsi-led RPF – did not interfere in the domestic affairs of Rwanda (SCR 846). The peacekeeping mission clearly supported the Rwandan government over the RPF, and the RPF would never see the UN forces as neutral.

The Rwandan government and the RPF signed a peace agreement in August 1993, and in early October the Security Council authorized a peacekeeping force to oversee its implementation, provide security in Kigali, investigate complaints about police and militias, coordinate relief assistance, and monitor the repatriation of Rwandan refugees. Although the Council authorized around 2,500 troops, few countries volunteered (Laegrid 1999). That month eighteen American soldiers were killed in Somalia, greatly decreasing Western interest in getting involved in another African conflict. The only wealthy countries with any interest in Rwanda were France and Belgium. France already had troops on the ground in an attempt to save the regime from the RPF advance. At RPF insistence, the peace agreement stated that all foreign troops had to leave the country by the time the UN peacekeepers arrived. So the UN mission was comprised of poorly trained and poorly equipped soldiers from African countries and soldiers from Belgium, Rwanda's former colonizer.

There were few positive signs. The RPF did not see UN troops sent as a result of French lobbying as neutral, and the Rwandan army did not see the Belgian troops in the UN mission as neutral. The parties made little progress in the formation of political institutions because they could not agree upon formulas for representation. Political violence increased in the final months of 1993 with sporadic assassinations and reports of weapons being distributed to citizens. Then the democratically elected president of Burundi, a Hutu named Melchior Ndadaye, was killed by Tutsi military leaders, escalating political violence in both Burundi and Rwanda. Around 300,000 refugees crossed from Burundi into Rwanda. The Rwandan government split the refugees into camps divided along ethnic lines, and they later recruited young men from the Hutu camps into the genocidal militias.

In January 1994 a high-ranking Hutu militia official reported to the UN commander that he had been ordered to plan for the extermination of the Tutsi community. He warned of an oncoming genocide to prevent the implementation of the peace agreement, that plans were being made to kill Belgian peacekeepers to get them to withdraw, and that secret arms caches were stashed around Kigali (Dallaire 2003). When the UN commander requested permission to search and capture those arms caches, the UN Secretariat denied the request. Such an operation was inconsistent with its peacekeeping mandate. The UN mission could not undertake an offensive mission against one side without undermining neutrality and endangering the consent of the Rwandan government required to continue the mission. Indeed, the mandate stated that it could use force only in cooperation with the local police. But in this situation, it was the local police who were stockpiling the weapons.

The situation was deteriorating. The Security Council could have pursued collective security, strengthened the UN mission, and authorized the use of force to protect Rwandan civilians. But most, including the United States, maintained a peacekeeping perspective, concluded that there was no peace to keep, and argued to end the mission. The Council compromised and on 5 April 1994 threatened to pull out in six weeks unless a transitional government was sworn in (SCR 909). The very next day the presidents of Rwanda and Burundi were killed when their plane was shot down trying to approach the Kigali airport. Although there is no conclusive evidence, most believe that officials in the Rwandan government killed their own president to instigate the genocide. Rwandan military forces set up roadblocks in Kigali before the news of the plane crash had been announced, and they denied UN observers access to the crash site. Radio broadcasts charged that the RPF and Belgian peacekeepers were responsible for the death of the president.

The genocide began the next day, with the systematic killing of opposition and pro-democracy politicians, both Hutu and Tutsi. Those also killed in the first wave were ten Belgian peacekeepers, journalists, human rights activists, lawyers, and civil servants. Thousands of Rwandans went to UN compounds for protection. The massacres reignited the civil war; RPF forces engaged the government forces and moved toward Kigali. The renewed conflict led to massive refugee flows. Over 250,000 (mostly Tutsi) refugees crossed the border into Tanzania within two weeks. These events put the UN mission in an impossible situation: how to be neutral and encourage the political process when one of the parties is committing genocide and the other is violating the ceasefire and continuing the civil war? The military operations of a peacekeeping mission were to be conducted only in cooperation with government forces, and now those forces were engaged in genocide.

The UN commander requested a collective security mandate with Chapter VII powers, but the Security Council was not going to authorize that so soon after Somalia. Instead the UN Secretariat told the mission to remain neutral and provide protection for refugees. The Hutu massacre of Tutsis increased in the following days, and the Tutsi-led RPF continued its offensive and crossed the demilitarized zone established by the peace agreement. This time there were no French forces to stop the RPF, and UN troops had no mandate to deter the attack. The peacekeeping mission could neither stop the genocide nor effectively intervene in the civil war.

When the genocide began, the Security Council again had to decide whether to continue interpreting the conflict primarily as a civil war between the government and the RPF or primarily as a humanitarian disaster because the Rwandan government was committing genocide against the Tutsis. Most on the Council continued to treat it as a civil war; indeed, there was little early recognition that the Rwandan government was supporting the genocide. Interpreting it as a civil war meant the peacekeepers had to leave – there was no peace to keep. Interpreting it as genocide would require a collective security enforcement mission to end the threat to international peace and security. Given the reality on the ground, what member states were willing to do, and the neutral rules of peacekeeping, the Security Council considered nonintervention the appropriate response.

There was no international condemnation during the first few weeks of the genocide; it was simply another African civil war. Belgian troops left the UN mission by 20 April. The United States refused requests to jam the radio broadcasts inciting the genocide. The Clinton administration circulated a memo forbidding use of the word "genocide." The Security Council took no action until 21 April, when it voted to keep a small UN force of 300 troops to act as an intermediary, attempt a ceasefire agreement, resume humanitarian operations, and provide security for those citizens who sought refuge at UN compounds (SCR 912). The Hutu militias, now certain that there would be no international intervention, increased the number of killings. There was immediate global pressure on the Council to reconsider.

On 29 April the Council rejected a resolution supported by five nonpermanent Council members calling the situation genocide and bolstering the UN mission. The United States argued that action should be taken by the Organization of African Unity. China and Russia feared that interventions based on human rights would encourage others to question the treatment of their own citizens. The United States presented an alternative of setting up safe havens outside Rwandan borders for refugees of the conflict. President Clinton ordered that American participation in UN missions must be in response to threats to international peace and security, must advance American interests at an acceptable risk, and must have adequate command and control procedures and an exit strategy. The United Kingdom was the only veto power willing to call it genocide and intervene.

There was overwhelming international pressure on the Security Council to act. On 17 May – six weeks after the genocide began – the Council authorized an arms embargo on Rwanda and expanded the UN mission to 5,500 troops so that it could provide safe conditions for refugees, help provide assistance by NGOs, and monitor border crossing points (SCR 918). Although still a peacekeeping mission, the Council authorized the use of force to protect civilians, resolving the contradiction with an expanded definition of self-defense. Prior to this resolution, similar protection mandates in Bosnia had always used Chapter VII powers. Even with this movement toward collective security, or perhaps because of it, only nine

African countries stepped forward to send troops. By the time all 5,000 troops arrived in October, the RPF had won the civil war and the genocide was over.

In May the RPF took control of Kigali. Government forces went south in front of the RPF advance, and France again wanted to intervene and prevent the RPF from taking total control of the country (Prunier 1999). So France offered to deploy troops to provide a "humanitarian safe zone" in the south-west corner of the country –where the Rwandan military forces were retreating. Security Council members recognized the offer as something other than purely humanitarian. France was more interested in preserving the Rwandan government and stopping the RPF offensive that it was in stopping the genocide. It wanted a mandate to prevent the RPF from entering the safe zone. When the Council approved the deployment of 2,500 French troops as peacekeepers (SCR 929), the five nonpermanent members who had been most enthusiastically endorsing stronger action against the genocide abstained.

By July an estimated 6,000 people per hour fled to the French safe zone. Most were Hutu, including militia members and ministers of the interim government. It is likely that the French protected and gave weapons to those who had perpetrated acts of genocide (Prunier 1999; Barnett 2002). The French never tried to disarm the Rwandan army or the militias, and never arrested a single suspected war criminal. The killings again increased when the Hutu extremists realized that the French were coming. Operation Turquoise raised troubling questions: Did the Security Council provide support for those who committed genocide? Did the French intend to fight the only military force capable of stopping the genocide? The RPF repeatedly announced that it was against French intervention: where was the attempt to maintain neutrality?

On 4 July the RPF announced that it would establish a new government based on the earlier peace agreements. In the following two weeks a million people fled to Zaire, the fastest migration in history. Most of the refugees were Hutu, including war criminals who had engaged in the genocide. The French and Zairian forces made no effort to separate the militia from civilians, and those who had engaged in genocide quickly controlled the camps. Nearly two million people were refugees in Zaire, Tanzania, and Burundi. Many struggled through cholera outbreaks. The refugee crisis provided the first television pictures of the conflict and sparked a massive global aid effort. (Television coverage in April was dominated by the South African election of Nelson Mandela and Serb assaults on Bosnian safe havens.) Again conflating the civil war and the genocide, the world community sympathized with the refugees, not understanding that they included war criminals. In one of the many ironies of this conflict, the unprecedented global relief efforts unwittingly helped to feed many of those who committed the genocide.

Another irony was that Rwanda was on the Security Council during the entire crisis. A Hutu extremist took the Rwandan seat in January 1994. Sitting in on the private discussions, the representative could convey to the Rwandan government that the veto powers were hesitant about intervention. For example, the day after the 15 April Security Council meeting in which the United States opposed intervention, the Rwandan government decided to extend the genocide to southern

Rwanda. As it became clearer that the government was implicated in the genocide, no one knew what to do with the Rwandan delegate. Even after the RPF military victory, there was no one from an accredited government of Rwanda to replace him. The Council did change protocol and did not allow the Rwandan delegate to assume the presidency. An RPF representative finally took the seat on the Council in December 1994.

The RPF installed a new government on 19 July. Both the civil war and the genocide were over, but the humanitarian disaster remained. On 22 July the United States announced that it would deploy troops to help the refugees in camps in Zaire, where the worst cholera outbreaks occurred (but also where the Hutu war criminals were). There continued to be more attention to conditions of the refugee camps as a result of the civil war than the carnage within Rwanda as a result of the genocide. When the veto powers recognized the magnitude of the horrors, they decided to engage in post hoc collective security enforcement by establishing an ad hoc tribunal to prosecute instances of genocide in November 1994 (SC 955) (see Chapter 6).

The inaction of the Security Council during the Rwandan genocide – and the widespread notion within the UN at the time that it was acting appropriately – was shocking. A later UN report on the Rwanda genocide concluded that the UN obligation to act transcended the traditional rules of peacekeeping: there should be no neutrality in the face of genocide, and the Security Council should have authorized a Chapter VII mandate (Ramcharan 2002). This growing support for a more robust Security Council approach to avoid another Rwanda led to more "third-generation" peacekeeping missions. But the Council has not fully adopted this approach. The Kosovo case illustrates another example of gridlock on the Council. And in Sudan, as in Rwanda, it seems content to prosecute offenders after the fact instead of acting to prevent ongoing genocide. It continues to be extremely difficult to fuse moral, political, and legal obligations to prevent humanitarian disasters within a collective security framework.

Kosovo

Kosovo was another pivotal episode in the post-cold war construction of collective security (Bellamy 2002; Daalder and O'Hanlon 2000). The Council deadlocked on whether to intervene given massive human rights violations by the Serb government of Slobodan Milošević against Albanian Muslims. The United States, Britain and France urged Council action, but Russia and China resisted. Russia did not want a Western use of force in what it considered its own sphere of influence; China did not want to set a precedent that "domestic affairs" can trigger Council action. In the end NATO acted without Council authorization, and used force in a humanitarian intervention to end the Serb atrocities. While Council debates about Bosnia and Rwanda were primarily about whether to pursue peacekeeping or collective security, the debate over Kosovo was about whether to pursue procedural or hegemonic collective security.

Kosovo is a province within Serbia, but Albanian Muslims constitute 90 percent of the population. When Yugoslavia began to fragment after the cold war, the Albanian Muslims began to agitate for more autonomy within Serbia, and many advocated independence. Serb President Slobodan Milošević responded to this movement with brutal repression, and the United States imposed bilateral sanctions on Serbia in May 1991. In October the Kosovo assembly declared independence, but only Albania recognized it as a new state. Western countries urged Serbia to respect minority rights and negotiate an autonomy status for the territory. In December 1992 the outgoing Bush administration sent a "Christmas Warning" to Belgrade that the United States would be willing to use force against the Serbs if they cause a conflict in Kosovo. The incoming Clinton administration reiterated this policy and issued a joint statement with Russia urging Serbia to respect international human rights standards.

The "Christmas Warning" receded into the background during the war in Bosnia, but in 1998 violence between Serbs and Kosovo Albanians escalated again. In March the Security Council attempted to minimize the violence by imposing an arms embargo on Serbia (SCR 1160). Russia voted for the resolution only because it did not authorize the use of force. China abstained because it considered the conflict an internal matter. Reports of massive human rights violations continued throughout the summer of 1998. In September the Council demanded that Serbia withdraw its security forces from Kosovo, enable human rights monitors to return to Kosovo, facilitate the return of refugees, and begin political negotiations with the Albanian Muslims (SCR 1199). Russia again supported the resolution because there was no explicit authorization of force if Serbia did not comply. China again abstained, arguing that the Council should not violate Serb sovereignty. Russia, China, and France all argued that another resolution would be necessary to authorize force.

The Serbs did not initially comply, and NATO prepared for airstrikes. Russia and China criticized NATO, arguing that the Council had not authorized any use of force. Despite this Council split, on 13 October Milosevic announced that Serbia would comply with SCR 1199 and agree to a ceasefire, troop withdrawals, return of refugees, international monitors, and a negotiated autonomy for Kosovo. When the Security Council negotiated another resolution, Russia threatened to veto any draft that authorized force if the Serbs did not comply. The Council passed an ambiguous resolution on 24 October that did not include the standard "all necessary means" phrase to authorize force (SCR 1203). Russia and China abstained even though they argued that the resolution did not explicitly authorize force if the Serbs did not comply. The United States, Britain and France all argued that SCR 1203 authorized NATO to use force.

While Serb forces in Kosovo withdrew to pre-March 1998 levels, reports of human rights abuses continued. On 15 January 1999, Serb security forces killed forty-five people in the "Racak Massacre," and Milošević refused to allow war crimes prosecutors access to the scene. He argued that Serbia had a right to respond to provocations by the Kosovo Liberation Army on its own soil. On 18 January NATO condemned the massacre as a flagrant violation of international humanitarian law. Britain and France announced that they were willing to send ground troops to reinforce a political settlement. On 31 January NATO warned Serbia to stop the offensive in Kosovo and begin peace talks by 6 February or face air strikes. Milošević agreed to negotiate in Rambouillet.

NATO threats to punish the Serbs if they would not agree to a settlement were complicated by the Kosovo Albanians, who were reluctant to sign any deal that did not include a referendum on Kosovo's independence. NATO could not bomb the Serbs for refusing to sign a peace agreement if the Kosovo Albanians also refused. But NATO did not support independence for Kosovo. On 18 March, under great Western pressure, the Kosovo Albanians signed the Rambouillet Accords, which guaranteed autonomy but not independence. Milošević, who had never attended the talks and had increased the number of Serb troops in Kosovo, began a new military offensive on 20 March. Consistent with Russia and China's position, Milošević argued that Yugoslavia had a right to use force to end a secessionist movement within its borders.

NATO began its bombing campaign four days later on 24 March. The United States argued that the overwhelming humanitarian crisis justified intervention even without explicit Security Council authorization. Echoing a later United States argument about the invasion of Iraq, Madeleine Albright argued: "Our explicit goal should be to transform the Balkans from Europe's primary source of instability into an important part of its mainstream." Clinton argued:

> We act to protect thousands of innocent people in Kosovo from a mounting military offensive. We act to prevent a wider war, to diffuse a powder keg at the heart of Europe that has exploded twice before in this century with catastrophic results. And we act to stand united with our allies for peace. By acting now, we are upholding our values, protecting our interests, and advancing the cause of peace . . . It is this challenge that we and our allies are facing in Kosovo. That is why we have acted now – because we care about saving innocent lives; because we have an interest in avoiding an even crueler and costlier war; and because our children need and deserve a peaceful, stable, free Europe.
>
> (Clinton 1999)

NATO argued that force was justified to avert a humanitarian catastrophe because there was no other alternative and the use of force was proportionate. Blair (1999) argued: "This is a just war, based not on any territorial ambitions but on values. We cannot let the evil of ethnic cleansing stand. We must not rest until it is reversed. We have learned twice before in this century that appeasement does not work. If we let an evil dictator range unchallenged, we will have to spill infinitely more blood and treasure to stop him later." These justifications imply that human rights violations were not domestic matters but legitimate concerns of the international community. NATO, now acting as a regional collective security organization, had the right to defend the stability of Europe. State sovereignty in the post-cold war world is limited because "legitimate" states ensure basic human rights. States that perpetrate ethnic cleansing forfeit their right to territorial integrity. No NATO country argued that their action was illegal but moral. All argued that international law supported it.

Russia and China vehemently disagreed, arguing that invoking a humanitarian crisis to justify armed intervention without Security Council approval violated the UN Charter. Russia, India, China, and others argued that international law did not authorize a group of states to use force against another state to punish it for human rights violations. Since there was no global consensus on the relative status of human rights versus state sovereignty, the NATO use of force was an attempt to impose Western rules on the global community. They argued that the use of force usurped both the Security Council's responsibility to maintain international security and the traditional notion of state sovereignty, thus undermining global order.

Russia, of course, also believed that NATO was directly threatening its national interests. NATO was using force within the former Soviet sphere of influence. Russian politicians from across the political spectrum condemned the war, claiming that NATO would next bomb Russia when it attempted to deal with separatist movements. An April 1999 survey showed that 56 percent of Russians said that NATO's motivations were military and strategic; only 14 percent said NATO acted to prevent atrocities against Kosovo Albanians. NATO's use of force in Kosovo increased Russian fears that the West was isolating it from regional and global security issues. It ended the Russian dream of a European security system without United States influence.

For Russia this was now more than a dispute about how to implement collective security. NATO was invoking rules of empire. Consider the following statements by the Russian foreign minister and top military leader (British Broadcasting Corporation 1998):

- "Russia is deeply outraged by NATO's military action against sovereign Yugoslavia, an action that is nothing short of undisguised aggression . . . Only the UN Security Council has the right to decide (if) the use of force should be taken to maintain or restore international peace and security."
- "The true aims are obvious. To impose on the world the political, military, and economic dictate of the United States."
- "What is in the balance now is law and lawlessness. It is a question of either reaffirming the commitment of one's country and people to the principles and values of the United Nations Charter, or tolerating a situation in which gross force dictates realpolitik."

Russia responded with policies invoking a rivalry security arrangement. It signed a joint defense initiative with Belarus. It held war games in the Balkans with an anti-NATO bent. It expelled NATO representatives from Moscow, suspended cooperation in the Partnership for Peace program, withdrew its mission from Brussels and NATO countries, and withdrew officers responsible for communication between Russian and NATO forces in Bosnia. The Duma postponed the vote on the START II nuclear arms agreement again. Russia even began talks with China and India to form a counterhegemonic alliance.

Russia became more humiliated and isolated as the bombing went on. On 7 April NATO announced that the bombing would end when Yugoslavia agreed to a verifiable ceasefire, the withdrawal of all Serb military and police forces in Kosovo, the stationing of an international military force, the safe return of Albanian refugees, and a willingness to implement the Rambouillet Accords. On 24 April NATO began to enforce an oil embargo by searching all ships entering Yugoslavia – and most of the incoming oil originated in Russia. On 25 April Russia was the only state in the General Assembly to vote against a resolution condemning "war crimes" against Albanians by Serbian forces in Kosovo. While Russia favored a limited UN monitoring mission after the conflict, on 29 April NATO proposed an "internationally protected area" in Kosovo, effectively controlled by allied forces as part of a broad and long-term peace-building mission. Yeltsin was desperately trying to save face. On 7 May 1999 the veto powers agreed that a future international force should be authorized by the Security Council and that Russia would be a part of the peacekeeping forces.

Then the United States bombed the Chinese embassy in Belgrade. Chinese officials alleged that it was deliberate and called it a "war crime." China suspended all military ties with the United States and ended all negotiations with the United States over human rights issues. China demanded an immediate halt to the bombing until the Security Council could consider further action in Kosovo. Chinese Premier Jiang Zemin said: "The US was using its economic and technological superiority to aggressively expand its influence, pursue 'power politics' and wantonly interfere in the internal affairs of other countries." Chinese leaders called the NATO campaign a "dangerous precedent of naked aggression," part of a "global strategy for world hegemony," a "new form of colonialism," an "aggressive war that is groundless in morality or law," and "part of a plot by the US to destroy Yugoslavia, expand eastward and control all of Europe" (Eckholm 1999). When the ICTY indicted Milošević for war crimes on May 27, China called the indictment an "American-led political scheme." On 3 June, China and Russia announced that they would form a "strategic partnership" to offset the global dominance of the United States.

The bombing continued into June, and eventually Milošević agreed to pull all Serb troops out of Kosovo. There was not one NATO casualty during the ten weeks of bombing. The Security Council subsequently authorized a post-conflict security presence in Kosovo (SCR 1244). The mandate was to maintain the ceasefire, ensure the military withdrawal, establish a secure environment for the return of refugees and displaced persons, and supervise de-mining. The Council also created an international civil authority to promote the establishment of "substantial autonomy" in Kosovo, perform administrative functions, develop institutions for democratic self-governance, support the reconstruction of key infrastructure, coordinate humanitarian and disaster aid, establish a local police force, protect human rights, and assure the safe return of refugees and displaced persons. This was the largest peace building mission the Council had ever authorized. Russia and China abstained.

NATO and Russia then had difficulty coordinating peacekeeping responsibilities. Russia wanted its own sector as part of the international military presence, and it sent 200 troops to control the Pristina airport on 12 June before NATO troops could arrive. A standoff between the Russian troops and NATO troops lasted for a few days until Russia and the United States could agree on the extent of Russian participation in the peacekeeping force. Russia did not get its own sector (even Italy got one), but the 3,600 Russian troops had operational autonomy within sectors led by the United States, France, and Germany in particularly sensitive areas where both Serbs and Albanians lived.

The Kosovo case illustrates the complexity of collective security. The international community was not ready to advocate humanitarian intervention as an accepted principle of world politics. Small countries do not necessarily want to live in a world where big countries routinely cite humanitarian conditions to justify military intervention. NATO force in Kosovo hierarchically asserted such a right. And NATO argued that it was legitimate for democratic governments to intervene to stop human rights abuses but conveyed that it would not be legitimate for countries like Russia or China to do the same. This is hierarchy: when we use force it legitimately enforces collective security rules, but when you use force it destabilizes the region. We have the legitimate authority to enforce the rules – even, in this case, without Security Council authorization. NATO force in Kosovo established an important precedent invoking hegemonic collective security that helped create the conditions for the subsequent United States invasion of Iraq.

And yet human rights norms had strengthened to such an extent that the international community did not wholly condemn NATO action in Kosovo. When Russia brought a resolution to the Security Council condemning the NATO bombing of Kosovo, it was defeated by twelve votes to three (only Russia, China, and Namibia voted in favor). In addition to the five NATO votes, Slovenia, Argentina, Brazil, Bahrain, Malaysia, Gabon, and Gambia voted against it. The General Assembly neither endorsed nor condemned the bombing. Secretary General Kofi Annan reflected this ambiguity. Against NATO he said: "Unless the Security Council is restored to its preeminent position as the sole source of legitimacy on the use of force, we are on a dangerous path to anarchy" (Miller, J. 1999). But against Russia and China he said: "Unless the Security Council can unite around the aim of confronting massive human rights violations and crimes against humanity on the scale in Kosovo, then we will betray the very ideals that inspired the founding of the United Nations." The Security Council still struggles to reconcile these positions.

Sudan

The ongoing conflict in Sudan, like Rwanda, includes both a civil war and a related but distinct genocide (United Nations 2005, Martin 2002, Mahmoud 2004, Udombana 2005). The civil war between the Muslim Sudanese government and Christian groups in the south began in 1983 and is the longest running conflict in Africa. The war is over a variety of issues: the most important ones are southern autonomy, the distribution of resources, and religious conflict. More than 2 million people have died during the conflict, and 4.5 million people have been forcibly displaced from their homes. The number of deaths from this civil war is greater than those in Angola, Bosnia, Chechnya, Kosovo, Liberia, Sierra Leone, Somalia, and Rwanda combined.

Sudan is the largest country in Africa with a population of 40 million people. Islam is the dominant religion in the north, while Christianity and animist religions are prevalent in the South. More than 130 languages exist among its ethnically diverse peoples. After gaining independence from the British in 1956, Sudan has been governed mostly by military regimes with short periods of democratic rule. A military coup in 1958 by General Ibrahim Abbud ended the first democratic regime. Abbud supported the spread of the Arabic language and Islam, and by 1963 resistance against these policies in the South led to armed rebellion. The lack of public order led to Abbud's resignation, and elections were held in 1965. The coalition government formed after these elections was again toppled by a military coup in May 1969. Led by Colonel Gaafar Mohamed Al-Nimeiri, the government adopted a one-party socialist ideology. In February 1972 Nimeiri signed the Addis Ababa agreement granting some autonomy to the rebels from the South, enabling a peace that lasted eleven years.

The civil war began again in 1983 for two reasons: (1) the government revoked the autonomy agreement in an attempt to control the oil-rich areas of the south; and (2) the government imposed Islamic law throughout Sudan. The Sudanese People's Liberation Movement (SPLM) took up arms against the government. The conflict worsened in June 1989 when General Omar Hassan El-Bashir, the current leader of Sudan, took over in a military coup. Bashir allied with Islamist groups, banned political parties, imprisoned critics, and re-established sharia law. He provided sanctuary for Osama bin Laden, strengthened ties to Iran, and facilitated a plot to assassinate Egyptian president Mubarak. The Islamist elements of the regime also issued a fatwa against African tribes in Darfur that became the basis for future government policies. The civil war raged for twenty years, until the government and the SPLA signed a tentative peace agreement on 27 May 2004.

United States policy throughout the 1990s was to support the southern groups in the civil war and pursue regime change against the government. In August 1993 it imposed sanctions on Sudan for sponsoring terrorism. In February 1994 it failed to convince the Security Council to condemn Sudan for aerial bombings of the south. In 1996 it led the movement to put sanctions on Sudan for facilitating the Mubarak assassination plot (SCR 1054) and then failing to extradite suspects (SCR 1070). After the 1998 Al Qaeda bombings of American embassies in Kenya and Tanzania, it fired cruise missiles against a pharmaceutical plant in Khartoum, making dubious allegations that it was engaged in producing chemical weapons and was linked to bin Laden. And in 1999 the United States passed the Sudan Peace Act to provide assistance to Sudanese opposition forces.

The genocide in Sudan is distinct from the civil war. It began in 2003 in Darfur, a western region that has not been part of the civil war. Ethnicity rather than religion dominates the genocide: while all tribes in Darfur are Islamic, the salient group identities are those who are Arab and those who are "African." Sudan's regime has paid and armed Arab militias, who have destroyed about 90 percent of the black African villages in Darfur. Arab supporters of the government have targeted Africans to obtain their land. While the civil war and the genocide are distinct, both include groups with grievances against the government about the lack of political representation and fair distribution of resources.

Darfur is the largest region in Sudan, about the size of France, with an estimated population of 6 million people. Darfur was a sultanate that fell under British control in 1917 and was then incorporated into Sudan. Most of the inhabitants live in small villages, and most economic activity is based on subsistence farming and cattle herding. Disputes often arose when nomads came across the land of the sedentary farmers. In the 1980s drought and desertification in northern and central Darfur increased tensions over scarce resources. Previous agreements about the movement of cattle were not respected as cattle herders often invaded the fields of the farmers in search of pasture and water. Migration into the more fertile areas of Darfur increased, and clashes between the Arab newcomers and the African locals developed. Most of the conflicts ended peacefully, however, through the efforts of an ancient tribal mediation system.

However, the central government abolished this tribal system and appointed leaders loyal to the regime. When these new leaders consistently ruled in favor of the nomadic Arabs over the sedentary Africans, the latter developed militias to protect tribal interests. In late 2002 they began attacking police offices, and in April 2003 they began attacking military installations. The government could not initially respond because its military resources were in the south. Given a military threat from two rebel movements and the lack of military capabilities in Darfur, the government exploited the existing tensions and called upon local tribes to assist in fighting the rebels. Given the encroaching desertification, Arab nomadic tribes wishing to acquire land signed up to fight along with convicted felons and foreigners from Chad and Libya. These "recruits" became what the civilian population would refer to as the "janjaweed," a term denoting an armed bandit on a horse or camel. Over the next three years, these militias destroyed villages, targeted civilians, killed over 300,000 people, and displaced nearly 2 million people.

The government and the rebel groups in Darfur signed a ceasefire agreement on 8 April 2004 and agreed to the presence of African Union (AU) peacekeeping troops. Sudan, however, did nothing to stop the janjaweed militias. The AU troops, with their own peacekeeping rather than collective security mandate, had neither the authority nor the resources to stop the killings. When the AU requested assistance from the Security Council, the veto powers had to decide whether to embrace a collective security approach. The United States wanted to threaten Sudan with economic sanctions. However, Russia and China were opposed to even mentioning the possibility of sanctions. On 30 July the Council required Sudan to allow humanitarian aid, respect human rights, and disarm the janjaweed militias within one month or face "further actions" (SCR 1556). It charged the UN peacekeeping mission in the south (monitoring the implementation of the peace agreement between the government and the SPLM) to cooperate more closely with African Union troops in Darfur.

Sudan did not change its policies in the following month and reports of human rights violations increased. United States officials now openly characterized the events in Darfur as "genocide" and advocated a shift from peacekeeping to collective security. But the other veto powers were reluctant to take the promised "further actions." China had extensive oil interests in Sudan (the China National Petroleum Company owned 40 percent of the Sudanese state-owned oil production) and was adamantly opposed to sanctions. Russia argued that the war on terrorism was a higher priority and threatening Sudan would antagonize the Arab world. France advocated the African Union deal with the problem without outside involvement. Only the British suggested the possibility of sending troops. The Council agreed to threaten the use of sanctions if Sudan failed to curb the ethnic violence, authorize a Commission to investigate the situation in Darfur, increase the number of human rights monitors in Darfur, and increase cooperation with the AU mission (SCR 1564). China abstained.

The Darfur Commission submitted its report in January 2005, documenting instances of murder, torture, forced disappearances, destruction of villages, rape, pillaging and forced displacement (United Nations 2005). The vast majority of the victims were black Africans. The Commission established clear links between the State and the janjaweed militias, including spending around $1 million per day on salaries. It concluded that the government and the janjaweed were responsible for war crimes and crimes against humanity (but not genocide). It compiled a list of perpetrators – including Sudan government officials, members of militia forces, members of rebel groups, and military commanders – and recommended that the Security Council refer the situation to the International Criminal Court (ICC).

Also in January 2005 the Sudan government and the SPLM signed a comprehensive peace agreement. This put the Security Council in an untenable situation. While there was now a peace to keep in southern Sudan, Darfur urgently required collective security. How can the Security Council pursue both peacekeeping and collective security in Sudan simultaneously? How to be a neutral monitor and implementer of a peace agreement in the south while charging the government with crimes against humanity in Darfur? Why would the government of Sudan continue the peace process ending the civil war with the UN playing a neutral peacekeeping role if the UN is also taking sides in the Darfur conflict? Should the Council risk the civil war peace agreement to pursue collective security in Darfur? Or should it de-emphasize the atrocities in Darfur in order to end the civil war?

Ensuing Council resolutions exhibited these tensions. One resolution established a complex peace-building mission of 10,000 troops to support the implementation of the peace agreement ending the civil war, facilitate the return of refugees, provide humanitarian assistance, protect citizens from violence, and help develop post-conflict governance institutions (SCR 1590). A second resolution imposed smart sanctions (travel bans, frozen assets, restricted arms sales) on those perpetrating crimes in Darfur, prohibited offensive military flights into Darfur, and prohibited sending military equipment into the region without prior notification of the Council (SCR 1591). Russia and China abstained. A third resolution authorized the ICC to investigate those identified by the Darfur Commission and directed all parties to cooperate with the investigation (SCR 1593).

This third resolution was a significant development in post-cold war collective security. As Sudan was not a member of the ICC, only a Security Council resolution could authorize an ICC investigation of the genocide in Darfur. The United States argued against the referral, consistent with its hostile approach to the ICC (see Chapter 6). It instead proposed a new court at the existing UN tribunal for Rwanda in Arusha, Tanzania, but France and the United Kingdom strongly resisted. The United States did not want to legitimize the ICC, but it also did not want to veto a resolution to prosecute war criminals. So it again lobbied for provisions that would exempt Americans from the tribunal's jurisdiction (the Council had granted these exemptions in 2002 and 2003 but refused in 2004). In return for adding this provision, the United States abstained (as did China). For the first time the Council authorized the ICC to prosecute state decision-makers who pursued genocide.

Sudan continues to resist most Council actions regarding Darfur. It has not complied with resolutions requiring humanitarian aid into Darfur. It has not co-operated with the ICC investigation. It has not consented to a UN peacekeeping mission to replace the AU peacekeeping mission. American advocacy of stronger action in Sudan has weakened since an April 2005 CIA debriefing of the head of Sudan intelligence, himself wanted for war crimes in Darfur, to gain information regarding Osama bin Laden. And the Sudanese government has been diplomatically effective in garnering Arab League support and currying favor with France and China, given their oil interests. The Security Council cannot bring itself to stop the genocide in Darfur.

Conclusions

These cases show that when the Security Council was unwilling to impose hierarchy, it could not provide (human) security. The Council was hesitant to use force in Bosnia and deadlocked over using force in Kosovo. It was unwilling to stop genocide in Rwanda, and continues that unwillingness in Sudan. There are few examples of the Council enforcing human rights rules without the consent of the relevant state (Fenton 2004). Many states, including Russia and China, do not want emerging human rights rules to influence their own domestic systems. And enforcement requires states to elevate human rights over other security interests, which is less likely to occur during the current war on terrorism (Foot 2005).

This is why Kosovo was such an important case. NATO argued that fifteen liberal democracies could legitimately intervene to protect human rights even without Security Council approval. Was this a legitimate assertion of hierarchy or an illegitimate degradation of Yugoslav sovereignty and the Russian sphere of influence? While clearly outside the bounds of the UN Charter, Russia and China could not get much of the rest of the world to condemn this use of force. *This is the only example of hegemonic collective security in the post-cold war world not widely criticized in the global community.* It was mitigated by two factors: (1) the United States had multilateral cover because it was a NATO operation; and (2) the rationale was explicitly humanitarian rather than a claim to be enforcing a Security Council resolution.

The use of force in Kosovo, however, has not successfully established a norm of humanitarian intervention. Any future humanitarian intervention without Council approval is bound to be controversial. The same NATO countries that used force in Kosovo would likely deny that others could regularly declare a humanitarian disaster and militarily intervene without Council authorization. So Kosovo remains in this gray area of normative legitimacy. It suggests the outer limits of hierarchical policies that the international community would accept. And it suggests how difficult it is to resolve the security–hierarchy paradox and pursue policies that avoid both too little and too much hierarchy.

9   Terrorism

Like weapons proliferation and human rights, terrorism also illustrates the security–hierarchy paradox. A world with too little hierarchy will be unable to deal with terrorism. States that rely on their own military capability – such as Israel in Gaza and the West Bank, Russia in Chechnya, or the United States in Afghanistan – only exacerbate the conflict. Like weapons proliferation, dealing with terrorism requires a certain amount of hierarchy: rules prohibiting terrorist acts; rules obligating states to arrest terrorists, prevent safe havens, exchange intelligence, and extradite suspects; and enforcement mechanisms against both states and nonstate terrorist groups that fail to comply. And like human rights, dealing with terrorism requires agreement on the definition of the term and which rules violations threaten international security. Dealing with terrorism requires a social rather than a material solution, hinging on a global construction of normative prohibitions against terrorism analogous to norms against slavery or genocide.

This chapter analyzes Security Council efforts to coordinate global counter-terrorism policies. Most of its actions have recognized the security-interdependent nature of terrorism and increased the level of hierarchy in world politics. For example, the Council has authorized sanctions against Libya, Sudan, and Afghanistan for failing to extradite terrorist suspects. It has authorized sanctions against Al Qaeda and all individuals and entities supporting Al Qaeda. In an unprecedented move, it has directed states to ratify existing multilateral treaties and report progress of their implementation to a subsidiary organ of the Council. These actions have strengthened collective security rules against terrorism.

But the Security Council has also recognized self-defense against terrorism as a legitimate claim justifying the use of force. This assertion invokes war and rivalry rules rather than collective security rules. It does not recognize the security-interdependent nature of terrorism. It treats terrorism as acts of war that require a military response rather than a transnational criminal act that requires multilateral crime fighting. It equates terrorists with enemy soldiers rather than criminals. This principle could lead to either too little or too much hierarchy. Too little hierarchy could result if many states adopted it; anti-terrorism efforts would then be a hodgepodge of local rivalries and wars rather than a coherent global effort. Too much hierarchy would result if the United States claimed a flexible notion of self-defense against terrorism – as in the Bush Doctrine – and denied that anyone else could legitimately assert such a claim.

A world with too much hierarchy will also be unable to deal with global terrorism. States must interpret global rules against terrorism to be fair, effective and legitimate. For the United States to encourage the multilateral cooperation necessary to counter global terrorism, it must not assert too much hierarchy. But it has invoked hierarchical security arrangements in four ways: (1) by protecting Israel from collective enforcement measures, implying that global security rules do not apply to Israel; (2) by treating the fight against terrorism as a war rather than crime; (3) by asserting that the traditional notion of self-defense does not apply to its own policies; and (4) by using force without Security Council authorization in Sudan, Afghanistan, and Iraq. United States policies have convinced many in the Middle East that it is pursuing an illegitimate empire. The security–hierarchy paradox again applies: the United States can only deal with the terrorist threat emanating from the Middle East by asserting less hierarchy in the region.

Global rules against terrorism

The Security Council rarely dealt with terrorism during the cold war (Boulden and Weiss 2004). Terrorism was not considered a strategic threat to the major powers. The vast majority of terrorist groups were associated with separatist movements, and most states considered the issue a domestic matter. Many developing countries considered terrorism an unfortunate but necessary tactic in struggles for national liberation. When the General Assembly addressed terrorism, it generally criticized the "state terrorism" of Israel and South Africa. The Council first used the term "terrorism" in 1985, condemning "all acts of hostage-taking and abduction" as "manifestations of international terrorism" (SCR 579). The Council next used the term twice in 1989 when it condemned "terrorist attacks against civil aviation" (SCR 635) and again condemned hostage-taking as terrorism (SCR 638). None of these resolutions invoked Chapter VII powers.

Most global rules against terrorism thus stem from twelve treaties and protocols rather than Security Council resolutions. Some of the agreements deal with particular aspects of terrorism: aviation safety, the protection of nuclear materials, the marking of plastic explosives, and suppressing the financing of terrorism. Others prohibit particular acts: aircraft hijackings and bombings; attacks on government officials and diplomats; hostage-taking; terrorist acts in airports, on ships, or on offshore oil platforms; and terrorist bombings. (A thirteenth treaty on nuclear terrorism is open for signature and ratification but not yet in force.) With the exception of China and the treaty on marking plastic explosives, the veto powers have ratified every agreement. These treaties establish state jurisdiction over terrorist acts regardless of the territory in which they are committed. They attempt to establish the principle that there should be no safe haven for terrorists. But they are relatively weak because they include no monitoring system or enforcement mechanism. The Security Council remains the only enforcement mechanism regarding terrorism.

The main obstacle to constructing rules against terrorism is the contested nature of the term (Saul 2005). There is no globally accepted definition of terrorism. No global terrorism treaty includes a definition. The dispute is over how to distinguish legitimate and illegitimate acts of violence. States legitimately use violence in many situations to maintain national security and/or domestic order. States also cross the line by violating international humanitarian law. But where is that line? And which acts across that line constitute state terrorism? In the same way, nonstate groups legitimately use violence in the context of overwhelming state oppression. Nonstate groups also cross the line and commit terrorist acts. But where is that line? What distinguishes legitimate struggle against oppression from illegitimate terrorist acts?

Most definitions say that terrorism is an intentional act of violence against persons and/or property, and it is intended to intimidate a population or influence government policy. Disputes include whether the definition should distinguish "innocent civilians" from military or police forces. Are attacks against state forces, or assassinations of state leaders, sometimes legitimate acts of violence? Can we coherently distinguish combatants and noncombatants in a variety of contexts? Another dispute is whether the definition should include state actions. Can governments commit terrorist acts? States use force illegitimately when they commit genocide, crimes against humanity, and war crimes. Is state terrorism a fourth category? And how do we distinguish state terrorism from war crimes? These questions continue to bedevil ongoing negotiations for a comprehensive convention on terrorism.

The Israeli–Palestinian conflict has greatly complicated this dispute. While those on one side interpret Palestinian acts of violence (particularly suicide bombers that kill Israeli civilians) as clear acts of terrorism, those on the other side interpret Palestinian resistance to Israeli occupation as a legitimate act of national struggle. Conversely, while one side interprets Israeli policies in the occupied territories as state terrorism, the other side considers Israel to be acting in self-defense. Each side wants a definition of terrorism that implicates only the other side. Given these difficulties there is no consensus within the international community about the meaning and scope of terrorism (Joyner 2004).

The United States has played a tremendous role in this debate, going to great lengths to shield Israel from Security Council action. It has cast the lone veto on a staggering forty Council resolutions targeting Israel on a wide variety of policies, including its settlements in the West Bank, military incursions into Gaza and Lebanon, assassination of Palestinian leaders, destruction of houses and infrastructure, killing Palestinian refugees, and building the infamous "security wall." The United States has not always protected Israel in the Security Council. Indeed, Israel has violated thirty-two Council resolutions since 1968, more than any other country (Ayoob 2004). (Turkey, with twenty-four violations, is second, Morocco (seventeen) is third, and Iraq (sixteen) is fourth.)

Many interpret this United States record in the Security Council to unfairly exempt Israel from collective enforcement. Israel regularly invades its neighbors. It does not follow Geneva Convention protections for persons in occupied territories. It does not accept the principle in international law that refugees have the right to return to their homeland. It has illegally seized territory through force, including Jerusalem. But everyone understands that the United States would veto any Chapter VII enforcement measure against Israel. American extension of its hierarchical privileges to Israel is an important part of the underlying context for terrorist attacks against the United States.

Israel, of course, argues that it is acting in self-defense. It argues in effect that the "normal" rules of global security do not apply because it is not in a "normal" situation – most of its neighbors have not recognized its right to exist throughout its history; its enemies are willing to disrupt Israeli life with suicide bombings, etc. It argues that the most brutal of war rules rather than collective security rules govern its security relationships. Its own survival trumps rules about self-defense, human rights, and refugees' right of return.

The United States, while not supporting all Israeli policies, tends to share the Israeli understanding that fighting against terrorism invokes rules of war rather than collective security rules. Rhetoric about a "war on terrorism" predates the current Bush administration. President Reagan's Secretary of State George Shultz declared a "war on terrorism" in the 1980s and cited preemption and the unfettered use of military power as necessary tools. On 21 August 1998 Secretary of State Madeleine Albright said that terrorists "have basically declared war on all Americans." Two days later President Clinton said: "this will be a long, ongoing struggle between freedom and fanaticism, between the rule of law and terrorism." The terrorist events of 9/11 merely reinforced this understanding for many Americans.

Around the world, however, terrorism is mostly understood as crime rather than war (Frederking *et al.* 2005). This dispute has tremendous theoretical and practical implications about global security rules and how to fight terrorism (Feldman 2002; Howard 2002). War requires the use of military force; crime requires multilateral cooperation regarding intelligence, extradition, etc. The problem with the war interpretation, of course, is that the "war on terrorism" is not really a war (Jervis 2005, Crawford 2003). Terrorism is a tactic not an enemy. Interpreting terrorism as war overestimates the importance of American military dominance and underestimates the importance of security interdependence. It denies the possibility that terrorists have legitimate grievances. Fighting terrorism requires a political rather than a military understanding of security, encouraging diplomacy, international criminal justice, intelligence sharing, and many other forms of cooperation. Interpreting terrorism as crime also emphasizes root causes: better relations with the Islamic world, reducing global poverty, and resolving the Palestinian issue. In summary, global rules against terrorism are relatively weak because there is little agreement on either the definition of the term or how to appropriately deal with the issue.

The United States, the Security Council, and Terrorism

United States policies have vacillated between the war and crime approach to terrorism, between invoking war/rivalry or collective security rules to achieve security against terrorism. On the one hand, the United States has been the driving force putting terrorism on the Security Council agenda (de Jonge Oudraat 2004). It has championed Council efforts to coordinate state policies, particularly resolutions invoking Chapter VII powers to deal with terrorist threats:

- *Iraq (1991)*. The Council included the renunciation of terrorism as a ceasefire condition on Iraq after the Gulf War (SCR 687).
- *Libya (1992)*. The Council directed Libya to surrender two nationals for trial in the Lockerbie case, later authorizing sanctions for noncompliance (SCR 731, 748, 883).
- *Sudan (1995)*. The Council directed Sudan to extradite three suspects to Ethiopia for the attempted assassination of Egyptian President Mubarak and to stop providing sanctuaries to terrorist groups, later authorizing sanctions for noncompliance (SCR 1044, 1070).
- *Al Qaeda (1998)*. The Council directed all states to punish the perpetrators of the bombings of United States embassies in Kenya and Tanzania (SCR 1189).
- *Afghanistan (1999)*. The Council directed Afghanistan to refrain from harboring terrorists and to surrender Osama bin Laden (SCR 1214, 1267), later authorizing sanctions for noncompliance (SCR 1333, 1390).
- *Al Qaeda (2001)*. The Council directed all states to punish the perpetrators of the 9/11 terrorist attacks (SCR 1368). It required all states to collaborate in a variety of ways to prevent global terrorism, establishing a Counter-Terrorism Committee to monitor implementation (SCR 1373).
- *Iraq (2005)*. The Council authorized multinational forces in Iraq to use force to prevent and deter terrorism, the first resolution explicitly giving states authority to use force against "terrorism" (SCR 1546).

On the other hand, the United States has used force four times in response to terrorism, and each time it claimed self-defense rather than seek Council authorization. The United States used force against Libya in 1986 for the bombing of a Berlin disco, against Iraq in 1993 for the attempted assassination of former President Bush, in 1998 against Sudan and Afghanistan for the bombing of American embassies in Kenya and Tanzania, and in 2001 against Afghanistan for the 9/11 attacks. The United States has pursued both war and crime approaches to terrorism.

The Security Council has authorized sanctions regarding terrorism four times with varying levels of support and success. The sanctions against Afghanistan and Al Qaeda, both passed unanimously, are discussed below. The first case of sanctions regarding violations of terrorism rules was against Libya, and the resolution included five abstentions, including China. Although the United States and the

United Kingdom did not act in good faith regarding these sanctions during much of the 1990s (see Chapter 4), they did play a role in ending Libya's support for terrorist groups. When the United States and the United Kingdom began direct negotiations with Libya in the late 1990s, it agreed to expel the Abu Nidal organization, break ties with radical Palestinian groups, close down training camps, and extradite suspected terrorists to Egypt, Jordan, and Yemen. (Libya also began to comply with global WMD rules in December 2003 in return for normalized relations with the United States and the United Kingdom, suggesting the wisdom of direct talks with "rogue states" such as Iran and North Korea.)

The second instance was travel sanctions against Sudanese leaders for failing to extradite suspects in an attempted assassination of Egyptian President Mubarak and for providing a safe haven to terrorists, including Osama bin Laden. Both China and Russia abstained. The sanctions were relatively weak; the Council did not even form a sanctions committee to monitor implementation. After Al Qaeda bombed American embassies in 1998, the United States retaliated with air strikes on a pharmaceutical plant in Khartoum it (wrongly) believed was producing chemical weapons for terrorist use. The United States did not seek Security Council authorization; indeed, when Clinton addressed the General Assembly regarding terrorism the following month, he did not even mention the Security Council. International response to this American use of force criticized the inappropriate target; few outside the Muslim world criticized the United States claim that self-defense justified the attack. Sudan eventually expelled bin Laden, who went to Afghanistan. The sanctions remained in effect until 2001 when Sudan agreed to cooperate in the war on terrorism.

The Security Council has passed a series of resolutions using the crime metaphor for terrorism, urging states to prevent the financing of terrorism; to bring perpetrators to justice; to deny safe haven by apprehending, prosecuting or extraditing terrorists, and to exchange information (SCR 1269, 1377, 1456). Other resolutions condemned particular terrorist attacks in Bali (SCR 1438), Moscow (SCR 1440), Kenya (SCR 1450), Bogota (SCR 1465), Istanbul (SCR 1516), and Madrid (SCR 1530). The most significant resolutions (discussed in the next section) bound states to implement existing treaty obligations and report the extent of their implementation to a subsidiary body of the Council (Schrijver 2004). Particularly since 9/11, Council efforts to strengthen collective security rules against terrorism have treated it as a global criminal justice operation.

But the Council has also indirectly legitimated the United States "war" on terrorism. On 12 September 2001 – the day after the attacks – the Council recognized the inherent right of self-defense as a legitimate response to terrorism (SCR 1368). It was the first time the Council formally recognized this claim. During the cold war, for example, actions like Israeli incursions into Lebanon or the United States bombing of Libya were considered illegal and widely condemned. By recognizing the right to self-defense against terrorist attacks, the Council was invoking war/rivalry rules rather than collective security rules. It could not criticize any future American use of force in Afghanistan for violating collective security rules. As the next two sections show, the world generally accepted American claims of self-defense in Afghanistan but not in Iraq. The United States "war" on terrorism, initially accepted by the international community, eventually undermined global collective security.

Enforcing rules against terrorism: Afghanistan

The veto power disputes regarding weapons proliferation and human rights primarily focused on how to implement collective security rules. Disputes arose when Russia, China, and France insisted on Security Council authorization of all enforcement measures, and the United States prioritized its unique role in maintaining international security. United States claims of self-defense, while present, were secondary. The veto power disputes over terrorism have been different because United States claims to self-defense were primary and assertions of enforcing international law or Security Council resolutions were secondary. So the veto power disputes over terrorism were primarily about whether war/rivalry rules or collective security rules were more appropriate to fight terrorism. But the implications for hierarchy were similar because the United States asserted a privileged notion of self-defense that no one else could claim. And thus the hierarchy–security paradox still applies. United States policies have both weakened its ability to generate the political collaboration necessary to fight a transnational security threat and undermined the rule of law by encouraging other states to act in similar ways.

The Security Council debates over terrorism began with Afghan support for Al Qaeda, a radical Islamic terrorist organization led by Osama bin Laden. Al Qaeda has a coherent ideological agenda: end the United States presence in the Middle East, end United States support for Israel, topple secular Arab and Muslim governments, and establish a pan-Islamic caliphate throughout the Muslim world. As a transnational organization it is not dependent on any one state for its resources or survival. Its activists are drawn from all over the world, including from the Muslim populations in Western countries, and it has links with two dozen Islamist terrorist groups. Its leader Osama bin Laden sought refuge in Afghanistan after Sudan expelled him under pressure from the United States.

Afghanistan has suffered nearly constant warfare since the 1979 Soviet invasion (Rashid 2001; Fawn 2003). A coalition of northern warlords and fundamentalist Islamic groups called the Mujahadeen, bolstered by $7 billion in US aid, resisted that invasion until the Soviets withdrew in 1989. The Mujahadeen were largely Pashtun, the dominant ethnic group that has ruled Afghanistan since the eighteenth century. The northern warlords were not Pashtun but mostly Uzbek, Tajik, Turkmen, Baluch, and Hazara. The northern warlords overthrew the pro-communist Najibullah government in 1992. In 1994 the Islamic fundamentalist Taliban began a campaign to rid the country of the warlords, establish law and order through Islamic law, and restore power to "good Muslims." About two-thirds of the Taliban were Pashtun, and they had attended Islamic schools in Pakistan that taught a sectarian version of Islam that considered other versions, particularly those practiced by the northern ethnic groups, to be heretical.

During the civil war with the northern warlords, the Taliban provided sanctuary for fundamentalist Islamic groups, including Osama bin Laden after he was expelled from Sudan. In return, these foreign militants fought with the Taliban periodically against the northern warlords. Russia, Iran, India, and central Asian republics, all threatened by these Islamic groups, supported the northern warlords. Despite this support, the Taliban captured Kabul in 1996 and slowly continued northward. By 2000 they controlled 90 percent of the country, all but two northeastern provinces. The Taliban had little international support; only Saudi Arabia, Pakistan, and the United Arab Emirates extended diplomatic relations. The Taliban never occupied Afghanistan's seat in the United Nations. The Taliban's human rights abuses, treatment of women, earnings from the opium trade, and protection of bin Laden earned them "rogue" status.

There was little Security Council response to the 1996 Taliban takeover of Kabul. China again opposed what it considered Council interference in domestic politics. A nonbinding resolution stated concern about the continuing civil war, human rights abuses, discrimination against women, and the plight of refugees (SCR 1076). But there were no resolutions during the next 18 months. In August 1998 Al Qaeda bombed United States embassies in Kenya and Tanzania. International condemnation was universal and swift, from Boris Yeltsin to Kofi Annan to Yassir Arafat. The Security Council also condemned the bombings but did not invoke Chapter VII powers (SCR 1189). The United States did not ask the Council to pursue enforcement measures against the Taliban for harboring Al Qaeda in Afghanistan.

Instead the Clinton administration, without seeking Council authorization, fired eighty cruise missiles into bin Laden's training camps on 20 August 1998. It notified only Britain and Pakistan prior to the attack. Clinton called the use of force both self-defense against imminent terrorist plots and retribution for the bombings of American embassies. Clinton called bin Laden an "imminent threat" who was seeking to acquire WMD. He also authorized attempting to kill bin Laden with the cruise missile attacks (Johnston and Purdam 2004). Both international and United States law authorized the targeting of enemy leaders, but only during wartime. In a statement announcing the attacks, Clinton said:

> America has battled terrorism for many years. Where possible, we've used law enforcement and diplomatic tools to wage the fight . . . We have quietly disrupted terrorist groups and foiled their plots. We have isolated countries that practice terrorism. We've worked to build an international coalition against terror. But there have been and will be times when law enforcement and diplomatic tools are simply not enough. When our very national security is challenged, we must take extraordinary steps to protect the safety of our citizens.
>
> (Clinton 1998)

Russian President Yeltsin denounced the bombings. The Duma called the strikes an act of aggression contrary to international law. The Chinese Foreign

Ministry also criticized the bombings, saying: "We insist that the international community make joint efforts to fight against terrorist activities in accordance with the principles of the UN Charter and international rules, on the basis of respect of a country's sovereignty and territorial integrity" (China Daily 1998). The dispute over this use of force was not about how to appropriately implement collective security. It was about whether war/rivalry rules or collective security rules were more appropriate. It was about whether terrorism was war or crime.

Despite this dispute the Security Council passed two resolutions (1193 and 1214) later that year condemning the Taliban for a litany of rule violations, including support for Islamic terrorist groups throughout the region, the assassination of Iranian diplomatic personnel, the murder of UN officials, and refusing to allow humanitarian organizations into Afghanistan. But the Taliban pressed on, recognizing the Chechen Republic in January 1999 in support of their attempt to break away from Russia. They also began broadcasts into Central Asian republics, encouraging Islamic revolution. Hostility toward the Taliban made unlikely allies of India, Iran, Russia, the United States, and Central Asian governments.

The veto powers slowly increased pressure on the Taliban. The Security Council unanimously imposed financial and travel sanctions in October 1999 for not handing over bin Laden (SCR 1267). The Council called for increased sharing of information, preventing terrorist groups from raising money, and denying such groups safe haven. In April 2000 Russia, China, and three Central Asian republics established an anti-terrorism center in Kyrgyzstan. Chinese President Jiang Zemin criticized the Taliban for using opium revenues to fund the separatist Uighur movement. Russia even threatened to use force against Chechen terrorist camps in northern Afghanistan. The United States, however, urged Russia not to bomb Afghanistan because it would risk broadening the Chechen conflict. The United States was again asserting a hierarchical security arrangement: while it could use force in self-defense against terrorist camps in Afghanistan, Russia could not do so.

Then Al Qaeda struck again, bombing the USS Cole outside Yemen on 12 October 2000. Again there was overwhelming condemnation of the terrorist act, and the Council gave the Taliban thirty days to shut down all training camps and extradite bin Laden (SCR 1333). It also strengthened the travel and financial sanctions against both the Taliban and bin Laden. These sanctions did not extend to Afghan territory controlled by the northern alliance (Russia, India, and Iran continued to arm the northern warlords). China again abstained. The United States delegate said: "The Taliban cannot continue to flout the will of the international community and support and shelter terrorists without repercussions. As long as the Taliban continues to harbor terrorists, in particular Osama bin Laden, and to promote terrorism, it remains a threat to international peace and security" (Crossette 2000).

Thirty days passed, and the Taliban did not hand over bin Laden. The United States and the Security Council failed to follow through on their warnings to Afghanistan. The outgoing Clinton administration focused its foreign policy efforts on the Middle East peace process, and the incoming Bush administration did not prioritize terrorism as a primary security threat. Beyond providing safe haven for Al Qaeda, the Taliban defied the international community throughout 2001 in many ways, including blowing up giant Buddha statues in March despite global efforts to save them. In May the Taliban ordered religious minorities to wear tags identifying them as non-Muslims and also ordered Hindu women to veil themselves. Yet the only Council resolution regarding Afghanistan during this time established a panel to monitor violations of the existing sanctions against the Taliban. Neither Al Qaeda nor the Taliban were in the headlines prior to the terrorist attacks on 11 September 2001.

The destruction of the World Trade Center in New York and the attack on the Pentagon in Washington DC presented another pivotal moment in the history of post-cold war collective security. Would this horrendous act of terrorism instill unity among the veto powers and reinvigorate collective security? Or would it reignite already existing disputes about whether and how to implement collective security? The veto powers would again have to decide whether terrorism was war or crime. Initial American statements exhibited these tensions. On 11 September Bush used the crime metaphor:

> The search is under way for those who are behind these evil acts. I've directed the full resources of our intelligence and law enforcement communities to find those responsible and to bring them to justice. We will make no distinction between the terrorists who committed these acts and those who harbor them.
>
> (Bush 2001a)

The following day he used the war metaphor, calling the attacks "acts of war" and the perpetrators "enemies" rather than "criminals."

> The deliberate and deadly attacks which were carried out yesterday against our country were more than acts of terror. They were acts of war. This will require our country to unite in steadfast determination and resolve. Freedom and democracy are under attack. The American people need to know that we're facing a different enemy than we have ever faced. This enemy hides in shadows, and has no regard for human life.
>
> (Bush 2001b)

In a 20 September address to a joint session of Congress, the war metaphor seemed to triumph. Without mentioning the United Nations, the Security Council, or international law, Bush demanded that the Taliban surrender Al Qaeda leaders and permanently close their bases. He also defined a "war on terrorism" in broad terms: "Our war on terror begins with Al Qaeda, but it does not end there. It will not end until every terrorist group of global reach has been found, stopped and defeated" (Bush 2001c).

Yet the Bush administration also realized that multilateral cooperation through the UN was necessary to sustain a global anti-terrorist coalition. The UN could help establish that terrorist acts were morally unacceptable. It could also help deny funds, materials, space, and shelter to terrorists. In the months after 9/11 the United States was multilateral in a number of ways. It aggressively worked for anti-terrorist resolutions in the Security Council. It paid back $582 million in back dues owed to the UN. It ratified two terrorist treaties (on terrorist bombings and financing terrorism). It worked with other wealthy countries to monitor the financial transactions of terrorist groups. In addition to the "war" rhetoric, there was some recognition that a collective security approach would be necessary to deal with global terrorism.

The Security Council itself also showed these tensions. Its initial resolution passed on 12 September only weakly invoked collective security rules (SCR 1368). Although it directed all states to bring the perpetrators to justice, it said that it was up to member states, not the Council, to respond to individual acts of terrorism. Most importantly, it recognized for the first time an inherent right of self-defense as a legitimate response to terrorism (SCR 1368). The international community had always rejected this claim in the past when it led to actions that violated the territorial integrity of other states (United States bombing of Libya, Israeli incursions into Lebanon, etc.) With this resolution the Council seemed to endorse a future United States war on terrorism. The Council members unanimously passed the resolution and accentuated its unity by standing rather than using the traditional showing of hands.

The Council's next resolution reverted to a collective security approach. On 28 September it directed states to implement the obligations in existing terrorism treaties (SCR 1373). Even nonsignatories must now prevent terrorist acts, deny safe haven to terrorist groups, suppress terrorist financing, prosecute terrorists, assist other states in their criminal investigations, and prevent the movement of terrorists across national borders. In another post-cold war innovation, it required states to report progress toward implementation of these policies to the Counter-Terrorism Committee (CTC), a newly created subsidiary organ of the Council. The CTC, however, has only partially strengthened rules against terrorism. While it has encouraged many states to ratify existing terrorism treaties, their implementation (intelligence gathering, freezing economic assets, etc.) is beyond the administrative capacity of many states. The CTC has no enforcement capability. It also has not tried to define terrorism, allowing states to define those acts inside their borders in widely divergent ways.

The Council also debated whether its approval was needed for any United States military intervention in Afghanistan. The other four veto powers all advocated a collective security approach, saying that the United States should request Security Council approval and eventually put bin Laden on trial. China, wary that the United States would use terrorism as a pretext to expand its military presence in key regions of the world, was unusually adamant, stating several conditions for any American military mission: it should be (1) based on "concrete evidence"; (2) military proportionate; and (3) authorized by the Security Council. The United

States met the first condition by presenting its evidence of Taliban culpability to its NATO allies and the Security Council. It tried to meet the second condition by explaining to Council members how its military plans were consistent with humanitarian concerns.

But the United States did not meet the third condition; it did not seek further Council approval for a military response. Invoking war rather than collective security rules, it argued that its response would be in self-defense. European countries supported this claim. NATO for the first time in its history invoked its collective defense clause, treating 9/11 as an act of war that justified an allied military response. (The United States also refused to accept NATO's offer of collective self-defense.) The European Union also voted that SCR 1368 recognizing an inherent right of self-defense against terrorism gave the United States a legal basis for military intervention. On 2 October British Prime Minister Tony Blair (2001a) advocated the use of force, even without Council authorization: "Our immediate objectives are clear. We must bring bin Laden and other Al Qaeda leaders to justice and eliminate the terrorist threat they pose. We must ensure that Afghanistan ceases to harbor and sustain international terrorism."

The United States began its military operation with missile strikes on 7 October. On that day the United States sent a letter to the Security Council justifying the use of force by citing the self-defense clause in Article 51 of the UN Charter. The letter did not cite any Security Council resolution authorizing the attack, and it stated that the United States "may find that our self-defense requires further actions with respect to other organizations and other states." As with the later use of force in Iraq, the use of force in Afghanistan was really a preventive war. There was no imminent threat of another attack. As Tony Blair (2001b) said on 19 October: "We took this action with great reluctance. We took this because we had no option but to make sure those that perpetrated the terrible atrocity of 9/11 are stopped from doing this again."

The United States met with the Council on 9 October to persuade members that its response was legitimate and proportionate. While the Council passed no resolution, every member at least rhetorically supported the use of force after this meeting. China thanked the United States for presenting evidence of Al Qaeda guilt and for promising that any strikes would avoid civilian targets (Narayan 2001). French President Jacques Chirac (2001) said: "France has stood shoulder to shoulder with the American people out of friendship, out of solidarity, but also because we knew that all democracies are in danger when one of them receives such a blow to the heart." Russia even provided logistical support, providing intelligence, aiding the northern alliance, allowing the use of its territory to transport supplies, and accepting American military bases in former Soviet republics Kyrgyzstan and Tajikistan to conduct the war.

Most international support, however, was limited and tentative. The European Union passed a resolution stating that eliminating the Al Qaeda network was a proportionate response, but not overthrowing the Taliban. China offered no military and little logistical support. Many others restricted their support to humanitarian efforts. Uzbekistan, Iran and Saudi Arabia refused access to their bases or air space in the invasion. Many others, including India, Egypt and Pakistan, made their logistical support conditional on further UN authorization. Foreshadowing the later Iraq episode, the international community would not support American uses of force that clearly went beyond the parameters of the UN Charter and procedural collective security.

What helped ease these tensions was agreement that the UN should play an important role in Afghanistan after the war. The United States asked the UN to help establish a broad-based government to replace the Taliban. Kofi Annan appointed Lakhdar Brahimi (author of the Brahimi Report) as his special envoy to begin internal Afghan coalition building. Over forty countries requested to speak to the Security Council on 13 November to advocate an active UN role in post-war political mediation and humanitarian relief. The Council urged Afghan factions to participate in UN-sponsored negotiations (SCR 1378). It gave Brahimi authority over the humanitarian, human rights, and political actions of the UN in Afghanistan. An enthusiastic Tony Blair said:

> The way that the world embraces and supports the new Afghanistan will be the clearest possible indication that the dreadful events of 9/11 have resulted in a triumph for the international community acting together as a force for good, and in the defeat of the evil that is international terrorism . . . Step by step, there must be the new world order that emerges from the worst terrorist outrage in our history.
>
> (Blair 2001c)

The military operation succeeded more quickly than expected, and this accelerated UN political efforts. The United States bombing campaign enabled northern alliance forces to capture half of the country and enter Kabul by 13 November. On 25 November the first American troops were on the ground, and Taliban rule ended by the first week of December with the fall of Kandahar. The negotiating Afghan factions named Hamid Karzai interim president of the provisional government. The Security Council on 20 December authorized an International Security Assistance Force (ISAF) to maintain security in Kabul and the surrounding areas (SCR 1386). It then extended the sanctions against Al Qaeda beyond Afghan territory (SCR 1390). UN peacekeepers were on the ground in January 2002. The invasion of Afghanistan was no longer a unilateral American act.

A detailed discussion of the post-conflict nation-building efforts in Afghanistan goes beyond the scope of this book. But their difficulties also illustrate the declining utility of United States military dominance. American forces could not penetrate south-east Afghanistan along the Pakistani border to capture bin Laden. Security around Kabul remained tenuous as Taliban forces resisted the new government. Karzai's vice president was assassinated in July 2002, and Karzai narrowly escaped multiple assassination attempts. To increase security around Kabul, NATO forces took control of ISAF in August 2003, its first mission outside

Europe. But Taliban resistance grew stronger as time went on. Taking cues from the Iraqi insurgency, Afghan militants began suicide attacks in late 2005. NATO forces took over all military operations in the summer of 2006 in an attempt to defeat the Taliban insurgency, leading to the fiercest fighting in the entire conflict. Despite some historic events – the adoption of a new constitution in January 2004, presidential elections in October/November 2004, and parliamentary elections in September 2005 – post-conflict nation building in Afghanistan is very much a work in progress.

There are three reasons why the United States use of force in Afghanistan was less criticized than other American uses of force not authorized by the Security Council. First, there was widespread agreement among the veto powers that the Taliban and Al Qaeda represented a threat to international security. In addition to 9/11, the Taliban supported secessionist movements in Russia and China. Second, the United States engaged in good faith consultation with the Council, particularly by providing evidence of Al Qaeda's guilt and incorporating other's insistence about proportionality into its battle plans. Third, the United States agreed that the UN should play a central role in post-war reconstruction. These factors mitigated the usual post-cold war tensions between the veto powers. Despite the primary American rationale of self-defense and its refusal to seek explicit Council authorization, the veto powers interpreted the American invasion of Afghanistan to loosely fit within a procedural collective security framework. While wary of possible long-term implications, they did not interpret this use of force to illegitimately assert American hierarchy.

The Afghanistan case suggests the tantalizing question of whether the 9/11 terrorist attacks could have helped resolve post-cold war Security Council tensions and facilitate the transition of global security rules from cold war rivalry to post-cold war collective security. The immediate influence of these attacks was to elevate common interests and reduce tensions between the veto powers (Gladkyy 2003). The United States helped create a joint NATO–Russia Council in December 2001, giving Russia a voice but not a vote within NATO. Russia stopped complaining about NATO expansion and the Anti Ballistic Missile Treaty. And in May 2002 the two agreed to reduce nuclear warheads. China supported a global coalition against terrorism, which would enable them to go after opposition groups, including the Uighur insurgents in Xinjiang. The United States agreed to recognize the separatists as a terrorist group. China also agreed to cooperate with Council initiatives on intelligence sharing, financial transactions, and law enforcement (Malik 2002).

But the veto powers missed an historic opportunity to strengthen the cooperation forged in the immediate post-9/11 environment. When the United States extended its war on terrorism to Iraq, relying on a particular notion of self-defense reserved for itself, the world again rejected the hierarchical implications of American policy. None of the three factors mentioned above – consensus on the nature of the threat, American willingness to accommodate the demands of the other veto powers, and agreement on an extensive UN post-conflict role – was present during the Council deliberations regarding Iraq.

Extending the war on terrorism to Iraq

The terrorist attacks of 9/11 increasingly led the United States to invoke war and rivalry rules rather than collective security rules. The Bush administration argued that traditional notions of deterrence (itself a rivalry policy) were not sufficient against terrorists and rogue states (White House 2002a). While (rational) states can be deterred by a retaliatory military capability, (irrational) terrorists and rogue states cannot. They strike without warning and without regard for the ensuing consequences. Thus the only effective response is to get them first. The best defense is a good offense. The 2002 National Security Strategy of the United States put it this way:

> The gravest danger to our nation lies at the crossroads of radicalism and technology. Our enemies have openly declared that they are seeking weapons of mass destruction, and evidence indicates that they are doing so with determination. The United States will not allow these efforts to succeed. We will build defenses against ballistic missiles and other means of delivery. We will cooperate with other nations to deny, contain, and curtail our enemies' efforts to acquire dangerous technologies. And as a matter of common sense and self-defense, America will act against such emerging threats before they are fully formed.
>
> (White House 2002b)

United States officials constantly stated that 9/11 changed everything. President Bush (2003) said: "My vision shifted dramatically after 9/11, because I now realize the stakes, I realize the world has changed." Secretary of State Colin Powell (2002) said: "It's a different world . . . it's a new kind of threat." National Security Adviser Condoleeza Rice (2002) said: "And after 9/11, there is no longer any doubt that today America faces an existential threat to our security – a threat as any we faced during the Civil War, the so-called 'Good War,' or the Cold War." And President Bush (2002a) again: "Containment is not possible when unbalanced dictators with weapons of mass destruction can deliver those weapons on missiles or secretly provide them to terrorist allies." The United States believed that radical Islamic terrorism, WMD, rogue states, and a relatively open international system combined to create a fundamentally new world with fundamentally different security challenges. Existing global security rules – whether formal alliances, collective security, or customary law on self-defense – had been superseded. This new world required new rules.

One new rule was a preventive notion of self-defense. A second was regime change for "axis of evil" countries with both WMD aspirations and connections to terrorist groups. And a third was the detention and torture of "enemy combatants" (see Chapter 8). Consider the characteristics of these rules. All violated international law and prior to 9/11 would have been considered aggressive, inappropriate acts that harmed global security. All are explicitly hierarchical; only the United States could follow these rules. All imply that global security would best be achieved by rules that recognize very few restrictions on American action around the world to fight terrorism. The United States expected the international community to recognize the reality of this new world and accept the necessity of these new rules. But this did not happen. The terrorist attacks of 9/11 did not fundamentally change world politics. The dispute over Iraq turned into the same argument: how to implement collective security and how much hierarchy should exist in world politics.

This dispute began when the Bush administration turned its attention away from Afghanistan (and bin Laden) and toward Iraq (and Saddam Hussein). President Bush famously included Iraq in the "axis of evil" along with North Korea and Iran in the January 2002 State of the Union address.

> North Korea is a regime arming with missiles and weapons of mass destruction, while starving its citizens. Iran aggressively pursues these weapons and exports terror, while an unelected few repress the Iranian people's hope for freedom. Iraq continues to flaunt its hostility toward America and to support terror. The Iraqi regime has plotted to develop anthrax, and nerve gas, and nuclear weapons for over a decade. This is a regime that has already used poison gas to murder thousands of its own citizens – leaving the bodies of mothers huddled over their dead children. This is a regime that agreed to international inspections – then kicked out the inspectors. This is a regime that has something to hide from the civilized world. States like these, and their terrorist allies, constitute an axis of evil, arming to threaten the peace of the world. By seeking weapons of mass destruction, these regimes pose a grave and growing danger. They could provide these arms to terrorists, giving them the means to match their hatred . . . America will do what is necessary to ensure our nation's security.
>
> (Bush 2002b)

Iran, Iraq, and North Korea, of course, were not an axis at all. Iran and Iraq were bitter enemies who fought a war over whether secular Arab nationalism or fundamentalist Islam would be the dominant social force in the Middle East. North Korea was not closely linked to either Iran or Iraq. It is not clear why these three regimes warranted emphasis. None had direct ties to Al Qaeda or were implicated in the events of 9/11. Syria was just as active as Iran in supporting Middle East terrorism, and Iran had just supported the Afghan northern alliance in its war against the Taliban. Pakistan was a more flagrant violator of WMD proliferation rules than North Korea and was a supporter of the Taliban prior to its 9/11 about-face. What these three countries had in common were suspected WMD programs and ties to terrorists.

The Bush administration increased warnings throughout 2002 that Iraq was next on its agenda in the war on terrorism (Gershkoff and Kussner 2005). Officials constantly hinted at connections to Al Qaeda and a clandestine nuclear weapons program. For example, in August Vice President Cheney stated that Iraq would "fairly soon" have nuclear weapons, and a nuclear-armed Iraq would "seek domination of the entire Middle East, take control of a great portion of the world's energy supplies, directly threaten America's friends throughout the region, and the subject the United States or any other nation to nuclear blackmail . . . The risks of inaction are far greater than the risk of action" (Burmiller 2002). Yet the United States went to the UN to build some legitimacy around this policy. President Bush challenged the UN on 12 September to take action against Iraq for its failure to comply with Security Council resolutions. Without mentioning weapons inspections, he warned that if the UN failed to act within a matter of weeks, the United States would act to enforce compliance.

There was immediate global pressure on Iraq to accept weapons inspections in order to avoid war, which Iraq did four days later on 16 September. The United States demanded that the weapons inspectors have unrestricted access to all sites in Iraq and that the Security Council authorize force if Iraq interfered. Russia, China, and France resisted. France preferred a two-step process with one resolution demanding inspections, and then a second resolution authorizing force. Russia and China strongly opposed the use of force and argued that inspectors could go into Iraq on the basis of existing resolutions. Russian Ambassador Sergey Lavrov argued:

> If we're not talking about the deployment of the inspectors but about an attempt to use the Security Council to create a legal basis for the use of force, or even for a regime change of a UN member state . . . then we see no way how the Security Council could give its consent to that.
>
> (Gordon 2002)

After six weeks of intense negotiations, the Council agreed to a vague resolution enabling everyone to declare victory (SCR 1441). For the United States and Britain, the resolution found Iraq in "material breach" of prior resolutions, set up a new inspections regime, and warned of "serious consequences" if Iraq failed to disarm. For the others, the resolution did not explicitly authorize force and committed the United States to the inspection process (Marfleet and Miller 2005, Byers 2004).

The United States could not unilaterally establish its preferred new rules. The veto powers – including Britain – wanted the process to go through the Security Council, and the United States urgently lobbied to get an authorization of force. With SCR 1441 the United States conceded to a two-step process in order to avoid a veto from either Russia or France. The United States then used SCR 1441 to argue that an authorization of force would be necessary if Iraq did not reveal all its weapons programs and disarm. Secretary of State Powell addressed the Security Council for ninety minutes on 5 February 2003 and asserted that Iraq was continuing to develop WMD and had links to Al Qaeda. United States officials argued that the February UNMOVIC report would force the Security Council to act. However, it contradicted much of Powell's arguments, reporting that Iraq was providing unprecedented cooperation, that they had found no weapons, and that they needed more time to complete their work and present comprehensive conclusions.

The lack of a smoking gun in the UNMOVIC report led to a bitter showdown on 14 February as most members resisted the United States demand for the Security Council to authorize force. French Foreign Minister Dominique de Villepin's statement in favor of continued inspections drew a rare burst of applause from the diplomats and staff behind the Council delegates. Russia and China proposed extending and strengthening the weapons inspections process. The United States delegates seemed stunned that even countries such as Chile and Angola preferred inspections to war. Then in an extraordinary meeting that ran over two days, representatives from sixty-one states addressed the Council and urged it to avoid war and continue the sanctions. The Council waited for the UNMOVIC report on 7 March, which again failed to conclude that Iraq was in material breach of SCR 1441. The United States circulated a draft resolution on 10 March giving Iraq a deadline of 17 March to comply with all Council resolutions. Only four members (UK, Spain, and Chile) were in favor. China, Russia and France pledged a veto. Chirac said: "We refuse to follow a path that will lead automatically to war as long as the inspectors don't say to us, 'We can't go any further'" (Sciolino 2003). The Council never voted on that resolution and never determined that Iraq was in material breach of its obligations after SCR 1441.

On 18 March Bush delivered a forty-eight-hour ultimatum to Hussein to leave Iraq or face war. On 20 March the United States began an air war against targets in Baghdad. In the following days American and British ground troops entered Iraq from the south (Turkey rejected the United States request for access to its military bases, preventing a two-front military strategy). In a letter to the Security Council, the United States gave two justifications for the use of force: (1) Iraq's material breaches of its disarmament obligations in SCR 687 and 1441 ended the ceasefire with Iraq and revived the authority to use force under SCR 678 – passed 12 years earlier; and (2) self-defense. Both were questionable legal arguments (Hmoud 2004, Crawford 2003). The first justification treated Security Council resolutions like treaties when they are executive decisions binding on all states, including the United States. If the Security Council established a ceasefire, then the Security Council must decide to terminate it. The Council refusal to authorize force when the United States requested it represented the will of the Council more than American claims that it was enforcing Council resolutions.

The second claim was also dubious because anticipatory self-defense is only applicable if an attack is imminent. Iraq did not declare war on the United States. Iraq did not launch a military attack on the United States. There was no evidence that Iraq aided or sponsored hostile acts amounting to acts of war. There were no links between Iraq, Al Qaeda, and 9/11. The international community overwhelmingly rejected the self-defense argument. The United States position was that we think Iraq had WMD; and we think that Iraq had ties to Al Qaeda; and we think that Iraq might give WMD to Al Qaeda, and we think that Al Qaeda might use those weapons against us. That long list of hypothetical connections did not constitute self-defense against an imminent threat. It constituted an illegitimate preventive war (Johnstone 2004).

Condemnation from Russia, China and France (and many others) was immediate and overwhelming. They denounced the war as illegal, destabilizing and inevitably creating more terrorism. They said that it contradicted global public opinion and had no Security Council mandate. The following statement by Putin on 20 March was typical of the criticism:

> This military action cannot be justified. If we allow international law to be replaced by the law of the fist, under which the strong is always right and is unlimited in the choice of means to achieve its goals, then one of the basic principles of international law, the principle of the inviolability of the sovereignty of states, will be put into question. And then no one, not a single country in the world, will feel secure.
>
> (Saradzhyan and Yablokova 2003)

It was possible that the post-cold war experiment in collective security was over. Consistent with realist criticisms, the great powers might have identified each other as rivals and marginalized the importance of collective security institutions. And consistent with radical criticisms, the world's countries might have rejected the hierarchy and inherent double standards of a hegemonic collective security arrangement. The United States might have ignored the UN in pursuit of empire, and the other great powers might have begun a counterbalancing alliance against the United States. The rupture over how to implement collective security rules against Iraq might have ushered in a new global rivalry.

But no one wanted that outcome. France, Russia, and China did not want to resist American policy to the extent that the United States would completely ignore the UN. They wanted the UN to play a role in the post-war administration of Iraq and the provision of humanitarian aid. They did not submit a resolution condemning the invasion and calling for the withdrawal of foreign forces as they would have done if a nonveto power had invaded a country. Indeed, no international body formally condoned or condemned the invasion. There was a tremendous disconnect between the rhetorical criticism of the United States and the willingness to use global institutions to thwart it. The United States was immune from collective enforcement measures. Global resistance to the American invasion of Iraq amounted to an unwillingness to join its "coalition of the willing." But in a world of security interdependence, as the United States was about to learn, that itself was a significant blow to American policy.

The United States also did not want that outcome. It could not protect its security interests by provoking a global alliance against it. The United States did not irrevocably break its commitment to collective security with its invasion of Iraq. Although much of the world dismissed the claim, it invoked a hegemonic collective security argument by asserting that it was enforcing Security Council resolutions. It could have more thoroughly damaged the Security Council by demanding a vote on that second resolution, losing that vote, and then invading

Iraq anyway. Instead, the debate remained within the parameters of world politics since the cold war: what is the appropriate way to implement collective security rules? The invasion of Iraq widened the differences among the veto powers on this question, but it did not make the question irrelevant by automatically constructing a new set of rules.

The United States tried to increase the legitimacy of its use of force by championing the "coalition of the willing" assembled to assist the military operation. Thirty-six countries beyond the United States and the United Kingdom took part in the allied coalition. Their contributions, however, were modest. Only eight countries sent more than 200 troops, and only South Korea sent more than 1,000 troops. Including British troops, coalition countries never had more than 20,000 troops on the ground. The number of American troops in Iraq varied from 130,000 to 160,000 throughout the conflict. The coalition steadily dwindled as well, with only twenty-one countries remaining in it in November 2006. Spain, New Zealand, Portugal, the Netherlands, Hungary, Norway, Ukraine, Japan, and the Philippines have all withdrawn their troops from Iraq. And South Korea, Poland and the United Kingdom – three of the more significant contributors – all announced sharp troop withdrawals in 2007. As the coalition shrank over time, the United States use of force in Iraq looked less like hegemonic collective security.

The United States toppled the Hussein regime relatively easily, with American forces advancing into Baghdad by 9 April. But the United States made crucial early decisions that would help ignite the future insurgency. The Bush administration ignored the advice of its military and did not send in overwhelming numbers of troops to ensure post-combat security. It had no post-conflict nation-building plan and no contingency plans about how to deal with a possible insurgency against its presence. It made few efforts to stop looting in Baghdad and other cities. It abolished the Baath Party and fired all top government bureaucrats and military officials with links to the Baath Party. By dismantling the institutions of the Hussein regime, ending all Sunni privilege in Iraq, and promising democracy to the majority Shia population, the United States made a Sunni insurgency against its occupation more likely. By July 2003 American military leaders recognized that they faced an organized enemy intent on fighting a guerilla war.

The United States soon learned that it needed the UN. Many "coalition of the willing" countries were not willing to participate in the post-war occupation without a Council resolution. Security Council sanctions still existed on Iraq, and most countries would not buy Iraqi oil without a resolution legalizing the occupation. So in May 2003 – two months after the invasion – the United States was back in front of the Security Council requesting it to act regarding Iraq. The Council recognized the United States and the United Kingdom as occupying powers under international law, gave them the authority to administer oil revenues, and terminated all sanctions against Iraq (SCR 1483). In return, the United States reluctantly agreed to a central UN role in humanitarian relief and the reconstruction of political institutions. By providing a legal framework for the post-war occupation of Iraq, the Security Council clearly violated the UN Charter. But it helped repair the breach among the veto powers. It is another example that the Council is a political organization protecting the interests of the veto powers, not a legal organization enforcing international law.

One consequence of SCR 1483 was that the UN was now cooperating with the American occupation. The UN established a headquarters in Baghdad to establish humanitarian aid and begin political negotiations for a transitional government. The Sunni insurgency against the occupation repeatedly targeted UN headquarters. In August 2003 a guerilla attack killed the top UN official in Baghdad, and Kofi Annan withdrew the UN staff because of the deteriorating security conditions. By that point, the United States realized that it needed the UN to stay in order to legitimize the occupation in the face of Iraqi resistance. It also needed the UN to facilitate political negotiations because key Iraqi players, particularly the cleric al-Sistani, would not talk to United States officials. In September, Bush called for a Council resolution authorizing a multinational force of coalition soldiers and requesting member states to provide troops and funds to help stabilize Iraq. The United States was realizing early on that it could not bring stability to Iraq without multilateral cooperation.

The Security Council again agreed to the United States request in return for some American concessions. On 16 October 2003 the Council authorized a multinational force in Iraq under "unified" (American) command (SCR 1511). While this provided political cover, few countries subsequently sent a significant number of troops to cooperate in the American occupation of Iraq. In return, the Council charged the Iraqi Governing Council – handpicked by the United States – to present a timetable for the drafting of a constitution, elections, and independence by 15 December 2003 (SCR 1511). Annan sent Lakhdar Brahimi to mediate between the Iraqi factions regarding the construction of an interim government and elections. The United States asked the UN to provide monitors to ensure the legitimacy of upcoming Iraqi elections but Annan again refused, citing the security conditions on the ground.

The Security Council passed two significant resolutions regarding terrorism in 2004, and they continued to illustrate the ambivalence between the war and crime metaphor for terrorism. The first was another concession to an American demand, giving multinational forces in Iraq the authority to use force to prevent and deter terrorism (SCR 1546). This was the first resolution explicitly giving states the authority to use force against "terrorism." It is unclear to what extent this supports American notions that it is at "war" or how important a precedent this resolution might become in future counterterrorist efforts. The other resolution, passed after Chechen terrorists occupied a school in Beslan, included for the first time a working definition of terrorism. Note how the definition explicitly begins with the crime metaphor:

> [Terrorist acts are] criminal acts, including against civilians, committed with the intent to cause death or serious bodily injury, or taking of hostages, with the purpose to provoke a state of terror in the general public or in a group of

persons or particular persons, intimidate a population or compel a government or an international organization to do or to abstain from doing any act.

(SCR 1566)

This limited political agreement among the veto powers, however, did little to help the United States maintain security on the ground in Iraq. The Sunni insurgency throughout 2003–4 targeted both coalition troops and Shia and Kurdish populations with car bombs, roadside bombs and suicide attacks. They would not accept an Iraq – democratic or not – dominated by the Shia. Their goals were to encourage coalition troops to leave and then win a civil war with the Shia to regain control of Iraq. The Shia, due greatly to the leadership of al-Sistani, showed great restraint against the Sunni attacks in order to prevent civil war. But other Shia elements resented both the American occupation and the Sunni attacks. In April and May of 2004 Shia militias loyal to the cleric Moqtada al-Sadr began to take on coalition forces. Throughout the rest of 2004 the United States was simultaneously fighting both Sunnis during periodic sieges on Fulljah and Shia militias loyal to al-Sadr in Najaf.

The nation-building efforts saw some success. Saddam Hussein was captured in December 2003 and later found guilty by an Iraqi court of crimes against humanity. The United States ended the legal occupation of Iraq in June 2004 and handed over sovereignty to an interim government headed by Prime Minister Iyad Allawi. Iraq held elections in January 2005 for a transitional parliament that would draft a new Iraqi constitution. Sunni participation was limited, and Shia political parties dominated the assembly. In April 2005 the parliament selected Kurdish leader Jalel Talabani as President and Shia leader Ibrahim Jaafai as Prime Minister. In August 2005 Shia and Kurdish parliament members, but not Sunni representatives at the negotiations, endorsed a draft constitution. This constitution was then approved in an October 2005 referendum, again with low Sunni support. December 2005 elections led to the first full-term government since the United States invasion. The new government could not form until April 2006, however, after months of deadlock led to a compromise candidate Jawad al-Maliki as prime minister and a coalition government that included parties loyal to Moqtada al-Sadr.

The violence between the Sunni and Shia continued to escalate throughout 2005–6. Car bombs, shootings, and other explosions all surged after May 2005. A February 2006 bomb attack on an important Shia shrine in Samarra finally triggered a more widespread civil war. In May and June an average of 100 civilians per day were killed in the violence. The United States military continued its failing efforts to train the Iraqi army – heavily constituted by Shia militia members – to ensure security in Iraq on its own. A majority of the American public no longer supported the war, and the rising violence in Iraq contributed to Democratic Party victories in November 2006. The domestic debate within the United States – whether to reduce or increase troops – presumed the war to be a unilateral venture. Adopting a collective security approach and asking the Security Council to authorize more multinational troops was not an option; few countries would be willing to send troops. While the Council made some efforts to legitimize the unauthorized invasion after the fact, it was unwilling to substantially support the military operation, preferring to let the United States learn a hard lesson about relying on military capability in a security interdependent world.

Conclusions

The United States war on terrorism in Afghanistan and Iraq illustrates the priority of security interdependence over United States military dominance (Johnson and Russell 2005). Why is the Taliban gaining strength in Afghanistan? Why can the United States not control the seven mile road from the Baghdad airport into the city? Why can the United States not capture bin Laden? The inability of the United States to translate its military dominance into real security is that politics and power are primarily social (Reus-Smit 2004). Political influence requires more than military force and coercion; it requires others to interpret your policies as legitimate.

The majority of the world's countries did not consider the use of force against Iraq a legitimate collective security enforcement action. They did not consider Iraq to be a threat to international security, particularly not one that warranted an abandonment of the UN Charter. They interpreted the United States to be invoking rules of preventive war and empire. The United States (again) asserted too much hierarchy and alienated those whom it needed in a world of security interdependence. The United States must consider this underlying context in which it is fighting its war on terrorism and how others will interpret its use of force. Continuing to claim that 9/11 fundamentally changed world politics may eventually convince others that global security is indeed constituted by rules of rivalry and/or war. But the United States would be the rival and/or enemy, and few would cooperate with its counterterrorist efforts.

The United States must emphasize the social nature of global security. Its "war" on terrorism is in reality a global counterinsurgency policy. The United States threatens fundamentalist Islamic movements through its support for Israel and secular Middle Eastern regimes, its troops and military bases throughout the region, and its Western values that challenge Muslim culture. These radical groups believe that they are acting defensively against Western intrusion into their land. The United States must concern itself with how the moderate Islamic world will interpret its actions. The security–hierarchy paradox again applies: policies that invoke empire make radical Islamic ideology seem plausible. The United States did exactly what Osama bin Laden wanted it to do after 9/11: overreact and pursue illegitimate, imperial policies in the Middle East.

If the terrorist attacks of 9/11 did not convince the United States that its military capability alone cannot keep its citizens safe, then the failures in Afghanistan and Iraq should teach that lesson. The United States cannot fight a war in the broad terms advocated by the Bush administration after 9/11. For military, political, and moral reasons, it cannot invade every country that sponsors terrorism. It can only tackle this security threat through the multilateral collaboration of others, facilitated by international organizations. And it must do so by strengthening collective security rules against terrorism, weapons proliferation, and particularly human rights. The terrorist pathology is "I am right, the ends justify the means, and I will use violence to achieve my political goal." The United States cannot fight this pathology by adopting it. The United States needs to realize that a strong human rights culture is the antidote to this terrorist pathology (Roth 2004). Human rights and security against terrorism are mutually reinforcing, not a zero sum game.

United States counterterrorist efforts, however, have not embraced this approach. Its "war" has convinced others to call their domestic opponents "terrorists" and trample on human rights. China characterized the Uighur separatists in Xinjiang and the Maoist insurgency in Nepal to be terrorist movements. Russia asserted that Chechen separatists are terrorists in that internal conflict. India considered Islamic militants in Kashmir to be terrorists. Indonesia called the Aceh and West Papua insurgencies terrorist movements. India, Egypt, Malaysia, China, Russia, South Korea, and Zimbabwe have all used domestic anti-terrorism legislation passed since 2002 to repress opposition groups. Even Milošević during his ICTY trial argued that he had a right to fight Albanian terrorists in Kosovo. The United States has been less willing to criticize the human rights records of states (Sudan, Saudi Arabia, Egypt, Pakistan, Uzbekistan, etc.) that cooperate in the war on terrorism.

The fundamental flaw of the Bush Doctrine is that it views power as material rather than social. It presumes that material superiority easily translates into political influence. It presumes that others will agree that the United States is a benign global leader. It ignores the social aspects of legitimacy. Asserting the universality of your ideals and flexing your muscles does not create legitimacy. This view of power leaves the United States with an impoverished set of policy options. Coercion is not the best approach in a world of security interdependence. It harms both American interests and global order.

The war in Iraq has greatly increased the transnational security problems of terrorism, weapons proliferation, and human rights violations. It has decreased the legitimacy of pro-Western regimes in the Arab world. It has brought more radical elements to power through democratic elections in Palestine, Iran, and Lebanon. To avoid this continuing spiral the United States must recognize the security–hierarchy paradox: the terrorist threat driving the Bush Doctrine can be effectively addressed only within a collective security arrangement. Trying to pursue absolute security by remaking the world in its own image is empire, and others will resist empire.

Conclusion

The Security Council has struggled to develop and enforce the hierarchical rules necessary to maintain international security. Sometimes the realist critique applies: the veto powers cannot agree on what the rules are, when to implement the rules, and how to enforce the rules given noncompliance. China does not want collective action against Sudan or North Korea; Russia does not want collective action against Iran; the United States does not want collective action against Israel or Pakistan. It is difficult to generate a consensus about when terrorism, weapons proliferation, and human rights violations warrant Council action. This is one-half of the security–hierarchy paradox: too little hierarchy harms global security. In a security interdependent world, we need global rules to deal with issues like terrorism, weapons proliferation, and human rights. It is possible that the difficulties in generating these rules will constantly weaken post-cold war collective security.

The other half of the security–hierarchy paradox is that too much hierarchy harms global security. The United States sometimes asserts such a hierarchical position – you have to follow the rules, but we do not – that it undermines international security. The United States does not want India and Pakistan to engage in preventive self-defense toward each other. The United States does not want China to unilaterally enforce Security Council resolutions without explicit authorization. The United States does not want Russia to cite terrorism or a humanitarian disaster and intervene into another country. The United States does not want Iran and North Korea to reject international weapons inspections. The United States does not want Syria or the Democratic Republic of Congo to torture prisoners. The United States does not want Sudan to escape ICC jurisdiction.

And yet the United States acts in these ways. It wants a security arrangement in which the rules always apply to others but not always to itself (or Israel). In this way the radical critique sometimes applies: collective security institutions do not maintain international security in the interests of all but protect the interests of the major powers, and particularly the most dominant country. It is possible that these inherent double standards will erode the legitimacy of collective security rules to such an extent that many countries will reject the hierarchy, follow United States precedents, and ignore the collective security rules. Here the realist and radical critiques converge: at some point others will see the United States as a rival and/or enemy, and the collective security arrangement will break down as rivalry and war rules (re)emerge.

These possibilities are important because contemporary security threats require a collective security arrangement. Organizing the world into competing alliances would once again elevate state sovereignty over the human security agenda. We would not be able to build long-term global stability on the basis of human rights, economic development, and democracy. We would not be able to coordinate policy to deal with disease, migration, climate change and refugees, let alone weapons proliferation and terrorism. States have constructed collective security rules because it is in their interests to do so. A world based on the principle that sovereign states can do what they want is no longer adequate to address global security issues. In a security interdependent world, states must increasingly cooperate with other states and international organizations/corporations to provide for the security of its own citizens.

The Security Council struggles to pursue this human security agenda. It recognizes that only political collaboration can bring about security in today's world. It tries to navigate a middle path between deadlock and American unilateralism, between too little and too much hierarchy. Sometimes it achieves that middle ground with post-cold war innovations such as smart sanctions, more robust peace-building missions, judicial tribunals, and subsidiary organs monitoring state implementation of Council resolutions. All are examples of the Council searching for effective and legitimate ways to implement collective security. Future efforts will include building from the "conflict diamonds" efforts and more closely collaborating with global industry to make commodity sanctions more effective. It is possible that the Security Council will stay on this middle path and maintain the centrality of collective security rules in world politics.

But this is largely up to the United States. It is difficult to construct collective security rules in a world in which one country is militarily so much more powerful than the others (Dunne 2003). That country could say that there will be no global rules (too little hierarchy) or it could say that the global rules exist but they do not bind its own policies (too much hierarchy). For collective security to succeed the United States must – like all good constructivists – emphasize the social world over the material world. It must not rely solely on its own military capability to either provide for its own security or guarantee the legitimacy of its hegemonic position in world politics (Ikenberry 2004, Leffler 2003). It must learn the lessons of the security–hierarchy paradox and realize that it cannot impose its will on the world. It must focus on maintaining the legitimacy of collective security rules and assert less hierarchy.

The danger is that American foreign policy based on realist premises of rivals and enemies could become a self-fulfilling prophecy and undermine global collective security rules (Buzan 2004). The United States could damage the institutions it needs to realize its own policy objectives. A successful fight against terrorism can only succeed with the help of others: intelligence sharing, financial tracking, police arrests, extradition, etc. The United States is more likely to elicit such cooperation within a security arrangement of legitimate, consensually developed global rules. And the best place to achieve that legitimacy is the Security Council (Voten 2005). If the United States learns the lessons of the security–hierarchy paradox, it will inevitably continue to combine efforts with others on the Security Council to achieve international security.

Bibliography

Adler, E. (1997) "Seizing the Middle Ground: Constructivism and World Politics," *European Journal of International Politics*, 3: 319–363.

—— and Barnett, M. (eds) (1998) *Security Communities*. Cambridge: Cambridge University Press.

—— and Haas, P. M. (1992) "Epistemic Communities, World Order, and the Creation of a Reflectivist Research Program," *International Organization*, 46(3): 367–390.

Ahrari, M. E. (1999) "The Beginning of a New Cold War?" *European Security*, 8(3): 24–132.

Al-Anbari, A. A. (2001) "The Impact of United Nations Sanctions on Economic Development, Human Rights, and Civil Society," in Gowlland-Debbas, V. (ed.) *United Nations Sanctions and International Law*. The Hague: Kluwer Law International.

Albright, M. (1999) "A New NATO for a New Century," *United States Department of State Dispatch*, April, p. 7.

Alker, H. (1996) *Rediscoveries and Reformulations*. Cambridge: Cambridge University Press.

Alusla, N. (2001) "The Arming of Rwanda and the Genocide," *African Security Review* 13(2): 137–140.

Alvarez, J. (2006) "Torturing the Law," *Case Western Reserve Journal of International Law*, 37 (1): 175–223.

Angelet, N. (2001) "International Law Limits to the Security Council," in Gowlland-Debbas, V. (ed) *United Nations Sanctions and International Law*, The Hague: Kluwer Law International.

Angell, D.J. R. (2004) "The Angola Sanctions Committee," in Malone, D. M. (ed.) *The UN Security Council: From the Cold War to the 21ˢᵗ Century*. Boulder, CO: Lynne Reinner.

Annan, K. (1999) *The Question of Intervention*. New York: United Nations Department of Public Information.

Arend, A. C. and Beck, R.J. (1993) *International Law and the Use of Force*. New York: Routledge.

Austin, J. L. (1962) *How to Do Things with Words*. Cambridge: MIT Press.

Aview, F. K. (1998) "Assessing Humanitarian Intervention in the Post-Cold War World Period: Sources of Consensus," *International Relations*, 14(2): 61–90.

Ayoob, M. (2004) "The War in Iraq: Normative and Strategic Implications," in Weiss, T. G., Crahan, M. E., and Goering, J. (eds) *Wars on Terrorism and Iraq: Human Rights, Unilateralism, and US Foreign Policy*. London: Routledge.

Bacevich, A. J. (2002) *American Empire: The Realities and Consequences of US Diplomacy*. Cambridge, MA: Harvard University Press.

Bahgat, G. (2003) "Iran, the United States, and the War on Terrorism," *Studies in Conflict and Terrorism*, 26(1): 93–104.

Bailey, S. (1994) *The UN Security Council and Human Rights*. London: St Martin's Press.

Bajpai, K. (2003) "US Nonproliferation Policy after the Cold War," in Malone, D. M. and Khong, Y. F. (eds) *Unilateralism and U.S. Foreign Policy: International Perspectives*. Boulder, CO: Lynne Reinner.

Barnett, M. (2002) *Eyewitness to a Genocide*. Ithaca, NY: Cornell University Press.

Barria, L. A. and Roper, S. D. (2005a) "Providing Justice and Reconciliation: the Criminal Tribunals for Sierra Leone and Cambodia," *Human Rights Review*, 7(1): 5–26.

—— (2005b) "How Effective are International Criminal Tribunals? An Analysis of the ICTY and the ICTR," *International Journal of Human Rights*, 9(3): 349–368.

Bellamy, A. J. (2002) *Kosovo and International Society*. London: Palgrave.

—— and Williams, P. D. (2005) "Who's Keeping the Peace? Regionalization and Contemporary Peace Operations," *International Security*, 29(4): 157–195.

Bennett, A. and Lepgold, J. (1993) "Reinventing Collective Security after the Cold War and Gulf Conflict," *Political Science Quarterly*, 108(1): 213–237.

Betts, R. K. (1992) "Systems for Peace or Causes of War? Collective Security, Arms Control, and the New Europe," *International Security*, 17(1): 5–43.

Blair, T. (1999) "Prime Minister's Speech to the Economic Club of Chicago." Available at: http://number-10.gov.uk/public/info/index.html (accessed 8 February 2005).

—— (2001a) "Prime Minister's Statement to Parliament on the September 11 Attacks." Available at: www.number-10.gov/output/ (accessed February 8 2005).

—— (2001b) "Press Conference Given by Prime Minister Tony Blair to Arab Journalists." Available at: www.number-10.gov/output/ (accessed 9 February 2005).

—— (2001c) "Prime Minister's Statement to Parliament on the War on Terror." Available at: www.number-10.gov/output/ (accessed 9 February 2005).

Boulden, J. (2001) *Peace Enforcement: The United Nations Experience in Congo, Somalia, and Bosnia*. Westport, CT: Praeger.

—— and Weiss, T. G. (eds) (2004) *Terrorism and the United Nations*, Bloomington, IN: University of Indiana Press.

Boutros-Ghali, B. (1992) *An Agenda for Peace*. New York: United Nations Press.

Bowen, N. (2005) "Multilateralism, Multipolarity, and Regionalism: French Foreign Policy Discourse," *Mediterranean Quarterly*, 16(1): 94–116.

Boyd-Judson, L. (2005) "Strategic Moral Diplomacy: Mandela, Qaddafi, and the Lockerbie Negotiations," *Foreign Policy Analysis*, 2(1):73–97.

Braun, C. (2004) "New Challenges to the Nuclear Nonproliferation Regime," *International Security*, 29(2): 5–49.

British Broadcasting Corporation (1998) "Russian Foreign Minister and Top Military Speak to Media on Kosovo Crisis," *BBC Worldwide Monitoring*, 30 March.

Brooks, S. G. and Wohlforth, W. C. (2002) "American Primacy in Perspective," *Foreign Affairs*, 81(1): 20–33.

—— (2005) "International Relations Theory and the Case against Unilateralism," *Perspectives on Politics*, 3(3): 509–524.

Burmiller, E. (2002) "Cheney says Peril of a Nuclear Iraq Justifies Attack," *New York Times*, August 27, A1.

Bush, G. H. W. (1991) "Address to the Nation Announcing Allied Military Action in the

Persian Gulf." Available at: http://bushlibrary.tamu.edu/research/papers/1991/ (accessed 13 June 2005).

—— and Scrowcroft, B. (1998) *A World Transformed*. New York: Knopf.

Bush, G. W. (2001a) "Statement by the President in His Address to the Nation." Available at: www.whitehouse.gov/news/releases/2001/ (accessed 13 September 2005).

—— (2001b) "Remarks by the President with the National Security Team." Available at: www.whitehouse.gov/news/releases/2001/ (accessed 13 September 2005).

—— (2001c) "Address to a Joint Session of Congress." Available at: www.whitehouse. gov/news/releases/2001/ (accessed 13 September 2005).

—— (2002a) "President Bush Delivers Graduation Speech at West Point," 1 June. Available at: www.whitehouse.gov/news/releases/2002/ (accessed 14 September 2005).

—— (2002b) "President Delivers State of the Union Address," 29 January. Available at: www.whitehouse.gov/news/releases/2002/ (accessed 14 September 2005).

—— (2003) "Press Conference Transcript," *New York Times*, February 1, A6.

Buzan, B. (1997) "Rethinking Security after the Cold War," *Cooperation and Conflict*, 32(1): 5–28.

—— (2004) *The United States and the Great Powers: World Politics in the Twenty-First Century*. Cambridge: Polity Press.

Byers, M. (2003) "Preemptive Self-defense: Hegemony, Equality and Strategies of Legal Change," *Journal of Political Philosophy*, 11(2): 171–190.

—— (2004) "Agreeing to Disagree: Security Council Resolution 1441 and Intentional Ambiguity," *Global Governance*, 10: 165–186.

Callamard, A. (1999) "French Policy in Rwanda," in Adelman, H. and Suhrke, A. (eds) *The Path of a Genocide*, New Brunswick, NJ: Transaction Publishers.

Carey, H. (2001) "US Domestic Politics and the Emerging Humanitarian Intervention Policy: Haiti, Bosnia, and Kosovo," *World Affairs*, 164(2): 72–82.

Checkel, J. (1998) "The Constructivist Turn in International Relations Theory," *World Politics*, 50(2): 324–348.

Chellaney, B. (1999) "Arms Control: the Role of the IAEA and UNCSCOM," in Alagappa, M. and Inoguchi, T. (eds) *International Security Management and the United Nations*. New York: United Nations University Press.

Chesterman, S. and Pouligny, B. (2003) "Are Sanctions Meant to Work? The Politics of Creating and Implementing Sanctions through the United Nations," *Global Governance*, 9(4): 503–518.

China Daily (1998) "US Urged to Observe Commitments," 2 September, p.1.

Chirac, J. (2001) "Fight against Terrorism and Afghanistan." Available at: www.dipomatie. gouv.fr/actual/declarations/bulletins/ (accessed 20 June 2005).

—— (2002) "Speech at the Tenth Ambassador's Conference." Available at: www. info-france-usa.org/news/statmnts/2002/ (accessed 10 July 2004).

Clarke, W. and Herbst, J. (1997) *Learning from Somalia: The Lessons of Armed Humanitarian Intervention*. Boulder, CO: Westview Press.

Claude, I. L. (1962) *Power and International Relations*. New York: Random House.

Clines, F. (1997) "Clinton says US will Wait and See as Iraqis Back Off," *New York Times*, 21 November, A1.

Clinton, W.J. (1994) "Clinton Address to the Nation on Haiti." Available at: www. clintonfoundation.org/legacy/ (accessed 3 June 2005).

—— (1998) "Address to the Nation on Terror." Available at: www.clintonfoundation.org/ legacy/ (accessed 3 June 2005).

—— (1999) "Address to the Nation on Airstrikes against Serbian Targets," *Weekly Compilation of Presidential Documents*, 35(12): 516–518.

Cohen, A. (1998) *Israel and the Bomb*. New York: Columbia University Press.

Colas, A. and Saull, R. (eds) (2006) *The War on Terrorism and the American "Empire" after the Cold War*. London: Routledge.

Cortright, D and Lopez, G. A. (1999) "Are Sanctions Just? The Problematic Case of Iraq," *Journal of International Affairs*, 52: 257.

—— (2004) "Reforming Sanctions," in Malone, D. M. (ed.) *The UN Security Council: From the Cold War to the 21ˢᵗ Century*. Boulder, CO: Lynne Reinner.

Crawford, N.C. (2002) *Argument and Change in World Politics: Ethics, Decolonization and Humanitarian Intervention*. Cambridge: Cambridge University Press.

—— (2003) "The Slippery Slope to Preventive War," *Ethics and International Affairs*, 17(1): 30–36.

Cronin, B. (2001) "The paradox of hegemony: America's ambiguous relationship with the United Nations," *European Journal of International Relations*, 7(1):103–130.

Crossette, B. (1997) "Russia and U.S. Square Off Over U.N. Sanctions on Iraq," *New York Times*, 25 November, A6.

—— (1998a) "At the UN, Tensions of Cold War are Renewed," *New York Times*, 18 December, A23.

—— (1998b) "UN Fails to Reach Consensus on Iraq Policy," *New York Times*, 24 December, A6.

—— (2000) "Tough Sanctions Imposed on Taliban Government Split UN," *New York Times*, 20 December, A20.

Daalder, I. and O'Hanlon, M. (2000) *Winning Ugly: NATO's War to Save Kosovo*. Washington DC: Brookings Institution.

Dallaire, R. (2003) *Shake Hands with the Devil*. New York: Carroll & Graf Publishers.

Deller, N. and Burroughs J. (2003) "Arms Control Abandoned: The Case of Biological Weapons," *World Policy Journal*, 20(2): 37–42.

Des Forges, A. (1999) *Leave None to Tell the Story*. New York: Human Rights Watch.

Deutsch, K. (1957) *Political Community and the North Atlantic Area*. Princeton, NJ: Princeton University Press.

Dobbins, J. (2005) *The UN's Role in Nation-Building: from the Congo to Iraq*. New York: RAND Publications.

Donald, D. (2002) "Neutrality, Impartiality and UN Peacekeeping at the Beginning of the 21ˢᵗ Century," *International Peacekeeping*, 9(4): 21–38.

Dougherty, B. K. (2004) "Right-sizing international criminal justice: the hybrid experiment at the Special Court for Sierra Leone," *International Affairs* 80: 311–328.

Doyle, M. W. and Sambanis, N. (2006) *Making War and Building Peace*. Princeton, NJ: Princeton University Press.

Duffy, G., Frederking, B. and Tucker, S. (1998) "Language Games: Analyzing the INF Treaty Negotiations," *International Studies Quarterly*, 42(2): 271–294.

Dugard, J. (2001) "Judicial Review of Sanctions," in Gowlland-Debbas, V. (ed.) *United Nations Sanctions and International Law*. The Hague: Kluwer Law International.

Dunne, T. (2003) "Society and Hierarchy in International Relations," *International Relations*, 17(3): 303–320.

Eckholm, E. (1999) "Bombing May Have Hardened China's Line," *New York Times*, 18 May, A11.

El Zeidy, M. M. (2005) "The Ugandan Government Triggers the First Test of the Complementarity Principle: An Assessment of the First State's Party Referral to the ICC," *International Criminal Law Review* 5: 83–119.

Elbe, S. (2006) "Should HIV/AIDS be Securitized? The Ethical Dilemmas of Linking HIV/AIDS and Security," *International Studies Quarterly*, 50: 119–144.

Erlanger, S. (1995a) "In a New Attack against NATO, Yeltsin Talks of a 'Conflagration of War,'" *New York Times*, September 9, A5.

—— (1995b) "Yeltsin Warns West on Bombing in Bosnia," *New York Times*, 8 September, A15.

Fawn, R. (2003) "From Ground Zero to the War in Afghanistan," in Buckley, M. and Fawn, R. (eds), Global Responses to Terrorism. London: Routledge.

Feldman, N. (2002) "Choices of Law, Choices of War," *Harvard Journal of Law & Public Policy,* 25(3): 458–485.

Fenton, N. (2004) *Understanding the UN Security Council.* London: Ashgate.

Ferguson, Niall. (2004) *Empire.* New York: Basic Books.

Finnemore, M. and Sikkink, K. (2001) "Taking Stock: The Constructivist Research Program In International Relations and Comparative Politics," *Annual Reviews of Political Science*, 4: 391–416.

Foot, R. (2005) "Human Rights and Counterterrorism in Global Governance: Reputation and Resistance," *Global Governance*, 11(3): 291–310.

Fortna, V. P. (2004) "Does Peacekeeping Keep Peace? International Intervention and the Duration of Peace after Civil War," *International Studies Quarterly*, 48(2): 269–292.

Frederking, B. (2000) *Resolving Security Dilemmas: A Constructivist Interpretation of the INF Treaty.* London: Ashgate.

—— (2003) "Constructing post-cold war collective security," *American Political Science Review* 97(3): 363–378.

—— Artime, M. and Sanchez-Pagano, M. (2005) "Interpreting September 11," *International Politics* , 42(1): 135–151.

Gershkoff, A. and Kussner, S. (2005) "Shaping Public Opinion: The 9/11-Iraq Connection in the Bush Administration's Rhetoric," *Perspectives on Politics*, 3(3): 525–537.

Ginifer, J. (2002) "Peace Building in the Congo: Mission Impossible?" *International Peacekeeping*, 9(3): 121–128.

Gladkyy, O. (2003) "American Foreign Policy and US Relations with Russia and China after September 11," *World Affairs*, 166(1): 3–22.

Gorbachev, M. (1987) "Reality and the Guarantees of a Secure World," *FBIS Daily Report: Soviet Union*, 17 September, 23–28.

Gordenker, L. and Weiss. T. (1993) "The Collective Security Idea and Changing World Politics," in Weiss, T. (ed.) *Collective Security in a Changing World.* Boulder, CO: Lynne Reinner.

Gordon, M. (2002) "US Plan Requires Inspection Access to All Iraq Sites," *New York Times*, 28 September, A1.

Gourevitch, P. (1998) *We Wish to Inform You that Tomorrow We Will be Killed With our Families.* New York: Farrar Straus & Giroux.

Graham, T. and LaVera, D. J. (2002) "Nuclear Weapons: The Comprehensive Test Ban Treaty and National Missile Defense," in Stewart, P. and Forman S. (eds) *Multilateralism and US foreign policy: ambivalent engagement.* Boulder, CO: Lynne Reinner.

Greig, J. M., and Diehl, P. F. (2005) "The Peacekeeping–Peacemaking Dilemma," *International Studies Quarterly*, 49(4): 621–645.

Habermas, J. (1984) *Theory of Communicative Action*, New York: Beacon.

—— (1987) *Theory of Communicative Action II*. New York: Beacon.

Hampson. F. O. and Malone, D. M. (2002) "Improving the UN's Capacity for Conflict Prevention," *International Peacekeeping*, 9(1): 77–98.

Hendrickson, R. C. (2001) "Article 51 and the Clinton Presidency: Military Strikes and the UN Charter," *Boston University International Law Journal*, 19(2): 207–230.

Hersh, S. M. (2004) *Chain of Command*. New York: Harper Collins.

Hienze, E. and Borer, D. A. (2002) "The Chechen Exception: Rethinking Russia's Human Rights Policy," *Politics* 22(2): 86–94.

Hirsch, J. (2004) "Sierra Leone," in Malone, D. M. (ed.) *The UN Security Council: From the Cold War to the 21ˢᵗ Century*, Boulder, CO: Lynne Reinner.

Hmoud, M. (2004) "The Use of Force against Iraq; Occupation and Security Council Resolution 1483," *Cornell International Law Journal*, 36(3):435–451.

Holum, J. (1997) "The CTBT and Nuclear Disarmament – The US View," *Journal of International Affairs*, 51(1): 263–279.

Hopf, T. (1998) "The Promise of Constructivism in International Relations Theory," *International Security*, 23(2):171–200.

Howard, M. (2002) "What's in a Name? How to Fight Terrorism," *Foreign Affairs*, 81(3): 8–13.

Hurrell, A. (1992) "Collective Security and International Order Revisited," *International Relations*, 11: 37–56.

Ikenberry, G. J. (2001) "America's Grand Strategy in an Age of Terror," *Survival*, 43(4): 31.

—— (2003) "State Power and the Institutional Bargain: America's Ambivalent Economic and Security Multilateralism," in Foot, R. MacFarlane, S. N. and Mastanduno, M. (eds) *US Hegemony and International Organizations*. Oxford: Oxford University Press.

—— (2004) "Liberal Hegemony or Empire?" in Held, D. and Koenig-Archibugi M. (eds) *American Power in the 21ˢᵗ Century*. Cambridge, UK: Polity Press.

International Commission on Intervention and State Sovereignty (2001) *The Responsibility to Protect*. Ottawa: International Development Research Center.

Jentleson, B. W. and Whytock, C. A. (2005). "Who 'Won' Libya? The Force–Diplomacy Debate and its Implications for Theory and Policy," *International Security*, 30(3): 47–86.

Jervis, R. (2005) *American Foreign Policy in a New Era*. London: Routledge.

Joeck, N. (1997) "Nuclear Proliferation and Nuclear Reversal in South Asia," *Comparative Strategy*, 16(2): 263–273.

Johansen, R.C. (2006) "The Impact of US Policy toward the International Criminal Court on the Prevention of Genocide, War Crimes, and Crimes against Humanity," *Human Rights Quarterly*, 28(2): 301–331.

Johnson, T. H. and Russell, J. A. (2005) "A Hard Day's Night? The United States and the Global War on Terrorism," *Comparative Strategy*, 24(1): 124–151.

Johnston, A. I. (2003) "Is China a Status Quo Power?" *International Security*, 27(4): 5–56.

Johnston, D. and Purdum, T. S. (2004) "Missed Chances in a Long Hunt for bin Laden," *New York Times*, 25 March, A1.

Johnstone, I. (2004) "US–UN Relations after Iraq: The End of the World (Order) as We Know It?" *European Journal of International Law*, 15(4): 813–838.

de Jonge Oudraat, C. (2004) "The Role of the Security Council," in Boulden, J. and Weiss, T. G. (eds) (2004) *Terrorism and the United Nations*. Bloomington, IN: University of Indiana Press.

Joyner, C. (2004) "The United Nations and Terrorism: Rethinking Legal Tensions between

National Security, Human Rights, and Civil Liberties," *International Studies Perspectives*, 5(2): 240–257.

Kampani, G. (2001) "In Praise of Indifference toward India's Bomb," *Orbis*, 45(2): 304–387.

Kane, T. (2001) "China's Foundations: Guiding Principles of Chinese Foreign Policy," *Comparative Strategy*, 20: 45–55.

Katshung, J.Y. (2006) "Prosecution of Grave Violations of Human Rights in Light of Challenges of National Courts and the International Criminal Court: The Congolese Dilemma," *Human Rights Review*, 7(3): 5–25.

Kegley, C. W. and Raymond, G. A. (2007) *After Iraq: The Imperiled American Imperium*. New York: Oxford University Press.

Kerr, D. (2005) "The Sino-Russian Partnership and US Policy toward North Korea: From Hegemony to Concert in Northeast Asia," *International Studies Quarterly*, 49: 411–437.

Klotz, A. (1995) *Protesting Prejudice: Apartheid and the Politics of Norms in International Relations*. Ithaca, NY: Cornell University Press.

Knight, W.A. (2004) "Improving the Effectiveness of UN Arms Embargoes," in Price, R. M. and Zacher, M. W. (eds) *The United Nations and Global Security*, New York: Palgrave.

Koskenniemi, M. (1998) "The Place of Law in Collective Security: Reflections on the Recent Activity of the Security Council," in Paolini, A. J., Jarvis, A. P., and Reus-Smit, C. (eds) *Between Sovereignty and Global Governance*. New York: St. Martin's Press.

Krahmann, E. (2005) "American Hegemony or Global Governance? Competing Visions of International Security," *International Studies Review*, 7(4): 531–545.

Krasner, S. D. (2004) "Sharing Sovereignty: New Institutions for Collapsed and Failing States," *International Security*, 29(2): 85–120.

Krasno, J. E. and Sutterlin, J. (2003) The *United Nations and Iraq: Defanging the Viper*. Westport, CT: Praeger.

Kratochwil, F. (1989) *Norms, Rules and Decisions*. Cambridge: Cambridge University Press.

—— (2001) "Constructivism as an Approach to Interdisciplinary Study," in Fierke, K. M. and Jorgenson, K. E. (eds) *Constructing International Relations: the Next Generation*, New York: M. E. Sharpe.

Krisch, N. (2003) "The United States and the International Criminal Court," in Malone, D.M. and Khong, Y.F. (eds) *Unilateralism and U.S. Foreign Policy: International Perspectives*. Boulder, CO: Lynne Reinner.

Kubalkova, V. (2001) "The Twenty Years' Cartharsis," in Fierke, K. M. and Jorgenson, K. E. (eds) *Constructing International Relations: the Next Generation*. New York: M. E. Sharpe.

Kupchan, C. (1994) "The Case for Collective Security," in Downs, G. W. (ed.) *Collective Security beyond the Cold War*. Ann Arbor, MI: University of Michigan.

—— and Kupchan, C. (1995) "The Promise of Collective Security," *International Security*, 20(1): 52–61.

Laegrid, T. (1999) "UN Peacekeeping in Rwanda," in Adelman, H. and Suhrke, A. (eds) *The Path of a Genocide*. New Brunswick, NJ: Transaction Publishers.

Lake, D. (2006) "American Hegemony and the Future of East–West Relations," *International Studies Perspectives*, 7(1): 23–30.

Leffler, M. (2003) "9/11 and the Past and Future of American Foreign Policy," *International Affairs*, 79(5): 1045–1063.

Loehr, R. C. and Wong, E. M. (1995) "The UN and Arms Control in Iraq: A New Role?" *Journal of International Affairs*, 49(1): 167–182.

Luck, E. (2003) "American Exceptionalism and International Organization: Lessons from the 1990s," in Foot, R. MacFarlane, S. N. and Mastanduno, M. (eds) *US Hegemony and International Organizations*. Oxford: Oxford University Press.

—— (2006) UN Security Council: Practice and Promise. London: Routledge.

Lynch, M. (2002) "Why Engage? China and the Logic of Communicative Engagement," *European Journal of International Relations*, 8(2):187–230.

Macrae, J. (ed.) (2002) *The New Humanitarianisms: A Review of Trends in Global Humanitarian Action*. London: Overseas Development Institute.

Mahmoud, M. E. (2004) "Inside Darfur: Ethnic Genocide by a Governance Crisis," *Comparative Studies of South Asia, Africa, and the Middle East*, 24(2): 3–17.

Malik, J. M. (2002) "Dragon on Terrorism: Assessing China's Tactical Gains and Strategic Losses after September 11," *Contemporary Southeast Asia*, 24(2): 252–293.

Malone, D. M. (1998) *Decision Making in the UN Security Council*. Oxford: Clarendon Press.

—— (1999) "Goodbye UNSCOM: A Sorry Tale in US–UN relations," *Security Dialogue*, 30(4): 393–411.

—— (2003) "US–UN Relations in the UN Security Council in the Post-Cold War Era," in Foot, R., MacFarlane, S. N. and Mastanduno, M. (eds) *US Hegemony and International Organizations*. Oxford: Oxford University Press.

—— and Thakur, R. (2001) "UN Peacekeeping: Lessons Learned," *Global Governance*, 7(1): 11–17.

Marfleet, B. G. and Miller, C. (2005) "Failure after 1441: Bush and Chirac in the UN Security Council," *Foreign Policy Analysis*, 1: 333–360.

Marten, K. Z. (2004) *Enforcing the Peace: Learning from the Imperial Past*. New York: Columbia University Press.

Martin, R. (2002) "Sudan's Perfect War," *Foreign Affairs* 81(2): 111–127.

Mazrui, A. (1996) "The New Dynamics of Security: The United Nations and Africa," *World Policy Journal*, 13(1): 37–42.

Mearsheimer, J. J. (1994/5) "The False Promise of International Institutions," *International Security*, 19(3): 5–49.

Medeiros, E. S. (2003) "China's New Diplomacy," *Foreign Affairs*, 82(6): 22–35.

Meernik, J. (2003) "Victor's Justice or the Law? Judging and Punishing at the International Criminal Tribunal for the Former Yugolsavia," *Journal of Conflict Resolution*, 47(2): 140–162.

Melvern, L. (2004) *Conspiracy to Murder: the Rwandan Genocide*. London: Verso.

Miller, J. (1999) "Annan Takes Critical Stance on US Actions in Kosovo," *New York Times*, 19 May, A11.

Miller, L. H. (1999) "The Idea and the Reality of Collective Security," *Global Governance*, 5 (3): 303–332.

Mingst, K. (2003) "Troubled Waters: The United States–United Nations Relationship," *International Peacekeeping*, 10 (4): 82–93.

Miskel, J. F. and Norton, R. (2003) "The Intervention in the Democratic Republic of Congo," *Civil Wars*, 6(4): 1–13.

Mitchell, A. (1996) "Raid on Iraq: US Launches Further Strikes against Iraq after Clinton Vows He Will Extract 'Price'," *New York Times*, 4 September, A1.

Mobekk, E. (2001) "Enforcement of Democracy in Haiti," *Democratization*, 8(3): 173–188.

Moon, C. I. and Bae, J. Y. (2005) "The Bush Doctrine and the North Korean Nuclear Crisis," in Gurtov, M. and Van Ness, P. (eds) *Confronting the Bush Doctrine: Critical Views from the Asia-Pacific.* London: Routledge.

Morphet, S. (2000) "China as a Permanent Member of the Security Council," *Security Dialogue*, 31(2):151–166.

Mullenbach, M. J. (2005) "Deciding to Keep Peace: An Analysis of International Influences on the Establishment of Third-Party Peacekeeping Missions," *International Studies Quarterly*, 49(3): 529–556.

Myers, S. L. (1998) "Albright Says U.S. Could Act Alone Against Baghdad," *New York Times*, 29 January, A6.

Narayan, A. (2001) "China Cautiously Supports US–British Air Strikes," *China Online*, 8 October.

Newman, E. (2001) "Human Security and Constructivism," *International Studies Perspectives*, 2(2): 239–251.

Nizamani, H. K. (2001) *The Roots of Rhetoric: Politics of Nuclear Weapons in India and Pakistan.* New Delhi: India Research Press.

Olonisakin, F. (1996) "UN Cooperation with Regional Organizations in Peacekeeping: the Experience of ECOMOG and UNOMIL in Liberia," *International Peacekeeping*, 3(3): 33–51.

Onuf, N. G. (1989) *World of our Making.* Columbia, NY: University of South Carolina Press.

—— (1998) "Constructivism: a User's Manual," in Kubalkova, V. (ed.) *International Relations in a Constructed World.* London: M. E. Sharpe.

—— (2002) "Worlds of Our Making: The Strange Career of Constructivism in International Relations," in Puchala, D. (ed.) *Visions of International Relations*, Columbia, NY: University of South Carolina Press.

Pack, M. (2005) "Developments at the Special Court for Sierra Leone," *The Law and Practice of International Courts and Tribunals*, 4: 171–192.

Pape, R. (2005) "Soft Balancing against the United States," *International Security*, 30(1): 7–45.

Paris, R. (1997) "Peace Building and the Limits of Liberal Internationalism," *International Security*, 22(2): 82.

Paul, T. V. (2005) "Soft Balancing in the Age of US Primacy," *International Security*, 30(1): 46–71.

—— Wirtz, J. J. and Fortmann, M. (eds) (2004) *Balance of Power: Theory and Practice in the 21ˢᵗ Century.* Stanford, CA: Stanford University Press.

Powell, C. (2002) "Interview with Colin Powell," *New York Times*, 8 September, p. 18.

Price, R. and Tannenwald, N. (1996) "Constructing Norms of Humanitarian Intervention," in Katzenstein, P.J. (ed.) *The Culture of National Security.* New York: Columbia University Press.

Prunier, G. (1999) "Operation Turquoise: A Humanitarian Escape from a Political Dead End," in Adelman, H. and Suhrke, A. (eds) *The Path of a Genocide.* New Brunswick, NJ: Transaction Publishers.

Puchala, D. (2005) "World Hegemony and the United Nations," *International Studies Review*, 7(4): 571–584.

Pugh, M. and Sidhu, W. P. S. (2003) (eds) *The United Nations and Regional Security: Europe and Beyond.* Boulder, CO: Lynne Reinner.

Rajaee, B. (2004) "Deciphering Iran: The Political Evolution of the Islamic Republic and

US Foreign Policy after September 11," *Comparative Studies of South Asia, Africa and the Middle East*, 24(1): 159–172.

Ramazani, R. K. (1998) "The Shifting Premise of Iran's Foreign Policy: Towards a Democratic Peace?" *Middle East Journal*, 52(2): 177–187.

Ramcharan, B. G. (2002) *The Security Council and the Protection of Human Rights*. The Hague: Martinus Nijhoff Publishers.

Rashid, A. (2001) "Afghanistan: Ending the Policy Quagmire," *Journal of International Affairs*, 54(2): 395–410.

Renou, X. (2002) "A New French Policy for Africa?" *Journal of Contemporary African Studies*, 20(1): 5–26.

Reus-Smit, C. (2004) *American Power and World Order*. Cambridge: Polity Press.

Rice, C. (2002) "A Balance of Power that Favors Freedom," 1 October. Available at: www. manhattan-institute.org/ (accessed 7 May 2005).

Risse, T. (2000) "Let's argue! Communicative Action in World Politics," *International Organization*, 54: 1–39.

Roberts, A. (2004) "The Use of Force," Malone, D. M. (ed.) *The UN Security Council from the Cold War to the 21st Century*. Boulder, CO: Lynne Reinner.

Rose, E. (2005) "From a Punitive to a Bargaining Model of Sanctions: Lessons from Iraq," *International Studies Quarterly*, 49(3): 459–479.

Roth, K. (2004) "The Fight against Terrorism: The Bush Administration's Dangerous Neglect of Human Rights," in Weiss, T. G., Crahan, M. E., and Goering, J. (eds) (2004) *Wars on Terrorism and Iraq: Human Rights, Unilateralism, and US Foreign Policy*. London: Routledge.

Rouleau, E. (1995) "America's Unyielding Policy toward Iraq, *Foreign Affairs*, 74(1): 59–72.

Ruggie, J. G. (1994) "Third Try at World Order? America and Multilateralism after the Cold War," *Political Science Quarterly*, 109(4): 553–571.

Sanderson, J. M. (1998) "Peacekeeping or Peace Enforcement? Global Flux and the Dilemmas of UN Intervention," in Paolini, A. J., Jarvis, A. P., and Reus-Smit, C. (eds) *Between Sovereignty and Global Governance*. New York: St. Martin's Press.

Sarooshi, D. (1999) *The United Nations and the Development of Collective Security: The Delegation by the UN Security Council of its Chapter VII Powers*. Oxford: Clarendon Press.

Saul, B. (2005) "Definition of 'Terrorism' in the UN Security Council: 1985–2004," *Chinese Journal of International Law*, 4(1): 141–166.

Schelling, T. (1960) *The Strategy of Conflict*. Cambridge: Harvard University Press.

Schmeman, S. (1993) "Raid on Iraq: Russia Urges the Security Council to Reconvene on the Iraq Fighting," *New York Times*, 19 January, A9.

Schrijver, N. (2004) "September 11 and Challenges to International Law," in Boulden, J. and Weiss, T. G. (eds) *Terrorism and the United Nations*, Bloomington, IN: University of Indiana Press.

Sciolino, E. (2003) "France to Veto Resolution on Iraq War, Chirac Says," *New York Times*, 11 March, A10.

Searle, J. (1969) *Speech Acts*. Cambridge: Cambridge University Press.

—— (1995) *The Social Construction of Reality*. New York: Free Press.

Sen, S. K. (1999) "He Who Rides a Tiger: The Rationale of India's Nuclear Tests," *Comparative Strategy*, 18(2): 129–137.

Sens, A.G. (2004) "From Peace-keeping to Peace-building: The United Nations and the

Challenge of Intra-state War," in Price, R. M. and Zacher, M. W. (eds) *The United Nations and Global Security*. New York: Palgrave.

Shearman, P. (2001) "The Sources of Russian Conduct: Understanding Russian Foreign Policy," *Review of International Studies*, 27: 249–265.

Sherman, J.S. (2000) "Profits versus Peace: The Clandestine Diamond Economy in Angola," *Journal of International Affairs*, 53(2): 699–719.

da Silva, P. T. (2004) "Weapons of Mass Destruction: the Iraqi Case," in Malone, D. M. (ed) *The UN Security Council: from the Cold War to the 21ˢᵗ Century*. Boulder, CO: Lynne Reinner.

Smithson, A. E. (1998) "Senate Emasculates Treaty," *Bulletin of the Atomic Scientists*, 54(4): 6.

Snyder, J. and Vinjamuri, L. (2003/4) "Trials and Errors: Principle and Pragmatism in Strategies of International Justice," *International Security*, 28(3): 5–44.

Stanton, G. (2004) "Could the Rwandan Genocide Have Been Prevented?" *Journal of Genocide Research*, 6(2): 211–228.

Takeyh, R. (2003) "Iran at a Crossroads," *Middle East Journal*, 57(1): 42–56.

Tannenwald, N. (2004) "The UN and Debates over Weapons of Mass Destruction," in Price, R. M. and Zacher, M. W. (eds) *The United Nations and Global Security*. New York: Palgrave.

Tostensen, A. and Bull, B. (2002) "Are Smart Sanctions Possible?" *World Politics*, 54: 373–403.

Tsygankov, A. P. (2001) "The Final Triumph of the Pax Americana? Western Intervention in Yugoslavia and Russia's Debate on the Post-Cold War Order," *Communist and Post-Communist Studies*, 34: 133–156.

Udombana, N. J. (2005) "When Neutrality is a Sin: The Darfur Crisis and the Crisis of Humanitarian Intervention in Sudan," *Human Rights Quarterly*, 27(4): 1149–1199.

United Nations (1992) "Items Related to the Situation in Somalia." Available at: www.un.org/Depts/dpa/repertoire/ (accessed 8 March 2006).

—— (1998) "Secretary-General Pledges Support." Available at: www.un.org/News/Press/docs/1998/ (accessed 27 July 2005).

—— (1999) "Secretary-General Reflects on Promise, Realities of His Role in World Affairs." Available at: www.un.org/News/Press/docs/1999/ (accessed 27 July 2005).

—— (2000) Report of the Panel of United Nations Peace Operations, New York: UN Department of Public Information.

—— (2001) "Statement by the President of the Security Council." Available at: http://daccessdds.un.org/doc/UNDOC/GEN/ (accessed 13 July 2005).

—— (2004) A More Secure World: Our Shared Responsibility, New York: UN Department of Public Information.

—— (2005) Report of the International Commission of Inquiry on Darfur. New York: UN Department of Public Information.

United States (2005) "The National Defense Strategy of the United States of America." Available at: www.defenselink.mil/news/Mar2005/ (accessed 10 March 2006).

Van Ness, P. (2005) "The North Korean Nuclear Crisis," in Gurtov, M. and Van Ness, P. (eds.) *Confronting the Bush Doctrine: Critical Views from the Asia-Pacific*. London: Routledge.

Van Walsum, P. (2004) "The Iraq Sanctions Committee," in Malone, D. M. (ed.) *The UN Security Council*, Boulder, CO: Lynne Reinner.

Vayrynen, R. (2003) "Regionalism: Old and New," *International Studies Review*, 5:25–51.

Vickers, R. (2003) *The Labour Party and the World: Volume 1*. Manchester: Manchester University Press.

Voten, E. (2005) "The Political Origins of the UN Security Council's Ability to Legitimize the Use of Force," *International Organization*, 59(3): 527–557.

Wallace, W. (2005) "The Collapse of British Foreign Policy," *International Affairs*, 82(1): 53–68.

Wallensteen, P. and Johnasson, P. (2004) "Security Council Decisions in Perspective," in Malone, D. M. (ed.) *The UN Security Council from the Cold War to the 21st Century*. Boulder, CO: Lynne Reinner.

Walt, S. (2002) "Beyond bin Laden: Reshaping US Foreign Policy," *International Security*, 26(3): 56–78.

Waltz, K. (2000) "Structural Realism after the Cold War," *International Security*, 25(1): 5–41.

Weiss, H. F. and Carayannis, T. (2004) "Reconstructing the Congo," *Journal of International Affairs*, 58(1): 115–141.

Weiss, T. G. (ed.) (1993) *Collective Security in a Changing World*. Boulder, CO: Lynne Reinner.

—— Crahan, M. E., and Goering, J. (eds) (2004) *Wars on Terrorism and Iraq: Human Rights, Unilateralism, and US Foreign Policy*. London: Routledge.

Weller, M. (1999) "The US, Iraq and the Use of Force in a Unipolar World," *Survival*, 41(4): 81–100.

—— (2002) "Undoing the Global Constitution: UN Security Council Action on the International Criminal Court," *International Affairs*, 78(4): 693–712.

Wendt, A. (1999) *Social Theory of International Politics*. Cambridge: Cambridge University Press.

Weschler, J. (2004) "Human Rights," in Malone, D. M. (ed.) *The UN Security Council from the Cold War to the 21st Century*. Boulder, CO: Lynne Reinner.

de Wet, E. (2004) *The Chapter VII Powers of the United Nations Security Council*. Oxford: Hart Publishing.

Wheeler, N. (2002) "Decision-Making Rules and Procedures for Humanitarian Intervention," *The International Journal of Human Rights*, 6(1): 127–138.

—— (2001) *Saving Strangers: Humanitarian Intervention in International Society*. New York: Oxford University Press.

White House (2002a) "President's Remarks at Graduation Exercise of the US Military Academy." Available at: www.whitehouse.gov/news/releases/2002 (accessed 11 February 2005).

—— (2002b) "National Security Strategy of the United States of America." Available at: www.whitehouse.gov/nsc/ (accessed 12 February 2005).

Whitney, C. (1998) "Chirac Wary of Quick Attack if Iraq Breaks Inspection Deal," New York Times, 7 February, A8.

—— (1999a) "French Prime Minister Assails US over Iraq Air Strikes," *New York Times*, 7 January, A6.

—— (1999b) "Allies are Cool to French Plan to Monitor Iraq," *New York Times*, 10 January, A9.

Williams, M. C. and Neumann, I. B. (2000) "From Alliance to Security Community: NATO, Russia, and the Power of Identity," *Millennium*, 29(2): 357–387.

Williams, P. D. (2002) "The Rise and Fall of the 'Ethical Dimension': Presentation and Practice in New Labor Foreign Policy," *Cambridge Review of International Affairs*, 15(1): 53–63.

—— (2004) "Who's Making UK Foreign Policy?" *International Affairs*, 80(5): 909–929.

Wilson, W. (1982) "Address to the US Senate, January 22, 1917," in Link, A. S. (ed.) *The Papers of Woodrow Wilson, Vol. 40*. Princeton, NJ: Princeton University Press.

Wohlforth, W. (1999) "The Stability of a Unipolar World," *International Security*, 24(1): 5–41.

Woodhouse, T. and Ramsbotham, O. (2005) "Cosmopolitan Peacekeeping and the Globalization of Security," *International Peacekeeping*, 12(2): 139–1546.

Wright, Clive. (2004) "Tackling Conflict Diamonds: The Kimberley Process Certification Scheme," *International Peacekeeping*, 11(4): 697–708

Yetiv, S. A. (1997) *The Persian Gulf Crisis*. Westport, CT: Greenwood Press.

Yilmaz, M.E. (2005) "UN Peacekeeping in the Post-Cold War Era," *International Journal on World Peace*, 22(2): 13–28.

Yong, D. (2001) "Hegemon on the Offensive: Chinese Perspectives on US Global Strategy," *Political Science Quarterly*, 116(1): 343–359.

Zhao, S. (ed.) (2004) *Chinese Foreign Policy: Pragmatism and Strategic Behavior*. London: M. E. Sharpe.

Zlobin, N. (2004) "Iraq in the Context of Post-Soviet Foreign Policy," *Mediterranean Quarterly*, 15(2): 83–102.

Index